David Sanders

1106 ...

Urbana, IL 61801

D0080817

Readings in Historic Preservation

Why? What? How?

This federal-style house on Chestnut Street in Salem, Mass. is an example of high-style American architecture. Vernacular buildings and districts of far less sophistication also play a significant part in any historic preservation program designed to provide an insight into America's past. *Courtesy of the National Trust.*

Readings in Historic Preservation

Why? What? How?

Edited by

Norman Williams, Jr. & Edmund H. Kellogg
Environmental Law Center
Vermont Law School

and

Frank B. Gilbert
National Trust for Historic Preservation

This volume is one of a series of publications issued under the aegis of the Environmental Law Center of Vermont Law School. The Center seeks to promote the interdisciplinary study of the law guiding the planning, management, and preservation of natural and historic resources in New England. It is entirely suitable, therefore, that two of the editors of this volume are among the "founding faculty" of the Center and its program.

The University of Arizona College of Law also contributed greatly to this volume, in particular by generously providing a large part of the necessary staff support.

Copyright © 1983, Rutgers—The State University of New Jersey
All rights reserved

Second Printing - - May, 1984

Published in the United States by the
Center for Urban Policy Research
New Brunswick, New Jersey

Library of Congress Cataloging in Publication Data

Main entry under title:

Readings in historic preservation.

    1. Historic buildings—United States—Con-
servation and restoration—Addresses, essays,
lectures. 2. Buildings—United States—
Remodeling for other use—Addresses, essays,
lectures. 3. Architecture and history—United
States—Addresses, essays, lectures. I. Williams,
Norman Jr., 1915- . II. Kellogg, Edmund
Halsey, 1912-   . III. Gilbert, Frank B.
IV. Rutgers University. Center for Urban
Policy Research.
NA106.R4   363.6′9′0973   82-1265
ISBN 0-88285-076-8   AACR2

Contents

PART I   BACKGROUND

1   HISTORICAL PERSPECTIVE

2   WHY HISTORIC PRESERVATION?

3   THREATS TO HISTORIC STRUCTURES AND SITES

PART II WHAT TO PRESERVE

4 CRITERIA FOR DECISIONS ON PRESERVATION – HISTORIC, AESTHETIC, AND PRACTICAL

PART III HOW TO PRESERVE

5 CRITERIA ON CONFORMITY WITH ARCHITECTURAL STYLES IN THE AREA

6   REHABILITATION, RESTORATION, RECONSTRUCTION OR STABILIZATION?

7   ADAPTIVE REUSE

8   PRESERVATION THROUGH AREA PLANNING

PART IV   A MAJOR PROBLEM, OFTEN OVERLOOKED

9   THE EFFECT ON THE POOR AND MINORITIES

Preface

This volume was originally compiled in 1976, when Norman Williams was first visiting at the University of Arizona College of Law. Dean Joseph Livermore noted that Historic Preservation Law was a rapidly developing and significant field of law and that the college should offer a course in this area. The result, after one term of absolutely fascinating reading, was the first collection of these materials, together with (longer) accompanying legal materials that will be published separately.

This volume reviews the principal substantive problems involved in historic preservation, with a good deal of historical background, and is intended to give officials, administrators, and lawyers dealing with preservation the necessary substantive background to understand the legal problems that arise. Although American courts have now accepted the need to deal with aesthetic problems through the legal process, the necessary legal regulations must be so phrased and administered that equal treatment can be assured to all. This requires clear standards understood by all. In order to draft and to deal with such standards, it is necessary to have a considerable understanding of the basic features of architecture, how it is threatened, and how it is preserved. These subjects are developed herein with numerous examples.*

The entire field of historic preservation, the substantive and legal problems involved, and the literature about it have developed rapidly in the last five years. Accordingly, the present volume has developed greatly since the original draft. Much of the difference can be attributed to the first-hand experience of two of the editors in the field of historic preservation—Edmund H. Kellogg with experience in both public and private preservation organizations in the United States and abroad, and Frank B. Gilbert, former executive director of the New York City Landmarks Commission and chief counsel for landmarks and preservation law at the National Trust for Historic Preservation. Both are also teachers of classes in Historic Preservation Law.

Equally important in producing this volume has been the assistance of Professor Robert Giebner, another of the recognized national authorities in the field, and a former member of the board of the National Trust. Indeed the original draft was derived almost entirely from his own library, which he generously made available along with his continuous and unfailing counsel and help in various ways.

---

*Because of space limitations, we have omitted material on architectural history, which is available in any one of several other books recommended on p. 141.

No law professor can be much better than the work of his student assistants, and we have been fortunate in those who have worked with us on these materials. Among those who have made special efforts have been Arthur Arguedas and Jeanita Belford, on the original collection of materials; Teresa Froncek Rankin, Josephine Falls, Kenneth Clark, and Rick Savino, on various intermediate rearrangements; and Terry Leahy, Caroleta Oliveros, and Elaine Paul on the final preparations for publication. In addition, the Vermont Law School, the University of Arizona College of Law, the University of Arizona Committee on Urban Planning, and the National Trust for Historic Preservation have all been unstinting in their support. It is customary to note here—and in this instance is notably true—that our wives have been most patient in putting up with everything that is involved in a legal publication.

Acknowledgments

Grateful acknowledgment is made for permission to reprint the following material:

Hachette, World Guides, *Spain*. Copyright by Hachette, 1980.

Historic Preservation Today. Dupont, "Viollet-le-Duc and Restoration in France," Summerson, "Ruskin, Morris, and the 'Antiscrape' Philosophy," Hosmer, "Private Philanthropy and Preservation," Lorentz, "Reconstruction of the Old Town Centers of Poland," Frin, "European Governmental Experience," Lancaster, "Some Thoughts on Preservation." The above material is excerpted from *Historic Preservation Today*, published by the National Trust for Historic Preservation and the Colonial Williamsburg Foundation. Copyright 1966 by the National Trust for Historic Preservation and Colonial Williamsburg, Incorporated.

The New York *Times*. Huxtable, "Resurrecting a Prophetic 19th-Century Practitioner," "A Fire in Galveston Ends Dispute on the Fate of Historic Building," Goldberger, "In Evicting a Stanford White Design, Virginians Gain Apparent Jefferson," Lindsey, "Urban Revival Poses Some Hard Choices." Copyright 1976/78/80 by the New York Times Company. Reprinted by permission.

With Heritage So Rich. Garvey, "Europe Protects Its Monuments," Whitehill, "Promoted to Glory. . . ," Tunnard, "Landmarks of Beauty and History." Copyright 1966 by Albert Rains and Laurance G. Henderson. Reprinted by permission of Albert Rains, Chairman, Special Committee on Historic Preservation, United States Conference of Mayors.

Lost America: From the Atlantic to the Mississippi. Copyright 1971 by the Pyne Press. Reprinted by permission of Constance M. Greiff.

Legal Techniques in Historic Preservation. Stipe, "Why Preserve Historic Resources?" McGee, "Administrative and Procedural Matters Before Boards of Review," Ziegler, "Implications of Urban Social Policy: The Quest for Community Self-Determination." Copyright 1972 by the National Trust for Historic Preservation.

A Future From the Past. Photographs copyright 1977 by Randolph Langenbach. Reprinted by permission of Randolph Langenbach.

Preservation and Conservation: Principles and Practices, Goldstone, "Administrative, Legal and City Planning Aspects of Historic Preservation Programs," Jacobs, "The Education of Architectural Preservation Specialists in the United States," Fitch, "On Formulating New Parameters for Preservation Policy." Copyright 1976 by the Preservation Press, National Trust for Historic Preservation.

A Historical Guide to Florence. Copyright 1973. Reprinted by permission of the author, John W. Higson, Jr.

What Time Is This Place? by Kevin Lynch. By permission of the MIT Press, Cambridge, Massachusetts. Copyright 1972 by the Massachusetts Institute of Technology.

"Fire Department Burns Down Historic House in Jersey County." Copyright 1977 by the Associated Press.

Conservation of Historic and Cultural Resources. This material is reprinted from PAS Report No. 244, copyright 1969 by the American Planning Association.

Guidebook for the Old and Historic Districts of Nantucket and Siasconset. Copyright 1967 by the Nantucket Historic Districts Commission, Nantucket, Massachusetts.

"Law and Contemporary Problems," Goldstone, "Aesthetics in Historic Districts," Newsom, "Blacks and Historic Preservation." Copyright 1971, 1972, by the Duke University School of Law.

Economic Benefits of Preserving Old Buildings. Lu, "Public Commitment and Private Investment in Preservation," Black, "Making Historic Preservation Profitable—If You're Willing to Wait," Chapman, "The Growing Public Stake in Urban Conservation." Copyright 1976 by The Preservation Press, National Trust for Historic Preservation.

Historic Preservation In Inner City Areas. Copyright 1971 by Van Trump, Ziegler and Shane, Inc.

Back to the City, A Guide to Urban Preservation, 1974. Courtesy Back to the City, Inc.

Business and Preservation. Copyright 1978 by INFORM, Inc. Reprinted as *New Profits from Old Buildings*, publisher McGraw-Hill Book Company.

Information: *Economic Analyses of Adaptive Use Projects, Guernsey Hall.* Copyright 1976 by The Preservation Press, National Trust for Historic Preservation in the United States.

Progressive Architecture. Reprinted from the November 1972 issue, copyright 1972 by Reinhold Publishing.

"The Arizona Daily Star." Copyright 1977. Reprinted by permission.

"Neighborhood Conservation and Reinvestment," February 26, 1978, published by Preservation Reports, Inc., Washington, D.C.

"Forum," published by the Council of Europe. Ragon, "From Pillage to Preservation," Houlet, "Adapting the Past to the Present," Dulieu, "Involving the Neighborhood."

Landmark Preservation. Reprinted by permission of the Citizens Union Research Foundation, Inc. of the City of New York.

Virginia Historic Districts Study. Reprinted by permission of Alice M. Bowsher, William T. Frazier and Jerome R. Saroff.

Preservation in the West. Reprinted by permission of the National Trust for Historic Preservation.

Historic Resources Survey Manual. Reprinted by permission of the New York State Office of Parks and Recreation, Division of Historic Preservation.

Connecticut Historic Preservation Plan. Reprinted by permission of the Connecticut Historical Commission.

Preservation News, the monthly newspaper of the National Trust for Historic Preservation, Poinsett, "What is Historic Preservation?" (July 1973), Leccese, "For God, For Country and. . . ," (June 1980), Knight, "State University Threatens Church," (May 1977), Editorial: "Demolition by Neglect," (March 1978). Reprinted by permission of the National Trust for Historic Preservation.

The Tannery. Reprinted by permission of TWB, Inc.

The Contribution of Historic Preservation to Urban Revitalization and Adaptive Use: A Survey of Construction Costs. Reprinted by permission of the Advisory Council on Historic Preservation.

Economic Benefits of Preservation, Preservation of Historic Adobe Buildings, Historic Structures Report (Delaware Water Gap), *National Benefits of Rehabilitating Existing Buildings*, and "Historic American Building Survey" (Black Historic Landmarks). Reprinted by permission of the United States Department of the Interior.

Opportunities for Historic Preservation. Reprinted by permission of the Southeastern Connecticut Regional Planning Agency.

Preservation and Rehabilitation of an Historic Commercial Area, A Demonstration Study of the Waterfront Historic District of New Bedford, Massachusetts conducted by the New Bedford, Massachusetts Redevelopment Authority in cooperation with the New Bedford City Planning Department and the Waterfront Historic Area League.

The Distinctive Architecture of Willemstad (1961). Reprinted by permission of J. Stanton Robbins and Lachlin F. Blair.

Cobble Hill Historic District Designation Report. Reprinted by permission of the New York City Landmarks Preservation Commission.

Revitalizing Older Houses in Charlestown. Reprinted by courtesy of the Boston Redevelopment Authority.

The Historical Preservation Program for New Mexico, 1973. Reprinted by permission of the State Planning Office, Santa Fe, New Mexico.

Comprehensive Land Use Plan for the Plantations and Unorganized Townships of the State of Maine. Reprinted by permission of the Department of Conservation, State of Maine.

Historic Districts, Murtagh, "Aesthetic and Social Dimensions of Historic Districts." Reprinted by permission of the National Trust for Historic Preservation.

The Urban Design Plan, Historic Hill, Newport, Rhode Island. Reprinted by permission of the authors.

Final Report on the Proposed McKnight Historic District, 1975. Reprinted by permission of the Springfield Historical Commission.

Beacon Hill Architecture Handbook. Reprinted by permission of the Beacon Hill Architectural Committee, Franklin Mead, Chairman.

Historic Preservation Plan for the Central Area General Neighborhood Renewal Area, Savannah, Georgia. Reprinted by permission of the City of Savannah. The publication was financed in part with funds from the U.S. Department of Housing and Urban Development.

Tucson's Historic Districts, Criteria for Preservation and Development. Reprinted by permission of the Planning Department, City of Tucson, Arizona.

Plan for the Creation of a Historic Environment. Reprinted by permission of Billy G. Garrett and James W. Garrison.

Preservation of the City's Character. Reprinted by permission of the Baltimore City Department of Planning, Larry Reich, Director.

Letter to Senator Frank Church. Reprinted by permission of the National Trust for Historic Preservation.

Letter from William Morris to John Ruskin. Reprinted by permission of the Beinecke Rare Book and Manuscript Library, Yale University.

Introduction

The idea of preserving the historical and cultural patrimony is not new—witness the fuss made locally over the desecration of the Grand Mosque of Cordoba in 1523, described in chapter 1—but the notion of historic preservation as a self-conscious organized movement is a product of the last two centuries. (After all, in Western Europe before 1800, there was not much, except neglect, to threaten the older historic buildings.) The organized movement for historic preservation in Europe, led by some rather romantically minded intellectuals, began in France and then in England in the mid-19th century. In the United States, the initiative came from citizen action at the local level; the familiar picture, and the dominant one until recently, has been one of a group of wealthy old ladies with high patriotic sentiments, organizing to save some specific building with some major historical association. As time went on, and particularly after the turn of the century, additional concerns became evident; for example, Indian antiquities in the Southwest. Public policy responded with measures to deal with such specific problems.

So matters went on, perking at a low level, for a century or more. The present movement for historic preservation is strikingly different, with a far broader range of interests and being more broadly based. Under this "New Preservation" (discussed at the end of chapter 1), the concern is with aesthetics as much as with historical associations, and with broad cultural implications even more. To take the obvious example, the important question is no longer whether Washington (or Lafayette) slept here; the question is how ordinary people lived out their lives, with the notion that preservation of the historical artifacts will make this clearer and thus supplement book learning. (The parallel is obvious to the historians' shift of interest to "social history.") Moreover, the interest is in matters of local and regional significance, rather than merely of national import; and considerations of saving artifacts from the historical past now play an important part in city planning generally, and particularly in the new (at long last!) rising field of neighborhood rehabilitation. Perhaps the most significant (and the largest) group now involved is young married couples, devoted to the urban life-style and working hard on neighborhood rehabilitation in historic central city areas—a far cry from the ladies who saved Mount Vernon

A further factor that has favored historic preservation over the past ten years is economics. Inflation has strongly affected the cost of building materials and therefore it pays well to reuse old buildings. Since 1976 tax considerations have sweetened this economic inducement.

All this has come into focus in connection with the environmental movement of the 1960s and 1970s. It is only natural, when one thinks of environmental protection, to take a look at buildings as well as at open lands; and so it is no coincidence that the National Historic Preservation Act dates from 1966. (The 1976 Bicentennial celebration no doubt also added to the sense of the historic past.) The courts have responded to all this with the same sort of sympathetic consideration, and as a result the late 1970s saw the rapid development of a large body of historic preservation law, some of it going far beyond what the most enthusiastic proponents would have hoped for a decade ago. As we move farther into the 1980s, historic preservation is beginning to reach the point where it is possible to settle down and work out the nitty-gritty of all sorts of problems, much of it at the administrative level. Yet major problems remain, not the least those involving long-standing conflicts with unsympathetic Federal development agencies, particularly those concerned with building highways and with urban renewal; and the vigorous reassertion of an unrestricted development ethic is bound to create more problems.

*Letter, William Morris to John Ruskin, dated May 26, 1880, Queen Square, Bloomsbury, London**

I do think we may save here and there some little fragment of art, and to my mind it would be worth the trouble, and years of our little Society's life, if we could but save one little gray building in England.

*By permission of the Beinecke Rare Book and Manuscript Library, Yale University.

Part I
Background

1.

Historical Perspective

4

Preamble

Historic preservation has probably been going on ever since there was something "historic" to preserve. It is interesting to note that Greek marble temples "preserved" in stone the old architectural forms (e.g., triglyphs and metopes), which had been present in their earlier wooden temples; the later rulers of Rome are known to have carried out preservation programs to maintain that city's more important buildings; and ancient Japanese wood temples have survived because parts were constantly replaced as they wore out. Among the earliest of the reasons for preservation efforts was the attempt by "upstart" Roman emperors to achieve acceptance by identifying themselves with earlier, "legitimate" rulers through association with old buildings. This motivation applied as well to Charlemagne who, in establishing his Holy Roman Empire, brought Roman workmen and parts of Roman buildings to Aachen (Aix la Chapelle), so as to stress his Romanness, and thus his legitimacy.

The reasons for the destruction of older buildings and the reasons for later attempts to preserve older buildings are dealt with in later chapters. It is sufficient here to say that developments in each country differed, and depended largely on each country's history, traditions, and legal system. In Europe, France and England were the leaders in the field. In France, the archaeologist Vitet, the architect Viollet-le-Duc, and the writer Prosper Mérimée, together with the Commission for Historic Monuments, began the modern preservation movement in the 1830s and 1840s. This occurred as French authorities became aware of the neglect that had befallen the country's famous landmarks since the Revolution. Because these pioneers had to start with little understanding of the problems of rehabilitation, they did many things now regarded as inappropriate. For example, they built new parts for buildings in a style they thought would have been "appropriate" instead of preserving so far as possible the original construction. Viollet-le-Duc, however, did save much architecture that otherwise would have disappeared and for this reason may be regarded as the father of modern preservation. In England, the general upheaval and fast geographical expansion of cities during the Industrial Revolution led to wholesale destruction of historic streets and buildings, which caused Ruskin, Morris, and others to realize the importance of ancient buildings and to start the British preservation movement.

In the United States, the preservation movement started later, perhaps because of the American attitude that newness is progress and is therefore better. The movement began with efforts to save buildings connected with famous people or events (e.g., Mt. Vernon, John Hancock's house, Old South Church in Boston). These efforts were not always successful, and were made only sporadically. The modern American preservation movement did not start until well into the twentieth century. It began with a federal law in 1906 to save archaeological remains on government-owned lands in the Southwest. Later steps included the Williamsburg restoration sponsored by John D. Rockefeller, Jr., in the 1920s; the Greenfield Village and Wayside Inn projects; municipal efforts starting with laws in Charleston, South Carolina, and New Orleans in the 1930s; the National Landmarks program, also in the 1930s, which ripened into the Historic American Buildings Survey and, eventually, into the establishment of the National Trust (1949) and the Historic Preservation Act of 1966.

Europe

The History of the Decline and Fall of the Roman Empire

Edward Gibbon

The spectator, who casts a mournful view over the ruins of ancient Rome, is tempted to accuse the memory of the Goths and Vandals, for the mischief which they had neither leisure, nor power, nor perhaps inclination, to perpetrate. The tempest of war might strike some lofty turrets to the ground, but the destruction which undermined the foundations of those mossy fabrics was prosecuted, slowly and silently, during a period of ten centuries; and the motives of interest that afterward operated without shame or control were severely checked by the taste and spirit of the emperor Majorian. The decay of the city had gradually impaired the value of the public works. The circus and theaters might still excite, but they seldom gratified, the desires of the people; the temples, which had escaped the zeal of the Christians, were no longer inhabited either by gods or men; the diminished crowds of the Romans were lost in the immense space of their baths and porticoes; and the stately libraries and halls of justice became useless to an indolent generation, whose repose was seldom disturbed either by study or business. The monuments of consular, or Imperial, greatness were not longer revered as the immortal glory of the capital; they were only esteemed as an inexhaustible mine of materials, cheaper and more convenient than the distant quarry. Specious petitions were continually addressed to the easy magistrates of Rome, which stated the want of stones or bricks for some necessary ser-

The interior of the Colosseum in Rome showing the results of having been used as a stone quarry for building materials for many centuries. *Courtesy of Italian State Tourist Office.*

vice; the fairest forms of architecture were rudely defaced for the sake of some paltry, or pretended, repairs; and the degenerate Romans, who converted the spoil to their own emolument, demolished with sacrilegious hands the labors of their ancestors. Majorian, who had often sighed over the desolation of the city, applied a severe remedy to the growing evil. He reserved to the prince and senate the sole cognizance of the extreme cases which might justify the destruction of an ancient edifice; imposed a fine of fifty pounds of gold (two thousand pounds sterling) on every magistrate who should presume to grant such illegal and scandalous license; and threatened to chastise the criminal obedience of their subordinate officers, by a severe whipping and the amputation of both their hands. In the last instance, the legislature might seem to forget the proportion of guilt and punishment; but his zeal arose from a generous principle, and Majorian was anxious to protect the monuments of those ages in which he would have desired and deserved to live. . . .

In the seventh year of his peaceful reign, Theodoric visited the old capital of the world; the senate and people advanced in solemn procession to salute a second Trajan, a new Valentinian; and he nobly supported that character by the assurance of a just and legal government, in a discourse which he was not afraid to pronounce in public and to inscribe on a tablet of brass. Rome, in this august ceremony, shot a last ray of declining glory; and a saint, the spectator of this pompous scene, could only hope, in his pious fancy, that it was excelled by the celestial splendor of the New Jerusalem. During a residence of six months, the fame, the person and the courteous demeanor of the Gothic king excited the admiration of the Romans, and he contemplated, with equal curiosity and surprise, the monuments that remained of their ancient greatness. He imprinted the footsteps of a conqueror on the Capitoline hill, and frankly confessed that each day he viewed with fresh wonder the forum of Trajan and his lofty column. The theater of Pompey appeared, even in its decay, as a huge mountain artificially hollowed and polished, and adorned by human industry; and he vaguely computed, that a river of gold must have been drained to erect the colossal amphitheatre of Titus. From the mouths of fourteen aqueducts, a pure and copious stream was diffused into every part of the city; among these the Claudian water, which arose at the distance of thirty-eight miles in the Sabine mountains, was conveyed along a gentle though constant declivity of solid arches, till it descended on the summit of the Aventine hill. The long and spacious vaults which had been constructed for the purpose of common sewers, subsisted, after twelve centuries, in their pristine strength; and the subterraneous channels have been preferred to all the visible wonders of Rome. The Gothic kings, so injuriously accused of the ruin of antiquity, were anxious to preserve the monuments of the nation whom they had subdued. The royal edicts were framed to prevent the abuses, the neglect, or the depredations of the citizens themselves; and a professed architect, the annual sum of two hundred pounds of gold, twenty-five thousand tiles, and the receipt of customs from the Lucrine port, were assigned for the ordinary repairs of the walls and public edifices. A similar care was extended to the statues of metal or marble of men or animals. The spirit of the horses, which have given a modern name to the Quirinal, was applauded by the Barbarians; the brazen elephants of the *Via sacra* were diligently restored; the famous heifer of Myron deceived the cattle, as they were driven through the forum of Peace; and an officer was created to protect those works of art, which Theodoric considered as the noblest ornament of his kingdom.

Spain (Hachette, World Guides*)

Córdoba

For nearly three centuries, the Chapter was satisfied with this interior arrangement.** But in 1523, it resolved to build a high altar, a sanctuary and a Capella Mayor, in the middle of the marvelous quincunx of the Arabian monument. On hearing the news, the Municipal Council was roused; it made an appeal to Charles V, and threatened every workman with death should he take part in the demolition of the mosque, adding, "that what they desired to destroy could never be replaced by anything of such perfection." The Royal Council intervened, declared the Municipal Council in the wrong, and entrusted Hernán Ruiz with the work. But when Charles V came to Andalusia three years later he visited the mosque and appeared very dissatisfied. "Had I known," he said to the Canons, "what you desired to do, you would not have done it, for what you are doing here can be found everywhere and what you possessed previously exists nowhere."

Viollet-le-Duc and Restoration in France†

Jacques Dupont‡

The name of Viollet-le-Duc has become a symbol of historic restoration. His work is universally known and has produced tributes of the highest admiration, as well as criticism of the most severe kind. The passions he provoked are not yet quelled. . . .

On his return from Italy in 1840, Viollet-le-Duc rapidly saw his career in outline. Newly aware of the monuments of France, he was still more struck by the science of their structure and the harmony

---

*Hachette, World Guides. *Spain*. Paris: Hachette, 1961, p. 720

**The Reconquista, the recapturing of Spain from Moorish control over a period of some seven centuries, ended with the conquest of Granada in 1492. The city of Córdoba, the capital of medieval Moslem Spain, was captured much earlier, in 1236. The Grand Mosque of Córdoba was the prime achievement of medieval Arabic architecture in the West, and even now remains one of the most extraordinary buildings in the world. After the reconquest of Córdoba, the Mosque was promptly renamed the Cathedral of Córdoba, and as such it was used for Roman Catholic services for nearly 300 years, with some minor renovations. However, in the mid-sixteenth century, an alteration was made which presents perhaps the oddest view in the history of architecture—a Spanish baroque church was built directly in the center of the Mosque.

†From the National Trust for Historic Preservation, *Historic Preservation Today*. Charlottesville, Va.: University Press of Virginia, 1966, pp. 3, 8-21.

‡Jacques Dupont is Inspecteur Général des Monuments Historiques, Paris, France.

Detail of Facade of Grand Mosque at Cordoba. The Christian Cathedral choir was inserted inside the Moorish building. *Courtesy of Spanish National Tourist Office.*

and method of their construction and decoration. His professional course was confirmed by his appointment as Inspecteur du Service des Bâtiments Civils, which included the care of the Archives and the Sainte Chapelle. He was also given the mission of restoring the Basilique de Vézelay by the Commission des Monuments Historiques.

Up to that time the passion for monuments of the Middle Ages was one shared only by archaeologists like Arcisse de Caumont, Ludovic Vitet, and Prosper Mérimée. And it was they who were to lead the subsequent fight for their preservation.

Until 1830, the maintenance of buildings from the Middle Ages was assumed by local architects. Their task was made more difficult because of the neglect into which the buildings had fallen after the Revolution; furthermore, most of these men were ignorant of the old construction techniques. The government of Louis Philippe tried to control these restorations and to establish a doctrine. On the twenty-fourth of October, 1830, Ludovic Vitet was appointed to the new post of Inspecteur Général des Monuments Historiques. To accomplish his purpose of halting vandalism and regulating the maintenance of the buildings, he chose architects who knew something of the ancient methods, understood their importance, could make correct drawings, and could take charge of upkeep and restoration. Vitet prompted the creation of the Commission des Monuments Historiques, of which he became chairman. His successor as Inspecteur Général, Prosper Mérimée, had little initial success. Because the architects were ill fitted for their task, many of the early restorations were dreadful.

Viollet-le-Duc, full of confidence, accepted at the age of 26 the responsibility of repairing Vézelay, "a task so delicate and dangerous that no architect, not even the masters Caristie and Duban, would undertake it." Hence began a series of long and varied works that nevertheless did not occupy all his time. Their importance lies not only in what he did but in what he inspired. He came to dominate a school and a period. Before him no doctrine had existed. "When we began to study the architecture of the Middle Ages no book existed to help us. We did not even dare to confess our interest, which seemed a deprivation of taste, but our instinct drew us towards the cathedrals."

Viollet-le-Duc henceforth devoted his life not only to effective restorations but also to the creation of a doctrine for historical restoration. It was a course that led him to write a great number of articles and books—chiefly the ten volumes of the dictionary of architecture, the six volumes of the dictionary of furniture, and the two volumes of talks on architecture which replaced the lectures that opponents forbade him to deliver at the École des Beaux Arts. In spite of unavoidable mistakes, his books have kept their literary, historical, and technical value, even though some drawings from his quick pen seem nowadays to have been born of a pseudo-Gothic nightmare. But it was through these works that the author clearly expressed his principal ideas.

First of all, Viollet-le-Duc considered architecture as the expression of the history of society, as material to be studied by the analytic methods familiar to the biological and physical sciences. The origin of each period and of each style lay in the preceding styles and periods, much as the earth layers studied by the geologist were built up by continual accumulation. On the one hand, of course, the monument must be appraised in relation to the society it reflects. But on the other, it must be considered in its anatomy, where every element takes its normal place. It was a new point of view. For Viollet-le-Duc structure and decoration were one. During the Middle Ages this was an essential concept, because no separation existed between them.

> Beauty is nothing more than the visible result of the wise use of the given material. In the most beautiful monument of the XIIth century you must not suppress an ornament; it is the consequence of a need fulfilled. You cannot lie with Gothic architecture; all sticks together. You cannot leave something to be finished by others. Ornament is a part of structure and can no more be divided from it than can muscle from flesh.

This outlook is quite new.

Considering a building of that period through its ornamentation would be similar to judging a book by its binding. The characteristic of this art is sincerity. If you need a wooden vault you will make that and not an imitation stone vault; if it is a ceiling, then the upper floor will suggest the decorations; beams and joints must be visible; a roof is made to protect, with a slope sufficient for the outflow of rain, and is not to be hidden behind an attic, as at Versailles.

From this intimate union of appearance and structure came the principle of the "ensemble." By it, Viollet-le-Duc meant everything that went into building and furnishing, from the foundation stones to tapestries, lights and small pieces. Artists contributed to an ensemble; the painter, sculptor, and glass worker were linked to the entire building. They would not think of looking at their picture, their statue, or their stained glass apart from the building they were made for. They saw themselves as members of a choir in which each one worked for a common harmony. They were obedient to a master of the works who was himself familiar enough with painting and sculpture to understand what help he could obtain from these arts to complement his own. This precious alliance disappeared when the architect was enclosed in "school" prejudices, when the sculptors made statues instead of statuary, and when painters made pictures instead of paintings. There were no major and minor arts during the thirteenth century. Every object was an object of art.

To understand and to respect this unity, the architect who would preserve old buildings had to understand the professions involved: those of the historian, the artist, and the engineer. Anthyme Saint-Paul, who generally has little use for Viollet-le-Duc, writes:

He had in a superior degree the knowledge essential to his job: of building materials—their quality and cost—of stone quarries and the means of extraction and transportation, of the methods of preparing mortars and coating, of the use and process of scaffolding, of the machinery, the drill, and the hand tools and crafts that went into the construction and decoration of buildings, and of the moral and material condition of the workmen. He had learned all—from his masters, from books, or from personal experience. By watching him create, in front of everyone, with a certainty that appeared geometrically unerring, by hearing his voice, sharp and short, as it led the way from idea to fact, by following his explanatory drawing, craftsmen received a revelation of their gifts and many raised their trade to art.

Viollet-le-Duc had the gift of selecting his assistants from all ranks and infusing in them his own enthusiasm. To evolve a theory for the preservation of historical monuments was not enough; he had to train workmen to be able to reproduce in modern times the old and forgotten techniques. In this his own cleverness with his hands served him well.

Now that we know the man and his intellectual background, we can better follow both the theory and the practice of his restorations. In theory, each building or each part of a building should be restored in its proper style, not only in appearance but also in structure. Few buildings, especially during the Middle Ages, were built all at one time, or if that had been the case they were subsequently, as a rule, notably modified by means of adjuncts or partial transformations. Before undertaking any repairs, therefore, it was essential to ascertain the exact age and character of each section and to draw up a report based upon definite documents or in the form of notes and sketches.

Further, at a given period, buildings varied according to regions. Those in Normandy differed from those in Provence. Each province had a style of its own, its peculiar methods of construction, and its particular materials. The architect should therefore know the types proper to each period and the style of each school.

Monuments, as a rule, have been repaired and enlarged throughout the ages, a fact that creates considerable embarrassment when the original parts and the modified sections need to be restored. Should we neglect the latter and reestablish the original unity of style, or must we restore the whole and maintain the later modifications? The decision in each case depends upon particular circumstances. But in general the decision must take into account respect for the original style, archaeological knowledge, and the quality of the addition.

For example: The vaults of a twelfth-century nave, having perished by accident, were later partly rebuilt following the current methods of the time. These latter vaults, in turn, are now in danger and require reconstruction. Should they be restored to their later or to their original form? The latter alternative, while presenting no disadvantage, permits a return to the unity of the building. The question is not one of maintaining an improvement to an originally faulty design but of realizing that the later vault was built following the then-traditional method, i.e., adopting for all repair the forms in practice at the time that repair was done. We now follow the opposite principle and restore each building in its own style.

But the new vaults that differ from the earlier ones may be very beautiful. They have allowed the addition of windows containing stained glass. They are combined with a system of outer construction of great value. Should one destroy all this for the satisfaction of reestablishing the pure lines of the primitive nave? Will all the stained glass be put in storage and will the outer flying buttresses remain useless?

Whatever the solution, we must always respect scrupulously every hidden clue that might lead to the discovery of successive changes. Some cathedrals of the twelfth century had no transept. During the fourteenth and fifteenth centuries, transepts were added by the suppression of two bays. It is always possible to find, even in careful work, marks of the original design and the restorer must be attentive to the preservation of these proofs.

Up to now the doctrine is wise. We become uneasy with some of the corollaries. When an architect has to rebuild, for example, that part of a monument of which nothing remains, he must indoctrinate his mind with the corresponding style and remember that each portion follows the same scale, that every fault of proportion will display a deformity. Again, one may be obliged to adapt an old monument to an appropriation entirely foreign to its original use in order to justify its upkeep by a governing body that refuses to spend money for a building without any use. Sometimes the solution is easy, as in making a library of the refectory of Saint Martin des Champs in Paris. In that case, Viollet-le-Duc preserved the fine architecture by the simple use of wooden shelves. But more often the architect must conform to a strict program imposed by the ultimate use of the building.

To accept a planned but incompatible use for a restored monument can be a steep price to pay for its preservation. Viollet-le-Duc confessed it to be a slippery slope, not to restore the building exactly, and one could take it only at the risk of otherwise losing the building entirely. At Narbonne, for instance, it was regrettable to have to transform the Bishop's Palace into a town hall by the addition of a new facade.

Although his opinions about construction may often be questionable, the technical advice Viollet-le-Duc set down is excellent. "Knowing that restoration inevitably unsettles old buildings, one must compensate for this curtailment of strength by giving power to the new parts, by perfecting the structure, by clamping walls, and by introducing greater resistances, for prolonging the life of the building is the true task of restoration." The architect must thoroughly know

the structure of the building, its anatomy, its temperament. He must make it live. He must be as familiar with it as if he had directed the original construction. With this knowledge he must also possess the knowledge of alternatives; if one fails, a second, a third, must be ready. Do not forget that monuments of the Middle Ages were not built like those of the Romans, where passive resistances are opposed to active forces. In the first, all parts are active; if a vault pushes, buttress and flying buttress must take the thrust; if an arch gets out of shape, curving it back is not sufficient for it then takes the thrust of other arches which react obliquely. In truth, you have to deal not only with inert vertical forces but also with forces opposed to each other.

These views, so evident and commonplace now, were new and quite indispensable to those who attempted to preserve from utter ruin the abandoned relics of the past.

Strangely, the Revolution—the cause of so much destruction—motivated the idea of the preservation of national monuments. It began to be understood that these, like the ancient monuments of Greece and Rome, were an integral part of history itself. So was launched the notion of Antiquités Nationales, up to then the province only of archaeologists like Gaignières or Millin. . . .

To begin with, an inventory was necessary. It was attempted by the Commission des Monuments, followed by the Commission Temporaire des Arts, which unfortunately became politically suspect—an inevitable corollary of preservation. The Commission failed to halt the destruction of the Royal Tombs in Saint Denis, prescribed by a decision of the Convention, but it gave birth, along with Alexandre Lenoir, to the Musée des Monuments where the wreckage was stored. It also was active in the saving of the Petit Château de Chantilly, the Château d'Écouen, the Basilique de Saint Denis, and in badly needed work in the cathedrals of Amiens and Chartres.

A powerful impulse arose aimed at preventing vandalism and favoring preservation. The publication of *Génie de Christianisme* by Chateaubriand, of the novels of Walter Scott, of *Notre Dame de Paris* by Victor Hugo, and of the two volumes in which Alexandre Laborde classified chronologically the monuments of France, all made public opinion sensitive and alive to these problems. The famous publication by Baron Taylor, *Romantic and Picturesque Travels Through Ancient France*, began in 1818. Norman scholars, accepting the challenge of their British colleagues, studied their province. Arcisse de Caumont wrote the outline of a rational exposition of medieval art. Founding the archaeological congresses, he gave them a spectacular tint of belligerence. Émeric-David, defender of medieval sculptors, and Didron, founder of the *Annales Archaéologiques*, had equal influence. Public opinion was led to demand the existence of a civil service to save the monuments abandoned after the Revolution. The government of Louis Philippe and his prime minister, Guizot, responded to this consensus in 1830 and created the Inspection Générale des Monuments Historiques with Vitet as head. . . .

If later on Viollet-le-Duc, emboldened by success, went too far, one must acknowledge that at least he possessed a knowledge of medieval architecture that had been ignored by his contemporaries.

His first job, the restoration of the church La Madeleine de Vézelay, was a great success and allowed him to apply the principles that have already been referred to. The building was tottering, and the most competent architects then working with Vitet and Mérimée had declined the task. Its state was so bad that all work of consolidation risked a final collapse. The causes of deterioration were many: mistakes of design at the beginning, the damage wrought by Protestants in 1589, which had been badly repaired, and the general neglect of the building during the seventeenth and eighteenth centuries.

Viollet-le-Duc began by making a complete survey of the church, in flat projection and cross section, in order to understand its structure. Then, with every precaution, he propped up the whole building. It is wrong to reproach him now for the repairs he made to the four ogival vaults of the nave, which were crumbling. He chose to rebuild three of them on the Roman type, similar to the original vaulting still existing, so as to maintain the unity of the nave. The fourth one he rebuilt in ogival shape as a testimony to the original design and to clear the entrance to the choir. He also had to fight against the tendency of the walls to draw apart and thus endanger the entire nave, and he had to rebuild the Gothic flying buttresses of the thirteenth century to take the thrust. At the apse, he lowered the roof of the ambulatory to permit more light to enter. On the façade, he had to remake the bases of the walls and porches. The southern tower was sinking and the central gable bending; this portion had to be dismantled and rebuilt, in the course of which he made a mistake by suppressing the reference of the high, narrow Gothic arcades that had been conceived to adorn the towers on

The Church of La Madeleine de Vézelay was the first of the major restorations by Viollet-le-Duc. *Courtesy of French Government Tourist Office.*

each side of the gable. If some capitals were remade on the interior, it was because their resistance had become too weak; the copies were as faithful as possible.

Minor mistakes do not destroy the overall merit of the man who safeguarded the church. Nowadays we would not dare to scuplt anew the spandrel of the central porch from the outline of the original; we would prefer to find its mangled remains. The nineteenth century never feared to introduce new sculptures. Perhaps we now have less audacity and only accept this necessity when it seems indispensable to the equilibrium of the architecture. Paul Léon says:

> The complete success of so dangerous a restoration made public the ability of the young architect. While the spire of Saint Denis was ruined by the mistakes of Debret, the unsteady church of Vézelay was saved by Viollet-le-Duc. This was a triumph for the doctrines upheld by the Service des Monuments Historiques, its commission, its inspectors, and its architects.

Following the challenge of Vézelay, the new school was able to apply publicly its methods at Notre Dame de Paris. The question there was one of restoring to this illustrious monument the glow it had lost after the Revolution. Jean Baptiste Lassus and Viollet-le-Duc proposed a wise scheme, followed by a report that expanded the principles of restoration: above all, respect the identity of material and shape, forbid molded constituents, avoid cast iron (unknown during the Middle Ages), abandon stone flags and mortars that hide the ailments of the building rather than cure them, and replace ruined parts with new ones containing no modification of form or proportion; reproduce ancient forms with "a religious discretion, and forsake every personal preference."

This was all very well stated, but Viollet-le-Duc had difficulty in following his own directions. He replaced the thirteenth-century windows (which were not harmonious) by rose windows of the twelfth century that were his own invention. He added a central spire, and for the western porches he made new statues inspired by those of the catheral of Bordeaux. We deplore these false statues, though we would probably also deplore an empty porch.

Inside the cathedral, seized by a mania for unity of style, he suppressed most of the classical decoration. Every painting placed by the guild of goldsmiths during the seventeenth and eighteenth centuries disappeared, and only mediocre altars and poor coloring remain in the chapels to hide unpleasant openings whose poor decoration completely ruined the whole building.

After his death, a reaction began to appear against Viollet-le-Duc and much criticism was leveled at his restorations. The slow influence of archaeologists began to impress the architects, and the works of Quicherat, de Lasteyrie, Brutails, and Lefèvre-Pontalis defined a new doctrine. As Paul Léon has put it, "A monument to be a testimony to the past must stay as the past has bequeathed it. To pretend to restore it to its original state is dangerous and deceitful; we must preserve buildings as they are, respecting the contribution of successive generations."

Ruskin, so strongly opposed to modern improvements, stirred up public opinion but he left unanswered the question of how we apply his theory of nonintervention while buildings are in daily use. Must we allow them to collapse without interfering? No, but careful maintenance can be sufficient. Architects for national monuments also now have enough assured income to permit the execution of urgent repairs that can prevent worse damage; and they can put back missing slates, keep the eaves clear, drain the walls, and by such attention largely circumvent the risk of more serious work.

The important monuments, those most threatened, were consolidated by Viollet-le-Duc and his pupils and later had only to be maintained. Subsequently, as the number of classified monuments increased and the money allowances decreased, the concept of upkeep took precedence for most buildings. In addition, technical progress assisted in the application of the new doctrine. New methods of preservation were able to avoid the dangerous and optional reconstruction of the past. An initial success that impressed public opinion, for example, was the strengthening of the central tower of the cathedral of Bayeux by the engineer Eugène Flachat, who underpinned the foundations of the piles.

The employment of concrete allowed the strengthening of an original structure without altering its appearance or form. The Inspecteur Général Anatole de Baudot was the forerunner of this technique about 1902. Since then it has acquired great merit. In this way Paul Selmersheim was able to restore on the spot the northern porch of Chartres while the southern had had to be taken down. At Reims, to release the rose crushed by the gable and to bind the towers, a simple concrete needle hiding the stonework was sufficient.

The advocates of care and maintenance could now be satisfied that preservation was triumphant, but subsequent events soon put into the background the theory that maintenance could be the ultimate answer.

During the first World War, more than a thousand monuments were severely damaged and the old problem of preservation was once again what it had been in the post-Revolutionary era. But to solve it a hundred years of experience, as well as the principles evolved by Viollet-le-Duc, were at hand. From that basis, the architect can, as an example, use the more possible of original stones (carved or not) and he can strengthen the structure's walls and piles by the injection of concrete. But his major care is still to rebuild the same architecture, guided by both exhaustive documentation and by photography.

Such preoccupations would have been laughable at the beginning of the nineteenth century when Viollet-le-Duc appeared on the scene. And if we have to give an opinion on his work and influence, it can only be done by referring back to that time when the monuments of the past had not yet been investigated and the concept of restoring was still quite unthinkable.

As the symbol of restoration, Viollet-le-Duc naturally incurred public censure for the liberties he took with it—especially later in his career. But is this quite fair? His intellectual background and his broad experience were unique at a time when neither scholar nor builder was able to help him, save Prosper Mérimée. His understanding of the problems, his knowledge, his capacity for hard work, his faith, his convincing gift for arousing enthusiasm in his fellow workers, whether carpenters or masons, his gifts as a writer and draftsman, all combined to make him the apostle of the preservation of monuments.

Resurrecting a Prophetic Nineteenth-Century Practitioner*

Ada Louise Huxtable

In any survey of out-of-favor architects least likely to be revived, the easy winner, until very recently, would have been Eugène Emmanuel Viollet-le-Duc. Probably no architect has been more consistently

New York Times, April 6, 1980, Section D, p. 31.

put down in this century; it is hard to look at a medieval monument in France, from the Cathedral of Notre Dame in Paris to the walled town of Carcassonne, without hearing imprecations against Viollet-le-Spoiler. He is the 19th-century French architect (1814–79) who spent his life elaborately reconstructing the buildings of the Middle Ages and who represents everything the 20th century has disdained: the over-restoration of monuments, the popularization of quasi-historical styles and, perhaps most unforgivable of all, the preeminence of the traditionalist in official art and culture. From the 1830s to the 1870s, Viollet-le-Duc was one of the most active, influential and respected architects in the Western world.

On second thought, that would probably make him a prime candidate for revival. In today's spirit of revisionism, scholars seem bent on standing history on its head, with the rediscovery prize going to the most unexpected choices. Last year was the centenary of Viollet-le-Duc's death, a moment when reputations have a way of beginning to rise. There has been talk of reassessment studies in progress. . . .

The controversial restorations form a long and impressive list: among them are the monuments of Vézelay, Sens, Amiens, Beaune, Avignon and Toulouse; there are churches, cathedrals, chateaux and hotels de ville. This work was based on the best archeological knowledge at that time, but the art and science of archeology have advanced immeasurably since then. Viollet-le-Duc overreacted, undeniably, and his confidence in his ability to recreate the past, to recapture the irretrievable, was boundless. But his concerns, as recorded in his writings, were often surprisingly sound and sensitive.

One must remember that that preservation philosophies of the 19th and 20th centuries could not be more unlike. Viollet-le-Duc's world wanted things put together the way they were, Humpty Dumpty fashion; he played the delicate and dangerous game of "restoring back." The 20th century stresses the value of whatever is left of the original fabric over everything else.

The important point is not how much of what we see today was put there by Viollet-le-Duc and his sculptors and artisans, but that without them, there would be little or nothing to see at all. France's superb medieval heritage was literally crumbling away, and sheer structural survival often made considerable rebuilding necessary.

Ruskin, Morris, and the "Anti-Scrape" Philosophy *

*Sir John Summerson * **

John Ruskin, William Morris, Philip Webb, and W.R. Lethaby all held very nearly if not absolutely identical views on the subject of the preservation of ancient buildings. Ruskin announced his views in 1849; Lethaby died in 1931. So I think we may say that for about eighty years a distinct philosophy

---

*From National Trust for Historic Preservation, *Historic Preservation Today.* Charlottesville, Va: University Press of Virginia, 1966, pp. 23–31.

**Sir John Summerson is Curator, Sir John Soane's Museum, London, England.

The Ramparts of Carcassone (Rehabilitated by Viollet-le-Duc). *Courtesy of French Government Tourist Office.*

of preservation was upheld. It was passionately upheld by these men and less passionately by great numbers of their followers. I much doubt if any living person adheres to it now. I also much doubt if many living people have a very clear idea of what this philosophy was. In the context of present conditions and problems it may appear rather curious; but it still has power.

The philosophy was invented—that is not too strong a word—by Ruskin, and here is a key passage from "The Lamp of Memory" in the *Seven Lamps of Architecture*:

> For, indeed, the greatest glory of a building is not in its stones, nor in its gold. Its glory is in its Age, and in that deep sense of voicefulness, of stern watching, of mysterious sympathy, nay, even of approval or condemnation, which we feel in walls that have long been washed by the passing waves of humanity. It is in their lasting witness against men, in their quiet contrast with the transitional character of all things, in the strength which, through the lapse of seasons and times, and the decline and birth of dynasties, and the changing of the face of the earth, and of the limits of the sea, maintains its sculptured shapeliness for a time insuperable, connects forgotten and following ages with each other, and half constitutes the identity, as it concentrates the sympathy, of nations: it is in that golden stain of time, that we are to look for the real light, and colour, and preciousness of architecture; and it is not until a building has assumed this character, till it has been encrusted with the fame, and hallowed by the deeds of men, till its walls have been witnesses of suffering, and its pillars rise out of the shadows of death, that its existence, more lasting as it is than that of the natural objects of the world around it, can be gifted with even so much as these possess, of language and of life.

The music of this passage is the music of a seventeenth-century sermon, as so much of Ruskin's earlier writing is: it is elevated, metaphysical, almost theological in tone and floats across to us with tremendous dignity the quite monstrous paradox that the emotional effect of a piece of architecture arises not from its form or the quality of its materials but from its antiquity. It is important to note that this declaration is made not as a plea for the conservation of buildings already ancient but as a fundamental truth about architecture. New buildings must be built to last indefinitely and must not depend for their impressiveness on anything that is perishable. In course of time they will acquire the marks of age and in those marks themselves there is meaning which, says Ruskin, "nothing else can replace and which it is our wisdom to consult and to desire."

In other words the art of architecture is the art of building ancient monuments; or, rather, of building structures which after several hundred years of exposure will be received as such by an unknown generation of men. "I think," says Ruskin, "a building cannot be considered as in its prime until four or five centuries have passed over it; and that the entire choice and arrangements of its details should have reference to their appearance after that period." He goes at considerable length into the question of "the picturesque," which he calls "parasitical sublimity." In modern jargon this might, I think, be paraphrased as "romantic overtones." Ruskin seeks to distinguish between these romantic overtones which arise from attention being given to accidents of decay, to the extent that these accidents acquire an emotional meaning entirely their own, and those which remain inherent to the building and ennoble it by expressing what is, to Ruskin, its chief glory—its age.

It is very important to understand this position of Ruskin's. I called his attitude, just now, a monstrous paradox, and it is not very difficult for us to dismiss it at once as pure nonsense. But wait. It may be nonsense to us in our material circumstances and intellectual climate. But consider Ruskin in his. He was living in an England many of whose institutions had scarcely changed since the time of Queen Elizabeth and the centers of whose towns consisted in very many cases entirely of medieval and Tudor buildings. When *we* think of such a town we think at once of obsolescence, of the "problem" of the city center, and of the rescue of parts of it as museum pieces. Ruskin in the 1840s did not see it so. These old buildings were not, technologically, much inferior—and, indeed, in substance and workmanship were often superior—to new buildings. The fact that they had stood for a very long time seemed only to confirm their excellence and their capacity to stand for a good deal longer. The rate of change in English towns and villages in the 1840s was still, by our standards, in-credibly slow. A huge vista of change, such as we are conscious of every moment of our lives, was then inconceivable.

Now these ancient time-resistant buildings had, at Ruskin's date, gradually been acquiring a new interest. A new sensibility toward them had developed through the writings of antiquaries and the engravings of illustrators: Sir Walter Scott, Carter, Britton, the elder Pugin, and Rickman. The younger Pugin they had utterly transported, even to a sort of mania. In Ruskin, too, the new sen-sibility was heightened to an extremity. Here were these buildings—neglected, despised, mutilated, but shining through everything and across four or five centuries as models of sound construction and exquisite ornament and sculpture. Once their ideal excellence was recognized it was not surprising that the sheer fact of age should carry overwhelming emotional significance. Had not something of the sort happened among the humanists of the fourteenth century, newly awakened to the architec-tural perfections of Rome?

The pattern of ideas in the passage we have just been considering is curiously logical. Ruskin has searchingly examined the sources of his love for medieval buildings. At the very center of them he has discovered, with absolute honesty and absolute conviction, the consideration that these buildings are old, that they have lasted. He has found that he cannot separate the mere intellectual certainty that they are old from the emotions induced by the presence of the buildings themselves, emotions which lead him to call them beautiful. The buildings look old. It is, in fact, the marks of age which cer-tify their antiquity and it is through these marks that he has learned to discover them as beautiful. Such has been, quite authentically, the pattern of appreciation. Then he takes the whole of this pat-tern and turns it upside down. Because the sheer age of buildings is, to Ruskin, the most moving aspect of them, therefore for a building to become moving as architecture it must be built with a view to becoming old; and it must be built of materials which will strongly and sympathetically take the marks of age. Of the actual forms which might accompany the application of this principle Ruskin declines to give any indication. There are, after all, the other six lamps to guide the architect in the way he should go.

Now, from this standpoint what view did Ruskin take of preservation? For the actual demolition of ancient buildings he would admit of no valid excuse whatever. "A fair building," he wrote, "is necessarily worth the ground it stands upon, and will be so until Central Africa and America shall have become as populous as Middlesex: nor is any cause whatever valid as a ground for its destruc-tion." In ratification of this uncompromising attitude he argued that there were positive moral obliga-tions both to the dead and to posterity. "It is . . . no question of expediency or feeling whether we shall preserve the buildings of past times or not. *We have no right whatever to touch them*. They are not ours. They belong partly to those who built them, and partly to all the generations of mankind who are to follow us." In an addendum to one of the *Lectures on Architecture* (1853) he developed this argument with quite fantastic ingenuity:

Putting aside all antiquarian considerations, and all artistical ones, I wish that people would only consider the steps and the weight of the following very simple argument. You allow it is wrong to waste time, your own time; but then it must be still more wrong to waste other people's; for you have some right to your own time, but none to theirs. Well, then, if it is thus wrong to waste the time of the living, it must be still more wrong to waste the time of the dead; for the living can redeem their time, the dead cannot. But you waste the best of the time of the dead when you destroy the works they have left you; for to those works they gave the best of their time, intending them for immortality.

So much for the ethics of demolition. But in Ruskin's mind there was a threat to ancient buildings much more terrible and much more evil than demolition. This was restoration. Demolition was the work of the ignorant mob—barbarous and crude. Restoration was the work of educated and responsible people, people who should know better. The indictment of restorers is one of the famous passages in the "Lamp of Memory":

> Restoration . . . means the most total destruction which a building can suffer: a destruction out of which no remnants can be gathered: a destruction accompanied with false description of the thing destroyed. Do not let us deceive ourselves in this important matter; it is *impossible*, as impossible as to raise the dead, to restore anything that has ever been great or beautiful in architecture.

What Ruskin mainly understood by restoration was a process very frequently employed in the 1840s and 1850s which consisted in the tooling away at decayed stone to reach a new, firm, and smooth surface. Naturally in this process moldings were distorted out of recognition, while all marks of handling and age were lost. And this loss of the visible marks of antiquity was to Ruskin the most dreadful fate which could befall any building.

If it were urged that restoration was often a physical necessity, Ruskin's answer was that proper care should prevent that necessity:

> Take proper care of your monuments, and you will not need to restore them. A few sheets of lead put in time upon a roof, a few dead leaves and sticks swept in time out of a water-course, will save both roof and walls from ruin. Watch an old building with an anxious care; guard it as best you may, and at *any* cost, from *every* influence of dilapidation. Count its stones as you would jewels of a crown; set watches about it as if at the gates of a besieged city; bind it together with iron where it loosens; stay it with timber where it declines; do not care about the unsightliness of the aid: better a crutch than a lost limb; and do this tenderly, and reverently, and continually, and many a generation will still be born and pass away beneath its shadow. Its evil day must come at last; but let it come declaredly and openly, and let no dishonouring and false substitute deprive it of the funeral offices of memory.

In all this, of course, we recognize the beginnings of the conservation ideology of William Morris' Society for the Protection of Ancient Buildings, the society he founded in 1877, twenty-eight years after the publication of the *Seven Lamps* and which, in reference to current restoration methods, he called the "Anti-Scrape." It was in 1877 that Ruskin, writing to Count Zorzi about the havoc that was being wrought at St. Mark's, Venice, put the principle that the Society was to embrace as its own:

> The single principle is, that after any operation whatsoever necessary for the safety of the building, every external stone should be set back in its actual place: if any are added to strengthen the walls, the new stone, instead of being made to resemble the old ones, should be left blank of sculpture, and every one have the date of its insertion engraved upon it.

For the internal support of St. Mark's, Ruskin suggested the use of sculptured and gilded wood. Iron bands, too, could have a picturesque effect; monastic ruins in the private grounds of English noblemen, he told the Count, with perhaps just the slightest hint that rank might count a little in this matter, were held together in this honest, practical way.

The idea of preservation by the propping and tying together of collapsing structures is somehow grotesque. It is interesting that in the letter to Zorzi, Ruskin lets slip the word "picturesque" without, this time, intending anything very precise and it suggests that this rough mode of preservation may have been sanctioned for him by the pictorial use of such devices, perhaps in the water colors of Samuel Prout whom he so much esteemed. Anyway, here was the beginning of [the] S.P.A.B. method, rationalized in the course of the Society's later activities and still upheld in principle, in all circumstances where its adoption is practicable, by most reputable restorers. The main difference between the modern attitude and Ruskin's is that the modern restorer preserves old material so far as possible as a matter of scientific conscience, because to replace old material with new is "bad archaeology." To Ruskin preservation of the old was something more spiritual; to bedevil old work by renewing it was a crime against the dead and the unborn. Perhaps it is only the words which are different.

Now if Ruskin was the author, as he certainly was, of the S.P.A.B. philosophy of restoration, he was also the grandfather of the Society itself. In the year that the Crystal Palace was reopened at Sydenham (1854) he published a pamphlet suggesting the formation of just such a Society, a society to watch over the welfare of ancient buildings and to publish at regular intervals reports on what was happening to them. Another twenty-three years were to elapse before William Morris took the steps which led to the formation of the S.P.A.B. and perhaps that interval of time was necessary for Ruskin's vision to descend into the air of practical politics, to become something capable of realization without inviting ridicule or contempt. In that interval, of course, restoration of the hated kind proceeded at headlong speed with Sir Gilbert Scott overhauling cathedral after cathedral and far less competent architects than Scott massacring country churches by the dozen.

To William Morris, Scott was the villain of the piece and it was the news that this architect was about to "restore" Tewkesbury Abbey that sparked his resolve to make concrete proposals for the new Society. We should perhaps pause here to consider how much of a villain Scott really was. The answer is quite simple. When Scott approached the restoration of a church he did so as a professional architect whose duty it was to remove decay, replace missing parts, and render the structure secure. He preserved old work when it was sound, replaced it when it was not. He had immense knowledge and if his restorations were a little harsh they were never ignorant. But restorations they certainly were. In his handling of old churches Scott saw them most decidedly as medieval buildings, which required that they be rendered back so far as possible to their original condition. This is where Morris so profoundly disagreed with him. For what was their "original" condition? At what precise point in time were they perfect and complete? Could one, by stripping off accretions and restoring missing parts, return the building to some ideal condition of completeness? Obviously not. The notion was philosophically unsound. A building was a long-drawn event in time and in that very fact lay its essential value to the present.

This was Morris' belief. He stated it first in a letter to the *Athenaeum*, in whose correspondence columns the subject had already been receiving attention. A month after the publication of the letter the new Society had held its first meeting, Morris himself acting as secretary, and an eloquent statement by him had been issued.

In the course of this statement Morris had to face what was to him a slightly embarrassing problem. If it was necessary to plead for the protection of ancient buildings, it was necessary to give some indication of what, in point of time, made a building ancient. Morris' own loyalty was to the Middle Ages but to plead exclusively for the medieval would have cut the ground from under his own philosophy and authorized that process of stripping ancient buildings which he so much deplored. His solution was slightly evasive:

> If . . . it be asked us to specify what kind or amount of art, style, or other interest in a building, makes it worth protecting, we answer: anything which can be looked on as artistic, picturesque, historical, antique, or substantial: any work, in short, over which educated artistic people would think it worthwhile to argue at all.

"It is for these buildings," he continued, commiting himself rather more deeply, "of all times and all styles, that we plead." All times and all styles! Was the odious seventeenth century, was Sir Christopher Wren, then to be admitted? Under pressure, yes; and the pressure came immediately from Thomas Carlyle. Carlyle was approached to join the new society through William Morgan. He was skeptical of its value, but one thing that caught his interest was the possibility of preventing the destruction of Wren's city churches, then under a grave threat from the Ecclesiastical Commissioners. He accepted membership on the implied condition that the Society interest itself in Wren. Morris was not pleased

This intervention on behalf of Wren somewhat distorted Morris' intentions. His Society was to stop the *restoration* of buildings, not to stop their demolition. "It seems to me," he wrote in a letter intended for Carlyle's eye, "not so much a question whether we are to have old buildings or not, as whether they are to be old or sham old." Actually to prevent the demolition of buildings, and seventeeth-century buildings at that, opened the door to a very different field of endeavor. It was one to which the Society soon became committed and to which it has been committed ever since. What, I wonder, would Morris have felt if he could have known that in 1962, his Society would be in alliance with an attempt to stop the demolition of the Greek Doric portico of Euston Station!

From Pillage to Preservation*

Michael Ragon

The First Conservationists

The papal decrees issued in the sixteenth century (and even in the fourteenth, though without much effect), which forbade the destruction of ruins and introduced fines for stone-cutters who transformed ancient marbles into lime, were probably the first measures designed to protect an architectural heritage of which there was not yet any clear idea.

The concept of "historic monument" apparently emerged only with the Romantic writers and painters of the early nineteenth century, who were, of course, fascinated by the Middle Ages and the Orient. In 1831 Victor Hugo published his novel *Notre Dame de Paris*, which soon became popular. It was both an exaltation of medieval Paris and a lyrical poem to the decaying Notre Dame Cathedral. The novel came as a timely eye-opener, for the previous year, at the request of Guizot, King Louis Philippe had set up the Historic Monuments Commission. Its first inspector general, Ludovic Vitet, saved the Saint Jean de Poitiers baptistry in the nick of time.

In 1833 he was succeeded by Prosper Mérimée, the author of *Carmen*, who in 1837 drew up a list of monuments for scheduling and protection. He had his friend, the architect Viollet-le-Duc, appointed to the conservation department. The latter's work as a "restorer" was immense, for it is to him that we owe the preservation of the cathedrals of Notre Dame de Paris, Chartres and Reims, the basilica of Saint Denis, the church of Vézelay, the ramparts of Carcassonne, and so on.

Paradoxically, the Second Empire, which enabled Mérimée and Viollet-le-Duc to develop an efficient service for the conservation and protection of the architectural heritage (not until 1882 was a

---

*From Council of Europe, *Forum*, 3rd Quarter 1979, p.11.

similar department set up in Great Britain), was at the same time just as destructive as the Rome of the Renaissance popes. Being dependent on transport, the voraciously expanding capitalist world was primarily concerned with building rectilinear roads across all its towns, whether new or old. For the sake of these thoroughfares, city centers were devastated and housing, parks, and urban art sacrificed.

Janus-Faced Capitalism

A new phenomenon was the spread of machinery to all sectors of activity. King William I of Holland converted the country house of the bishop princes of Liège into engineering works. The royal pavilions at Marly, in France, became cotton mills. In Paris, the old aristocratic district of Marais (whose poor inhabitants are now being displaced for the benefit of its restoration) was laid waste in the interests of business and small-scale industry. An example had been set in high places, for Baron Haussmann, the Perfect of Paris, blithely razed medieval Paris for the sake of rectilinear thoroughfares. Very soon the Haussmann methods extended beyond Paris. At Rouen, for instance, in order to build two straight roads—"rue de L'Impératrice" and "rue Impériale" (nowadays called "rue Jeanne d'Arc" and "rue Thiers" respectively)—500 houses, two churches and the most famous site in the city, "rue du Gros Horloge," were destroyed.

Although not so grotesquely, all modern states have shown the same Janus face up to the present day. They have displayed as much thoughtlessness in destroying the masterpieces of the past as scrupulousness in carrying out spectacular schemes for the protection of decaying monuments. They have devastated with one hand and restored with the other—and with the same apparent good faith, especially as it was not the same ministers or officials who were responsible for the two types of operation.

Europe Protects Its Monuments*

Robert R. Garvey

Each European country has its own approach to historic preservation. Each has its own legislation, its own techniques and methods. . . .

Sweden probably has the oldest legislation in the world with regard to ancient monuments. Such

*From U.S. Conference of Mayors, Special Committee on Historic Preservation, *With Heritage So Rich*. New York: Random House, 1966, pp.151–60.

monuments were placed under the protection of the law in 1666. As early as 1630 King Gustavus Adolphus II had created a post as Director General of Antiquities, who was to record and collect runic inscriptions and other ancient stones and objects. Some of these inscriptions and stones are reproduced in Sweden's earliest historical documents, such as Erik Dahlberg's great pictorial work on Sweden from the end of the seventeenth century. Though the law formally protected ruins and various prehistoric antiquities, it was actually for a long time impossible to prevent their destruction. Distances in Sweden were great; and the staff was small and communications had not developed. Attempts were made, with the aid of the parish ministers, to compile lists of the ancient monuments, but these lists were very incomplete.

It was not, however, until the early nineteenth century that interest in monuments for their historical and artistic value became the rule. The movement is said to have started in the papal states in 1819—the year of the pontifical edict of Cardinal Pacca, which was the first example of modern legislation passed for the protection of our cultural heritage. The initiation of the new movement is also marked in that same year by the restoration of the arch of Titus formerly encased in the medieval fortifications of Rome. Most of our modern methods are based on these first two examples of legislative and technical protection.

In France, a Commission des Monuments Historiques was created in 1837. The noted author, Prosper Mérimée, appointed General Inspector of Historic Monuments of France in 1841, particularly applied the two principles of legislative and technical protection and devoted himself to the conservation of ancient French monuments.

Very important was the attitude of the Greek governments after independence from Turkey had been secured. A law of 1839 declared all remnants of antiquity and the middle ages to be national property.

Today, nearly every country has a Monuments Protection Act as part of its national legislation (Great Britain and the Commonwealth, France, the Netherlands, Italy, etc.).

Great Britain and the Commonwealth

England and Wales began their preservation of ancient buildings or sites with the Ancient Monuments Protection Act of 1882. This listed 29 monuments—all earthworks, stone circles and the like—of which the most important was Stonehenge. They were listed in the schedule of the Act, from which the term "scheduling" ancient monuments is derived.

In general, before a national service can impose regulations affecting private property, the property must be "scheduled." This is a legal form of notifying the owner that owing to cultural, historic or artistic values, a given site or building cannot be modified without previous authorization from the competent services.

The Commissioners of the Board of Works, as the Ministry of Public Building and Works was then called, could accept, with the monument owner's agreement, either guardianship or a transfer of ownership, when they felt the monument's preservation was of public interest by reason of its historical, traditional or artistic interest. Thereafter the monument was maintained by the Commissioners.

The Queen was also given power, by Order of the Council, to add similar monuments to the list.

The matter was carried a little further by the Ancient Monuments Protection Act of 1900. It was passed for the purpose of covering medieval buildings as well as prehistoric remains. This Act defined a monument as "any structure, erection or monument of historic or architectural interest" other than an inhabited dwelling house.

This Act led to the first acquisition of buildings other than those considered prehistoric remains: for example, Deal Castle in 1904 and Richmond Castle, Yorkshire, in 1910.

Prior to the Act, the Commissioners already had responsibility for certain buildings, but these were more in the nature of surviving parts of former royal palaces, for which the Board of Works had always been responsible. The Acts of 1882 and 1900 were limited since they applied only to those buildings or sites which the government considered important enough to accept the financial liability for their upkeep. An attempt to list ancient monuments in general was not made and published until 1921 and comprised 139 monuments in England and 70 in Wales. However, the Commissioners of Works were empowered to prepare and publish such a list of monuments (whose preservation was considered to be of national importance), with the advice of the Ancient Monuments Boards for England, Wales and Scotland, under the Act of 1913.

This Act was amended in 1931 by the substitution of the period of three months notice of intention to demolish or alter a scheduled Ancient Monument. After this, confirmation by Parliament was only required where an objection to the order was made. In the other cases, the order remained in force indefinitely. The Act of 1931 also provided that preservation orders be registered in the Local Land Charges Registry.

The Act of 1933 simplified the procedure by enabling the Minister of Works, with the advice of the Ancient Monuments Board, to issue an interim preservation notice which is valid for 21 months. At the end of that time, such notice would expire unless a preservation order was substituted for it.

As a result of the War and the aerial bombardment, public opinion began to be very concerned about the preservation of ancient monuments. A provision was therefore inserted in the Town and Country Planning Act of 1944 enabling the newly-constituted Minister of Town and Country Planning to prepare, for the guidance of the local planning authorities, lists of buildings of special architectural or historic interest. Although the Town and Country Act has twice suffered repeal since 1944, this particular section has been twice reinstated. The former Ministry of Town and Country Planning was renamed the Ministry of Housing and Local Government.

The listing of buildings of special architectural or historic interest is still proceeding and the whole of England and Wales has not yet been investigated. The term "special architecture," which applies to an overwhelming proportion of the buildings listed, has been interpreted to cover almost all surviving buildings dating from earlier than about 1700 and most significant buildings erected between that date and 1830. The interest in Victorian buildings in recent years has caused coverage of a limited number of nineteenth or early twentieth century buildings of definite quality and character.

The buildings selected are divided into two lists and three grades.

Grades I and II are both included in the Statutory List. (The difference between the two grades is the degree of architectural or historical interest.) Grade I buildings are of such interest that demolition is not allowed under any circumstances. Grade II buildings are those of such interest that they ought not be destroyed. When a building is listed in either of these grades, a notice is served to the owners and occupiers informing them that they must give the local planning authority two-months notice of any intention to demolish or to alter the building in any way that would seriously affect its character. This notice must be passed on by the Local Planning Authority to the Minister of Housing and Local Government, who offers observations thereon during the two months. At the end of the two months, the owner is free to pull the building down or alter it unless a building preservation order has been issued.

In the case of alterations, the two-month period enables negotiations to be made between the owner and the local authority, sometimes resulting in a mutually satisfactory method of doing the work. No compensation is payable under the order, but if the owner can prove that the order deprives him of reasonable beneficial use, he can compel the local authority to buy it from him.

Grade III, the Supplementary List, buildings are the more modest ones. They are those which would qualify for inclusion in Grade II, but have depreciated in quality. Grade III imposes no obligation on the owner or occupier. In Scotland, the whole procedure for listing a building would be similar, but separately administered.

The Ministry listing today suffers from the lack of clerical staff to convert the provisional lists into statutory and supplementary lists. However, given a substantial increase in clerical staff, the Ministry listing could be in perfect working order in a few years.

Establishing the official inventory, however, is more difficult. Special consideration is not only given to the individual quality of each building, but to its relation with other buildings. Churches are given special consideration because of record purposes, but legal provisions of the Act do not apply to them as long as they are in ecclesiastical use.

The provisions for listed buildings of the Town and Country Planning Acts are largely negative. They can prevent demolition but do not insure maintenance. The Historic Buildings and Ancient Monuments Act of 1953 was a positive step, however. Always before, the authorities could prevent demolition, but could not insure maintenance. During the years following the War, it became increasingly obvious that without state aid some of the larger country houses would die from the heavy taxation and high costs of maintenance. Under the law of 1953, the Minister of Works was authorized to make grants toward the maintenance or repair of buildings of outstanding interest and their contents—with the condition that there was limited public access to the building. The Act also included monies toward the upkeep of any amenity lands. The Minister was further authorized to acquire them or to assist the local governments in doing so. Historic Buildings Councils for England, Wales and Scotland were set up to advise the Minister in making such grants. The majority of the buildings aided by grants have been inhabited dwelling houses. . . .

Generally speaking, however, the part played by private or voluntary action through nongovernmental agencies in the preservation of historic buildings has equaled, if not exceeded, the efforts of the government. Most important of these nongovernmental bodies is the National Trust for Places of Historic Interest or Natural Beauty, which was founded in 1894. The Trust is now the largest landowner in the country, acquired mostly through gift or testamentary bequest. In its early days, the Trust was chiefly concerned with the protection of unspoiled stretches of coastal scenery, fenland, downs and moors. Domestic architecture, and in particular the great country homes of England up until 1940, seemed in little danger and in no need of protection. However, since 1940, taxation radically altered their position. Owners can no longer maintain their houses. Famous buildings which survived the cannonades of Cromwell's armies, the financial panic of the South Sea Bubble and the changes of the Industrial Revolution, were seemingly rendered to the tax collector overnight.

The National Trust evolved its "Country House Scheme." This scheme enables an owner to give a house of architectural or historic interest to the Trust, together with a capital sum (or a rent-producing estate) to provide an endowment for maintenance. Because the Trust is registered as a charity, neither the property, nor the capital endowment for maintenance, are liable for death duties, and the income derived from the endowment is wholly free of tax. With this income the Trust maintains the fabric of the house, the contents of the state rooms (pictures, tapestries, etc.) and the gardens. At the same time, the Trust arranges for the donor and his heirs to continue living in the house rent-free, provided they allow public access to the gardens and state rooms on an agreed number of days every year. In this way, by a single operation, many houses and gardens are opened for the enjoyment of the public, are preserved intact as homes rather than as museums, and suffer no severance of the family connection which lends many houses much of their fascination and interest.

Another device has established close cooperation between the government and the National Trust. Estate taxes can be paid in part by the transfer of acceptable properties to the Treasury which in turn transfers such properties to the Trust.

A number of other bodies such as County Archaeological Societies also own and administer other, mostly smaller, historic buildings such as the remains of castles or abbeys.

The Society for the Protection of Ancient Buildings, which was founded by William Morris in 1877, is the oldest of the societies formed expressly for the preservation of buildings, as distinct from land. This Society has become known in recent years as the most active body, dealing with private operations, to save ancient buildings from demolition both by public propaganda and by giving advice on the manner of restoration and possible adaptation to other uses. The Georgian Group, founded in 1937, was an offshoot of the Society for the Protection of Ancient Buildings. It concerns itself with buildings dating from the Elizabethan to the early Victorian period and is a champion of these, just as the SPAB is of those of the earlier dates.

Both societies have recently been complemented by the formation of the Victorian Society, which fulfills the same purpose with regard to Victorian and Edwardian buildings. It has made striking progress in reducing public prejudices in the last two years. Other societies active in the field of preservation are the Ancient Monuments Society and the Council of British Archaeology, which acts as the coordinator of all local archaeological societies.

In addition, there are now more than five hundred local preservation or civic societies interested in the preservation of the character, amenities or historic buildings of areas which may vary in size, from a village to a large borough or county. The Civic Trust, founded in 1957, is the coordinator of the local preservation societies and its principal objectives include encouraging high quality in architecture, planning, etc.; preservation of buildings of artistic distinction or historic interest; and the protection of the beauties of the countryside.

France

France was the first country to show marked progress in the preservation of her monuments. Her legislation on the subject today is the most extensive. The present legislation dates back to 1913, with modifications through the years.

Buildings are designated for listing into two categories by the Minister, acting on the advice of the Commission des Monuments Historiques—monuments *classés* and monuments *inscrits*. *Monuments classés* are the whole or part of any building or land of public interest from the point of view of history or art. Buildings or land of lesser importance than the *monuments classés* are considered *monuments inscrits*, nevertheless have sufficient archaeological interest to render their preservation desirable. The restrictions, in either case, include not only the buildings or land designated, but also the field of visibility around them up to 500 yards.

After the owners of the buildings designated are informed of such and the designation is entered in the land charges register, the owner is entitled to a contribution from the state toward the upkeep, if his building has been designated as a *monument classé*. This matter is usually settled by a private negotiation between the owner and the Minister who provides the extent of the listing. The owner of a building can also request a listing as *classé*, after which his request is given due consideration by the Minister and his Commission. If the owner, on the other hand, objects to the classification of his building as a *monument classé*, he may appeal to the Conseil d'État, which decides his case. The owner can also claim compensation for inconveniences caused by this classification of his building.

In the case of *monuments classés*, no alteration, restoration or demolition may take place without the Minister's consent (very similar to Great Britain). When permission is granted, the Minister's own architects supervise the work, and in some instances, the Minister's staff actually performs the work at the state's expense.

The owner's consent to the designation of a *monument inscrit* is not required. The owner is only obligated to give the Minister four-months notice of any proposed modifications of the building. If the Minister disapproves the plan, the owner's only recourse is to get his building approved for designation to *monuments classés*. French legislation further provides that the state can contribute up to 40 percent of the cost of upkeep of *monuments inscrits*.

The law of 1930 set up a Commission des Sites, Perspectives et Paysages in each department together with a Commission Supérieure in Paris. Their purpose is to list national monuments and sites whose preservation is of public interest from the artistic, historic, scientific, legendary or picturesque point of view. Here again, owners of the land are notified of the designation and must give four-months notice of proposed work to be done that would affect the appearance of the monument or site. The owner can appeal to the Commission Supérieure and then the Conseil d'État if he disagrees with the classification by the Commission des Sites. He can also claim compensation if he suffers a loss from the classification.

The foregoing legislation applies only to single buildings, and until 1962, France had no procedure for the protection of ancient towns or villages as a whole. This law, the Malraux Law, as it is often referred to, André Malraux being the minister of Cultural Affairs under DeGaulle, created a Commission National des Secteurs Sauvegardés. It is hoped that in time the law of the Commission will be applied to about 1,000 historic towns and villages, but first pilot projects are being made in 14 places.

The purpose of the law is to substitute a positive approach to the problem for the State's negative actions of past years (protection through prohibitions and regulation). The law is designed to assist owners by a means of a system of loans and subsidies. The method of doing this existed in the urban renewal procedure already in use by the Ministry of Construction.

Before the passage of this 1962 law, urban renewal tended to destroy those areas in a town considered unhealthy, and build in their place modern living quarters. It has, therefore, now been decided that wherever the Ministry of Cultural Affairs considers the conservation of ancient areas in towns or villages to be necessary, the funds allocated to urban renewal for those areas shall be applied instead to the restoration and development of the existing buildings.

Because of this, the technical services of the Ministry of Cultural Affairs work with the urban renewal services of the Ministry of Construction to determine the areas in a town which should be safeguarded. This delimitation is accomplished by taking into consideration the historic, archaeological, artistic and picturesque elements of the areas in question. They, in general, correspond with the original nuclei of the towns, from which expansion developed.

After the "protected area" in any town or village has been designated, the local authority does have the right to object. If the designation is still felt to be justified, a decree by the Conseil d'État will be necessary. Actually, however, the French government attaches special importance of the winning of local agreement in plans for preservation and development, since such programs would be practically inconceivable without the collaboration of the authorities immediately concerned. In fact, the arbitrary classification of an area without local agreement might quite possibly result in a stalemate.

Following the designation, the Ministries concerned have two years to prepare a plan for the area. During these two years, no new buildings may be erected nor can existing ones be eliminated or altered without the approval of the Direction de l'Architecture in the Ministry of Cultural Affairs. The proposed plan when in final form—complete with special architectural directive—will be considered for approval by the Commission Nationale des Secteurs Sauvegardés. After adoption, the plan is carried out under the supervision of the Direction de l'Architecture of the Ministry of Cultural Affairs. The procedure affecting individual monuments classés or inscrits, if they should fall within the proposed plan, will remain unaltered.

The 1962 law contains other unusual provisions, besides that regarding the financing of such restoration. The law also provides for compulsory powers of acquisition and eviction, since the owners of buildings in almost all small towns and villages of France could not afford the cost of extensive restoration. By using the urban renewal funds for replacement of substandard housing for this restoration, the state can provide up to 80 percent of the cost of restoration. If the owners cannot or will not provide the remaining 20 percent, they can be expropriated by agreement, or by compulsion, if necessary.

Buildings acquired in this manner form a collective enterprise undertaken on communal initiative. The owner can resume ownership upon payment of the proportion of cost due from him after the restoration is completed. If this is not agreeable, the building will be sold, again with the right of option to the previous owner. Tenants, in the same manner, can be evicted with six-months notice for the duration of the restoration, and will be found temporary accomodations elsewhere. Upon completion of the work, the tenants may return. In some instances, however, they are unable to pay the increased rent due to the improvements of the building. In this case, permanent alternative accommodations will be found for them. Obviously, this is more difficult in villages than in towns, and in these cases it is a part of the enterprise of the state to aim at creating new kinds of activity which would raise the standard of living of old tenants, enabling them to pay increased rents.

The Netherlands

The first historic monuments procedures were not compiled until 1903. The present law dates from 1961. It provides that upon the advice of the State Commission for the Care of Monuments, the Minister of Education, Arts and Sciences may list sites, buildings or objects not less than 50 years old. The local authorities are the recipients of the lists and following their consideration, they may request of the Minister that certain proposed buildings be omitted from the list. The owners of the buildings make many similar objections, but these are heard by the courts rather than by the Minister himself.

In the Netherlands, too, demolition, alteration or repair of a listed building is subject to permission by the Minister of Education. If the Minister grants approval, restoration is conducted under the supervision of the State Service for the Care of Monuments by private architects obtained by the owner. According to the means of the owner and according to the importance of the building, the owner may obtain a subsidy for the maintenance of the building.

An important special provision of the relatively new law allows the Minister to list town and village views comprising groups of immovable objects, including trees, roads, streets, squares, bridges, canals, waterways and ditches which, in conjunction with one or more of the monuments belonging to the group. constitute a picture of public interest because of the beauty or character of the whole. . . .

Sweden

The Swedish Antiquities Act states that all ancient monuments are protected wherever they are. It is forbidden to destroy them, cover them over, plant on them or do any damage to them by building or in any other way. There is an important regulation to the effect that there shall belong to an ancient monument as large a piece of ground as is necessary for the preservation of the monument with regard to its nature and importance.

The Central Office has the right to carry out all kinds of investigations and excavations. The Office can also give permission for the removal of ancient monuments if they cause the landowner or a tenant hindrance or inconvenience out of all proportion to their importance. To this permission the Office can attach conditions, including the expense of excavation.

The Act also states that a proprietor or a tenant is to make inquiries well in advance as to whether ancient monuments will be affected by the work to be undertaken.

In short, one can say that the Swedish Antiquities Act is based upon the idea which prevailed throughout the eighteenth century, that the landowner has no right to use ancient monuments.

In Sweden, the preservation of monuments of historic interest relates mostly to those buildings owned by the state.

The ruins of old churches, castles and other buildings are regarded as ancient monuments and are consequently protected by the law. Buildings belonging to the state are managed by the National Board of Building and Town Planning and the oldest and most valuable of these buildings are recorded on a special list of historic buildings owned by the state. In the preservation of these buildings, the National Board of Building and Town Planning has to consult the Director General. Approximately the same rules apply to the ancient churches and their fittings.

Legal protection for old and valuable buildings in private possession is not so complete. Under the town planning and building regulations the local authorities have the duty to protect historically valuable buildings *as far as possible* and to see that they are not destroyed or damaged unless it is an imperative necessity. The restrictions in the regulations mean that they can only be applied where there is special interest in the matter and this is unfortunately not very often the case.

A new law for the protection of historic buildings was passed in 1960. Under this law a building in private possession which is particularly noteworthy can be registered by the Director General. Because of restrictive wording of the law, however, only some few buildings can be protected, and above all there is no possibility of legally protecting a street, a square or any other environment containing old buildings, of varying value individually but valuable as a whole.

A privately-owned building that preserves the individuality of the architecture of past times or the memory of a historically important event and that, considering this fact, is to be regarded as particularly remarkable, may by the Director General of the Central Office and of the Museum of National Antiquities be proclaimed a historic building. This may be done after consulation with the Board of Works, the Nordic Museum and Local Authorities. The provisions can extend to the surroundings of the buildings. The owners are notified of the listing and the listing is registered with the land register. Owners must obtain permission before they carry out any alteration to the buildings. If they neglect the maintenance imposed on them, the work can be done by the local authority and the cost reclaimed from the owners. But if the value of the building is reduced by the listing, the owner can claim compensation. If the owner does not wish his building listed, he can appeal to the Minister of Education. . . .

In a world that is so rapidly changing, where countries that have recently acquired independence are developing rapidly, mention should be made of the necessity for international action in the field of preservation and restoration of monuments.

National action cannot give to our cultural heritage as a whole the care it needs to survive the coming centuries. UNESCO has, therefore, undertaken to prepare a series of international instruments, which take the form of either international conventions or recommendations and additionally operates a bureau in its control that encourages and activates programs designed to assist in the international aspects of the preservation of monuments.

Conventions are submitted to member states for ratification while recommendations are used as a basis for draft national legislation and other national programs.

Thus an international convention of the "Protection of Cultural Property in the Case of Armed Conflict" was drawn up during the course of an intergovernmental conference convened in the Hague in 1954 (fifty countries are now parties to the convention), and two recommendations have been adopted by the General Conference and circulated among the member states of UNESCO. They are "The Recommendation on International Principles Applicable to Archaeological Excavation" and the "Recommendation Concerning the Safeguarding of the Beauty and Character of Landscapes." Another recommendation entitled "The Preservation of Cultural Property Endangered by Public or Private Works" is in preparation.

In 1958, UNESCO created the International Center for the Study of the Preservation and Restoration of Cultural Property to encourage international cooperation in activities in the conservation of the cultural patrimony of all nations—the great treasures common to humanity. Since its creation the Rome Center has operated in close harmony with UNESCO, ICOM, and other institutes and specialized groups in Italy and elsewhere. The Center operates a program consisting of expert consultation, publications, education and training.

The International Council on Monuments and Sites (ICOMOS) was established in 1965 by action of representatives of 26 nations at the request and suggestion of UNESCO. The purposes of ICOMOS are:

1. To promote the study and to encourage the preservation and development of monuments and sites.

2. To arouse and develop the interest of the authorities and the general public of all countries with respect to their monuments, sites and cultural heritage in general.

3. To constitute the international organization representing the administrative departments, institutions and persons interested in the preservation and study of monuments and sites. . . .

United States participation in ICOMOS has taken the form of a National Committee composed of 12 active members representing the principal organizations concerned with the preservation of historic properties in the United States.

United States

Penn Central Transportation Co. v. City of New York *

"Over one half of the buildings listed in the Historic American Building Survey, begun by the Federal Government in 1933, have been destroyed. . . . **

Lost America From the Atlantic to the Mississippi †

Constance M. Greiff

When the first European settlers set foot on the American continent, they began to destroy as surely as they began to build a new civilization. In the act of building, they eroded the wilderness. And in their quest for more land, they first disrupted and then destroyed the man-made traces of the aboriginal civilizations that preceded theirs. By the late seventeenth century the Indian villages of coastal Virginia and the Carolinas had, like most of their inhabitants, been eradicated.

The early arrivals at each new American frontier wasted no more thought on the abandonment or destruction of their own first shelters than they did on those of the Indians. There was no nostalgia, no desire to preserve the crude huts of Plimoth Plantation or the rude caves hacked out of the banks of the Delaware at Philadelphia. They were deserted, with no regrets, as soon as the settlers could erect more substantial housing. Some of the one- and two-room houses built along the eastern seaboard and in the Mississippi Valley during the seventeenth and early eighteenth centuries were more enduring. Their survival, occasionally intact, more often integrated into or as an adjunct to a later structure, generally depended on whether they were well-built and continued to be useful as shelter.

The design of buildings is unique among the arts. Art historians and critics may elevate architecture to equal status in the trilogy of the artistic pantheon. The standard fine arts curriculum may read—as if in one breath—painting, sculpture and architecture. But unlike a picture or a statue, a building must continue to justify itself on more than artistic grounds—especially so in America. It must continue, in some way, to be functional if it is to survive. And only recently have Americans begun to accept the notion that function might include the provision of visual delight, variety in the townscape, or a sense of place and identity. The basic criterion for the choice between survival and destruction has been—as it often continues to be—economic. A building has to earn its keep.

---

*438 U.S. 104, 108, n. 2(1978).

**For a different estimate on the extent of destruction, see page 40 *infra*.

†Princeton, N.J.: Pyne Press, 1971, pp. 1-7.

That simple dictum has governed the attitude of most Americans toward architecture. In any contest between Mammon and Clio and whatever gods or saints watch over architects and their creations, Mammon has usually won hands down. Consider the case of Ben Franklin and his fine Philadelphia townhouse, erected in 1765 on a mid-block lot extending from Market to Chestnut Streets. Franklin sowed the seeds of the building's destruction by having it placed at the end of a cul-de-sac entered from Market Street, reserving the valuable lots on either side of the entrance for commercial development. After his death in 1790, the house was occasionally occupied by descendants. More often it was rented, at first to M. LaCheva Frieve, the Portuguese ambassador, and then, with ever-declining status, as a school, boarding house and coffee house. The address by the second decade of the nineteenth century was, obviously, no longer a fashionable one for a residence. Nevertheless, the property was valuable since it lay near the heart of the city's financial and commercial district. Some of the busiest docks in what was still the country's major port were less than four blocks away. The country's most important financial institution, Stephen Girard's Bank, was even closer. The one obstacle to more lucrative development of the Franklin land was the house. Accordingly, in 1812, Franklin's heirs had the building demolished, continued the alley through from Market to Chestnut, and lined it with a double row of small, and presumably profitable, brick tenements. In turn, these were superseded by taller buildings in the second half of the nineteenth century.

The destruction of older buildings, in successive layers, in order to build anew on the same site, has certainly not been confined to Philadelphia. Major areas at the core of almost every American city rise today on the buried remnants of their past. They have been, to use a term currently fashionable in another context, recycled, not once, but many times. If Paul Revere, or rather his ghost, had returned to Boston in 1850, he would have had almost as much trouble recognizing parts of his city as he would today. The State Street that he carefully delineated as the background for his engraving of the Boston Massacre had itself been massacred. The decorous and dormered Georgian buildings of colonial Boston were gone. Their place had been taken by monumental Grecian temples to commerce, of which the most striking, the Merchant's Exchange and the Suffolk Bank, were the work of the greatest of Boston's Greek Revival architects, Isaiah Rogers. By the third quarter of the nineteenth century, these, in turn, were coming down, to be replaced by larger and more exuberant Victorian buildings. And, now, the process continues as those give way to the steel and glass constructions of a new classicism. Through it all the one constant reference point has been the Old State House, built in 1713 as a replacement for the Town House of 1657 that burned in 1711.

When Ben Franklin's house was razed in 1812, no voice was heard deploring the loss of the home of the father of half the cultural institutions of Philadelphia and the godfather of the Revolution. The idea of preserving the home of such a man as a public shrine simply did not occur to anyone. With equal equanimity, in the same year, Philadelphians witnessed the demolition of the original wings of Independence Hall, and the substitution of a pair of fireproof buildings designed by Robert Mills. In 1816, however, indignant protest was expressed at a loss of one part of this historic hall. It was occasioned by the stripping of the original decoration from the rooms in which the Declaration of Independence had been signed and the Constitutional Convention had sat. The project was evidently a colossal boondoggle, undertaken, according to the *Democratic Press*, to project a job for one of the county commissioner's relatives. John Read, Jr., a member of the city's Select Council, expressed the distress and outrage of himself and a number of his fellow citizens:

It would have particularly gratified us, to have perceived entire, every ornament & decoration, which had been placed in the building, by a correct architectural taste, particularly in that department of it, in which the declaration of independence, & the federal Constitution, were devised and completed. But we were too late to stop the manation, which had begun and progressed, before our knowledge of it, and when we sought to recover the pannelling and ornaments, to replace them, we were told that they were defaced and sold."

The sense of loss was not confined to the inhabitants of Philadelphia. In 1819 Col. John Trumbull, the painter, visited the building and noted, "the alterations which have been made in the Room where Congress actually sat on the famous 4th of July are such that the picture [his "The Declaration of Independence"] cannot be hung in it. . . . The spirit of innovation [had] laid unhallowed hands upon it, and violated its venerable walls by modern improvement, as it is called."

Independence Hall was, of course, a singular building. Dismay at the violence done it did not extend to any desire to protect other American architectural monuments. It was not until midcentury that the preservation, or rather salvation, of old buildings began to merit serious consideration. By then, at the height of the romantic era, the nation's own past was beginning to exert a strong attaction. Already, in the 1820's, Washington Irving and James Fenimore Cooper had published highly romanticized versions of regional history and folklore. Serious attention was also being paid to the collection and preservation of the raw material of the country's history. Citizens' groups in state after state founded historical societies. Massachusetts, in 1791, and New York, in 1804, were a precocious vanguard of the movement. It was probably the visit of the Marquis de Lafayette, in 1824, with its evocative associations with the Revolution, that gave impetus to the founding of state historical societies in Pennsylvania (1824), Connecticut (1825) and Michigan (1826). The roster continued to grow through the first half of the century, joined by Virginia (1831), Georgia (1839), Maryland (1844), New Jersey (1845), and others.

Concomitant with the effort to assemble the documentary record, there arose some interest, however flickering and feeble, in the sites at which the drama of American history had been played out. Even in the early years of the nineteenth century the loss of a few key buildings was simply not acceptable. When Princeton's Nassau Hall burned in 1802, alumni and friends of the college promptly raised the money to rebuild it. Congress, returning to the hulk of the Capitol after the War of 1812, briefly debated starting afresh on the flats near the Potomac. Fortunately it was decided to rebuild on the hill that the city's designer, Pierre L'Enfant, had likened to "a pedestal waiting for a monument." Philadelphians, rallying from their shock over the destruction of the interior of the Assembly Room of Independence Hall, commissioned John Haviland to undertake the first of a series of restorations in 1824.

So there were scattered votes against the abandonment of important buildings that had been damaged. But there were no advocates for buildings that were simply either old or beautiful.

The first organized attempt at saving a building came, appropriately enough, from Massachusetts, which, as one of the oldest and most thickly settled areas on the eastern seaboard, was following one of the basic and seemingly inexorable laws governing the fate of architecture. Those areas that have the most to lose, lose the most. Their losses are perhaps less tragic than those of an area like, for example, Memphis, Tennessee, which having had few buildings to begin with, have accomplished the destruction of the little they had.

Massachusetts' pioneering preservation campaign was waged in 1847. A group of private citizens in Deerfield attempted to preserve and move to another site the oldest house in town, the last remaining building, which had even survived an Indian attack on the village in 1704. A broadside was printed, letters were written to the local paper, and solicitations were made to raise the sum of $400. Like New England's most famous subsequent early venture in preservation, the 1863 campaign to save the Hancock House in Boston, and like countless succeeding efforts, the Deerfield project was a failure. Not enough people cared; certainly not enough were willing to provide funds to prevent the destruction of an old landmark.

Some few tentative steps toward preservation were more successful. In 1850, New York State acquired, almost by accident, Washington's Headquarters, the Jonathan Hasbrouck House, at Newburgh. In 1856 the State of Tennessee purchased Andrew Jackson's home, the Hermitage.

The preservation of the old houses along the main street of Old Deerfield, Massachusetts is the result of private benefactions. Most of the earliest preservation work in the U.S. was done on this basis. *Courtesy of Historic Deerfield, Inc., Deerfield, Massachusetts.*

And in 1853, the first successful private nationwide preservation organization was formed. This was the Mount Vernon Ladies' Association, dedicated to the single-minded purpose of preserving and restoring the home of the Father of His Country.

The trumpet-call might be sounded for a few singular buildings. In general, the nineteenth-century response to the loss of the country's visual heritage was at most mildly elegiac. Change, newness, in a word "progress," were accepted as synonyms for "better." A New Year's greeting issued to the customers of the Philadelphia *Public Ledger* in 1860 is typical. Oddly enough, the building shown, Latrobe's waterworks, must have been deeply impressed in the city's consciousness. When the greeting was issued it had been gone from the Philadelphia townscape for over 30 years. With a bow to the past, but faith in the future, the *Ledger* welcomed 1860:

> Yon Marble Hall—Irreverently Styled
> "The Pepperbox"—Was, Once, Our City's Pride;
> Around It, Lofty Trees and Verdure Smiled—
> Now Swept Away By Time's Unsparing Tide.
> Alas! 'Tis Sad—With Every Fading Year—
> To See Our "Ancient Landmarks" Disappear!
>
> Increase of Population On the Banks
> Of Schuylkill Must The Water Soon Pollute;
> Then Fairmount's Buildings, Mounds and
>   Rough-hewn Tanks
> Will Pass Away, Its Waterwheels Be Mute.
> Thus—Though Improvements Mark Each Changing Year,
> 'Tis Sad to See Old "Landmarks" Disappear.

Plus ça change, plus c'est la meme chose. The same sentiments, couched in less flowery terms perhaps, the same pious obeisance to familiar landmarks, open space, pure water can still be heard when the planning boards, the chambers of commerce and the booster clubs get together to discuss future growth. And the kicker's apt to be the same too. The amenities of the townscape are considered expendable in the name of "improvement"—for which read short-term economic gain.

For that matter, few preservationists in the late nineteenth century and the early years of the twentieth century exhibited any interest in the quality of either the natural or the man-made environment. Patriotic societies, family associations, occasionally government agencies, focused on single buildings, pursuing aims more patriotic than aesthetic. They—and their successors who still constitute a strong force in the preservation movement—were ruled by what might be termed the George-Washington-Slept-Here syndrome. The buildings in which they were interested were those in which great men had lived or great events, preferably of the Revolutionary period, had transpired. These were to be preserved, and perhaps restored, so that the visitor to such sacred precincts might be infused, by some mysterious process of osmosis, with the patriotic virtues of former inhabitants.

No one would deny that these pioneering preservationists, often in the face of enormous obstacles, saved an important body of American buildings. But because their aims were narrow, and because nobody else had any aims at all, whole facets of the American cultural heritage began to disappear. By the end of the nineteenth century the urban Dutch buildings of New York City and Albany had vanished, along with most traces of Swedish colonization along the lower Delaware. Other reminders of the multiplicity of national strains woven into the fabric of American life were also being obliterated or severely decimated—the remnants of French settlements along the Mississippi, of the Spanish along the Gulf coast, the unique farmhouses developed by the Dutch on Long Island and in northern New Jersey.

If buildings other than those associated with heroic figures were not protected, it was probably because they simply weren't old enough to capture the public fancy. The appreciation of architecture operates under a grandfather clause, or perhaps it might be more accurate to say a great-grandfather clause. Aesthetically, the generation gap has been with us for a long time. We tend to denigrate the tastes of the generation or two immediately preceding our own at the same time that we are attracted to the life style of their predecessors, first, perhaps, as merely amusingly quaint, and then as the object of serious study and admiration. So Americans of the first half of the nineteenth century looked far beyond their own beginnings to the remote past of ancient Greece and Rome, of medieval Europe, even of Egypt for their models. The buildings of their own past were viewed with contempt as examples of crudity and bad taste. The mid-century attitude toward buildings of the eighteenth century, in other words, was not very different from that of Lewis Mumford in 1924, when he called those of the 1880's "disreputable." They were objects to be discarded, or, if not, in an era which was more conserving of materials and less bound by the cost of labor than ours, lost by "modernization" into a totally new form. Calvert Vaux' project, published in *Harper's New Monthly Magazine* in 1855, was only one of many contemporary schemes for transforming what he characterized as an "ugly . . . old-fashioned homestead" which could not "be contemplated by the rising generation with anything like satisfaction" into a country house which was at least tolerable according to mid-Victorian standards of taste and suitability.

The Philadelphia Centennial Exposition of 1876 introduced the average American to more than the wonders of the art of such far-off places as Japan or Turkey, or Norman Shaw's version of Tudor England. The celebration of a hundred years of national life embraced, however tentatively, the arts and artifacts of the colonial period as well as its political and military history. The Connecticut pavilion, according to one contemporary, was "intended to represent a colonial homestead of a generation ago," and displayed some examples of early Connecticut furniture. Even more fascinating to visitors was "The New England Farmer's Home," complete with hostesses in period costume, and furnished with authentic pieces.

The sparks ignited by the Centennial flickered fitfully sometimes, but never quite went out. The summer of 1877 was the occasion of a by now almost mythical walking tour in the course of which colonial buildings along New England's coast were sketched by a group of young architects, two of them on holiday from the drafting-room of Henry Hobson Richardson, the Messrs. McKim and White. In 1879 the American Institute of Architects appointed a committee to study colonial building practices. Over the next several decades the interest in colonial, Georgian and Federal buildings grew so intense that it sometimes posed a threat to the objects of its own admiration. No museum would become party to the vandalism involved in cutting a painting into six separate pieces so that the component parts might be viewed by a wider audience. But no such scruples afflicted some of the early devotees of the work of America's colonial architects and builders. Not only buildings scheduled for demolition, but those left standing, were stripped of their paneling and other decorative detail. Houses such as Philadelphia's Stedman-Powel House (now beautifully restored on the exterior) and Stamper-Blackwell House were raped of their interiors, the former for installation in the Philadelphia Museum of Art and the American Wing of the Metropolitan Museum, the latter for Winterthur. It was a practice all too common among museum and private collectors in the 1920's and 30's.

If an excess of zeal was sometimes more damaging to early buildings than benign neglect, the burgeoning interest in the colonial period brought benefits as well. Its architecture and decorative arts became the object of serious study. One symbol of that strong interest was John D. Rockefeller, Jr.'s decision, in 1926, to restore a large area of a colonial village. In so doing, he and his associates were confronted with the fruits of a century and a half of neglect of the country's architectural heritage.

Even in an area as relatively undisturbed as Williamsburg, the sleepy, abandoned capital of colonial Virginia, buildings had gone whose loss, now that they were appreciated, was felt too keenly to be borne. The decision was made to rebuild.

Yet such a loss can never really be recouped. A reconstruction is not a fully adequate substitute for the original. It's as if the Louvre, having failed to recover the stolen Mona Lisa, had hung a good silkscreen print in its place and told the public that it was just as good as the real thing. At Williamsburg, where approximately half the buildings are reconstructions, one is constantly confronted with shadow and substance and the distinctions become blurred. There is, for example, the niggling question of what Capitol is it? Not, actually, the one in which Patrick Henry made his impassioned speech or George Mason introduced Virginia's Declaration of Rights. It is, rather, an earlier building, gutted by fire in 1747. The second Capitol, built on the foundations of the first, but in quite different form, had also been gone for almost a century when the reconstruction began. The earlier version was chosen, partly because it was more distinguished architecturally, partly because better documentary evidence of its original appearance was available.

Even in so ambitious a program as Williamsburg's, the aims remained narrow. Besides preserving the "beauty and charm of the old buildings and gardens of the the city," Mr. Rockefeller saw Williamsburg as valuable for "the lesson it teaches of the patriotism, high purpose, and unselfish devotion of our forefathers to the common good." What Williamsburg presents is upper-class WASP history. The streets are clean; the slave cabins and outhouses have been suppressed. It is history without depth and without continuity. The clock has stopped and the past has been enshrined behind glass. And having put history in its niche, one can admire it and forget it. There is no spillover of history or art as a living presence able to enrich our daily lives. At the same time that Rockefeller money from one hand was saving Williamsburg, funds from the other were accomplishing the work of destruction. In the 1930's the Standard Oil Company erected a gas station on the site of Charleston's Gabriel Manigault House. The station bears a plaque which reads: "In order to preserve the architectural traditions of Charleston, the brickwork and woodwork of the demolished Gabriel Manigault House 1800 AD were used in this station."

This is not to single out Williamsburg and/or the Rockefellers for censure. Certainly Williamsburg and the museum villages that followed it have performed two services that cannot be too highly valued. Their research departments have become centers for the collection and dissemination of knowledge on the identification, care, and restoration of the materials of the past. And by presenting that past in tangible and dramatic form, they have aroused admiration for at least certain aspects of the nation's heritage. What Williamsburg does exemplify and epitomize are American attitudes toward that heritage. By the end of World War II, after nearly a century of preservation effort, those attitudes were well-established. The remaining great public monuments and stately mansions of the eighteenth and early nineteenth century were virtually exempt from destruction. The rest was fair game.

The situation began to assume crisis proportions in the post-war years. In the 1930's, the Historic American Buildings Survey had been established to record the country's architectural patrimony. By the early 1960's, some 20 to 25 percent of the buildings listed had been destroyed or seriously altered. And the HABS had concentrated on buildings prior to 1830. Nobody was counting the numerically far greater losses among late nineteenth and early twentieth-century buildings.

The acceleration of loss was, in large part, an unintentional byblow of Federal programs planned, ironically, to improve the country's quality of life. After a decade of depression and half a decade of war there was a pent-up need for roads, schools, housing, factories; in short, for construction of all

The present Governor's palace at Williamsburg is the result of a painstaking restoration, having been rebuilt on the original foundations after a fire. *Courtesy of the National Trust.*

kinds. A series of bills provided both public funds and aid to private industry in fulfilling those needs. There were, in sum, not millions, but billions for new construction and destruction to make way for it, and only pennies for the protection of the man-made environment.

Landmark Preservation*

John S. Pyke, Jr.

> Today there is a great awakening of interest in history and things historical. The American public is becoming proud of its heritage. Whether it is the fact that a period of prosperity is giving us more leisure time to pursue cultural interests, or whether we are simply coming of age as a nation, is hard to say. Whatever the case may be, the fact is that historical sites, old buildings, forts, covered bridges, and other visible manifestations of our past way of life are enjoying an unprecedented degree of attention from the public at large.
> —Alan Burnham in *New York Landmarks* (1963).

The awakening of interest in things historical should not obscure the fact that a lively concern for conserving our historical and architectural heritage has existed for the last 100 years. As the number of buildings surviving from an earlier period has diminished, organized efforts to preserve historically and architecturally valuable buildings have naturally increased.

Beginnings

The father of our country may also be said to be, indirectly, the father of the landmarks preservation movement. One of the movement's earliest successes in the United States came in 1850 when New York State acquired Hasbrouck House in Newburgh as a public museum at a cost of $8,391.02. Hasbrouck House had been General Washington's headquarters during the last two years of the Revolutionary War; it was there that General Washington, while awaiting word that the British had capitulated, spurned the suggestion that he become the new nation's "King."

In 1853 the Mount Vernon Ladies Association, the first preservation organization in this country, was founded to purchase and maintain George Washington's home on the Potomac. With privately raised funds the Association acquired title to the property in 1858 after both the federal government and the Commonwealth of Virginia had refused to purchase it. For more than a hundred years the Mount Vernon Ladies Association has continued to maintain the landmark and its success has stimulated countless other preservations throughout the country.

---

*New York: Citizens Union Research Foundation, 2nd ed., 1972, pp. 7-8.

The urban wing of the preservation movement got its start with the campaign to save the Old South Meeting House in Boston. While officially a Congregational Church, the Old South Meeting House also had functioned as a public meeting house since its construction in 1729. It was the site of many historically important gatherings, including the boisterous political meetings leading up to the Boston Tea Party in 1773.

After the Church's congregation deserted the structure in 1875, it was sold at auction for commercial purposes following unsuccessful attempts to sell it to the Massachusetts Historical Society. Demolition workers were actually on the premises when a postponement of the demolition work was obtained. A public meeting to discuss the building's future was hurriedly called and those who attended were urged to preserve this visible reminder of Boston's proud past. Committees quickly formed to purchase the building and the site. Through contributions, both large and small, and a mortgage taken by a local insurance company, a dramatic rescue was effected. Over the years the mortgage was paid off by holding a variety of events in the building, including lectures, fairs and political and social functions.

The preservation movement took its most spectacular turn in 1926 when John D. Rockefeller, Jr., decided to undertake the complete restoration and reconstruction of an entire town, Colonial Williamsburg. By 1969 almost 80 million dollars had been spent to restore more than 80 major structures and reconstruct 45 others. The work is still proceeding.

By recreating a town at the finest period of its history and operating it solely as a museum, the Williamsburg preservationists popularized an approach to landmarks preservation that has captured the public imagination.

In 1929 Henry Ford embraced the Williamsburg approach of creating an open-air museum by establishing Greenfield Village, a make-believe town formed by moving over 100 reconstructed and restored seventeenth, eighteenth and nineteenth century buildings to a site in Dearborn, Michigan. Other village restoration and reconstruction projects include Old Sturbridge Village in Massachusetts, Schoenbrunn Village in Ohio and New Salem State Park in Illinois.

Many cities have recognized the opportunity for applying the broad vision of the planners of village restoration projects to the preservation of urban historic districts. The City of Providence, Rhode Island, made a major contribution to the methodology for planning the preservation and renewal of areas of historic architecture with the publication of its College Hill Demonstration Study in 1959. Funded in part by the federal government, the College Hill Study provided a useful example of how public and private planning might be coordinated.

Private Philanthropy and Preservation *

Charles B. Hosmer, Jr.

Pattern of Successful Preservations Work Before 1926 **

Number of Buildings	Patterns
45	Bought as headquarters by historical or patriotic group
29	Saved as museum by private group organized for that specific purpose

Providence was one of the first American cities to provide for the rehabilitation and protection of its historic areas. *Courtesy of the National Trust.*

Number of Buildings	Patterns	(Continued)

21....... Given to local group by private individual
16....... Restored and opened by private individual
13....... Leased to private group as custodian by city or state
13....... Restored by public campaign, though church-owned
10....... Bought by private organization, opened for nonmuseum use
9....... Saved by public campaign, then administered by city or state
9....... Bought as historic site by city
9....... Bought with private donations by regional preservation group
8....... Bought as historic site by state
7....... Given to regional preservation group by private individual
6....... Bought by city as part of park (not as historic site)
6....... Given to city by private individual
5....... Saved by family association as museum
4....... Restored by private campaign, though state-owned
4....... Bought by college or academy (not always for preservation)
4....... Saved by several organizations (helping one small historical group)
4....... Given to state by private individual
4....... Bought by private individual as part of biographical chain of houses
3....... Bought by federal government
3....... Bought by museum, sometimes just for woodwork
3....... Given to local group by family
2....... Bought by county government
2....... Bought from state by city, later restored
2....... Bought and exhibited by corporation
2....... Given to college by private individual
2....... Saved in fragments by private individual
1....... Transferred from city to state administration
1....... Given to nation by private group
1....... Endowed by private individual
1....... House abroad endowed by private group
1....... Own birthplace restored by private individual

*From National Trust for Historic Preservation, *Historic Preservation Today.* Charlottesville, Va: University Press of Virginia, 1966, pp. 157-58.

**The analysis of patterns is based upon work done for my dissertation, "Old Houses in America: The Preservation Movement to 1926" (Columbia University, 1961). The geographical distribution is also drawn from that source, from a number of published works such as Dorothy and Richard Pratt's *A Guide to Early American Homes* (both *North* and *South*), and from the membership list of the National Trust for Historic Preservation.

Virginia Historic Districts Study*

Alice M. Bowsher, William T. Frazier, Jerome R. Saroff

Profile of Preservation Group Leadership

A profile of the leadership of preservation groups in Virginia offers a useful perspective on the 13 groups. Such a profile was developed from a section in the questionnaire relating to the personal backgrounds of the officers.

The profile shows that the occupation of the principal officers in these groups (not just the respondents) is likely to be one of the jobs traditionally classified "white-collar-professional" (doctor, banker, teacher, etc.). However, a large number of the officers were housewives (32 percent) or were retired (21 percent). It is noteworthy that none of the officers was from the occupations traditionally classified "blue collar."

Of the preservation group officers and two staff interviewed, nine were male and four female. All were white. The majority were between 40 and 60, had graduate degrees, and were in upper income brackets of $20,000 or more.

The profile indicates that leadership in local private preservation efforts in Virginia comes from upper-middle-class white citizens with the wealth, education, and cultural background to devote time to historic preservation activities.**

Preservation in the West†

John L. Frisbee

The Historic Preservation Movement in the Western United States

The preservation movement is not new to the Western states but it has not developed as rapidly there as it has in the Eastern states. As early as the 1880's, serious efforts had been made to preserve

---

*1975, pp. 43-44
**In light of this profile, it is interesting that one preservation group has recently conducted a drive specifically to broaden its membership base, with the intention of increasing its effectiveness in the community.

†Washington, D. C.: National Trust for Historic Preservation, 1972, pp. 2, 22-24.

the Governor's Palace in Santa Fe. But as Charles Hosmer notes in *Presence of the Past* (New York: G.P. Putnam's Sons, 1965), preservation in the West in early years was spotty. It was confined essentially to California, specifically southern California with its Spanish missions. The contributions of Pearl Chase in Santa Barbara, beginning in the 1920's and continuing through today, should be recognized. If Charleston and New Orleans are considered the birthplaces of area preservation in the South and East, then Santa Barbara deserves similar designation as the birthplace of preservation in the West.

People require time to develop proper perspective on their heritage. Perhaps it is also necessary for them to suffer tragic losses of significant landmarks before they become aware that the need to preserve is directly related to increased land use and technological development. The period of greatest technological and population growth in the West has been in the years subsequent to World War II. The increasing emphasis upon historic preservation parallels that development.

Although remnants of prehistoric cultures and the periods of early Spanish and Russian colonization do exist, the greatest proportion of surviving tangible links with man-made culture in the West dates from the latter half of the 19th century. It is only in recent years that houses, shops and utilitarian structures of the late 19th and early 20th centuries have been recognized as having historical and architectural value. Their existence is increasingly endangered by the demands of intensified land use. Groups and individuals throughout the Western states are awakening to the critical need to preserve what remains of their architectural heritage.

Over the years, the emphasis in the Eastern preservation movement has shifted from the house museum and the outdoor museum village to the broader approaches of district and area preservation with the related legal and economic considerations.

In the West, a variety of approaches has been carried out concurrently, with perhaps less direction than in the East. There are tendencies to consider the preservation of old structures primarily in terms of historical museum use and to reconstruct or fabricate before retaining existing structures. These tendencies pervade the broader approaches of area preservation and the use of historic properties for general community benefit.

Other problems, while not wholly limited to the West, are essentially regional in nature. Perhaps because the main thrust of the preservation movement has been in the East, the National Trust has not had extensive involvement in problems peculiar to the West. Whereas the preservation movement in the East concentrated its efforts on buildings and structures, many more preservation concerns in the West are site- and object-oriented. The National Trust must expand its services to assist in this type of preservation work. Certainly aboriginal art, artifacts and archaeological sites explain much about early cultures in the American West. Equally significant are natural landmarks, historic trails and early settlements of the white man in the West. Efforts must be made to interpret, develop and protect these sites and objects.

Ghost Towns. The preservation of ghost towns is one distinctive regional problem in the West. Several surviving ghost towns have been incorporated into state and national park systems. The California Department of Parks and Recreation has assumed control of the ghost town of Columbia. The Montana Department of Fish and Game is purchasing and restoring portions of Bannack, where the state's first gold strike was made. The Nevada State Parks Department is purchasing and plans to restore the ghost town of Berlin. The Arizona State Parks Department has taken a similar approach to the early 20th-century copper-mining town of Jerome. The National Park Service is planning the acquisition and restoration of portions of the historic gold rush town of Skagway, Alaska.

In many instances, establishing an outdoor village museum is a suitable approach to the preservation of a ghost town, especially when the town is accessible to the general public, is of sufficient historical merit and has a substantial number of surviving buildings. A number of ghost towns have not been completely abandoned. Many enterprising businessmen have capitalized on the romantic

Shakespeare, New Mexico, just south of Lordsburg (1947). National Park Service, Dept. of the Interior, Western Archaeological Center, Tucson. *Ghost Towns in New Mexico.*

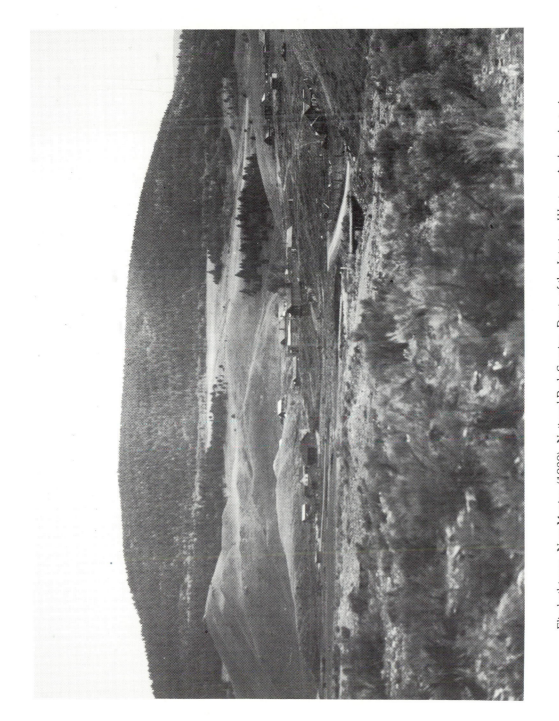

Elizabethtown, New Mexico (1939). National Park Service, Dept. of the Interior, Western Archaeological Center, Tucson. *Ghost Towns in New Mexico.*

history of Western gold and silver-mining communities. Several towns in the Motherlode Country of California; Virginia City, Nevada; and Virginia City, Montana, are today largely dependent upon tourism. Jacksonville, Oregon, a dying town a decade ago, now owes its livelihood to the 150,000-200,000 tourists who visit the town each year.

There are inherent problems in the outdoor museum village approach to preservation. It can lead to excessive commercialism and consequent erosion of the historic environment. Virginia City, Nevada, is a classic example of the overcommercialization of a historic town. Little control has been exercised over signs, and restoration has not been extensive. Property owners and tenants along the town's main street have done little more than paint the facades of their buildings and hang out signs. Many of the structures are in substantial need of repair and restoration. However, the gold and silver towns of the West were noisy, bustling communities with garish signs. Every shopkeeper was out to take the miners for their money. In some respects, then, Virginia City may be more evocative of the 19th-century West than an outdoor village museum would be. The fine line between appropriate atmosphere and tasteless commercialism is not always an easy one to draw.

In any case, most ghost towns do not meet the necessary criteria for being made into outdoor village museums. The costs involved also limit the number of ghost towns that can be developed in this manner. However, there are a large number of ghost towns well worth preserving. Other means must be found to protect and restore them.

Where the setting and climate are conducive, individuals may buy properties in ghost towns and use them as summer and weekend homes. This has been done in Jarbridge, Nevada, and Silver City, Idaho. Where other similar towns survive, this may well be the best approach to preservation. To ensure that the popularity of this approach will not lead to environmental erosion, individuals should be encouraged and assisted by preservation professionals in executing sympathetic restorations.

One problem associated with the restoration of houses in ghost towns for personal use is the fact that, in a number of cases, ghost towns are located on federal land. An individual can purchase a structure but not the land on which it is located. There may also be a problem in obtaining clear title to land, because of numerous title transfers. A person might have legal title to a piece of property while another holds title to the mineral rights. This can be a deterrent to those who might otherwise be interested in purchasing and restoring a historic property for personal use.

As a last resort, preservationists can attempt to simply stabilize the best surviving buildings in a ghost town and leave them unused. This is, of course, a temporary solution. Its success is largely dependent on whether or not the site is policed both during and after stabilization.

Isolation has been a key reason for the survival of ghost towns. However, jeeps, trail bikes, snowmobiles and helicopters preclude the isolation of most sites today. Often, important historic properties are located great distances from population centers. Consequently, it is difficult to police them and they become targets for vandals and souvenir hunters. Many ghost towns have been destroyed by such individuals. Isolated structures often must be moved for their own protection. While this may affect their integrity, it is often necessary for their survival.

Through the National Historic Preservation Fund, the National Trust has provided some assistance in preserving part of a historic ghost town. In June 1972, the National Trust granted a loan to the Western Montana Ghost Town Preservation Society to purchase a miners' fraternity hall and adjacent saloon in Elkhorn, Montana. The National Trust could further assist such preservation efforts by developing guidelines for the preservation and use of sites and structures in isolated environments.

Archaeological Sites. The questionnaire response of the Museum of Northern Arizona in Flagstaff sums up some of the problems of archaeologists in the West. The museum noted that the greatest threat to archaeological sites comes from souvenir hunters and vandals. By removing objects from such sites, these individuals are destroying the integrity of the sites and eliminating the possibility of thorough professional investigation. The museum stated that the National Trust could be extremely helpful in educating both adults and children about the diversity of the nation's cultural history and the importance of its archaeological sites.

Indian rock art presents another significant archaeological problem. Techniques must be devised to conserve petroglyphs in their original locations wherever possible. Petroglyphs are often defaced by target shooters and amateur artists. At present, they can be protected only by moving them to museums or prohibiting the public from getting near them. Neither approach is an adequate solution.

The National Trust has recommended to appropriate groups in Utah, Arizona and New Mexico that these three states join with Colorado and submit to the Four Corners Commission (a state-federal economic development commission operating in those four states), a proposal calling for a thorough study of means to protect the petroglyphs. Before any significant programs can be developed, basic research of protection and restoration methods must be accomplished.

Promoted to Glory. . . *

Walter Muir Whitehill

The first phase of historic preservation was concerned with the associative value of buildings; the second was quite as much concerned with their inherent architectural significance, irrespective of what had or had not taken place within their walls. This change of direction is explicit in William Sumner Appleton's statement of the purpose of the Society for the Preservation of New England Antiquities, which he organized in 1910 as "to save for future generations structures of the seventeenth and eighteenth centuries, and the early years of the nineteenth, *which are architecturally beautiful or unique,* or have special historical significance. Such buildings once destroyed can never be replaced."

---

*Special Committee on Historic Preservation, U. S. Conference of Mayors, *With Heritage So Rich,* 1966, p. 40.

Historic Resources Survey Manual*

New York State Board of Historic Preservation

The "New Preservation"

But as change has permeated nearly every aspect of twentieth century life, so have new ideas about historic preservation been formulated and assimilated. Increasingly since World War II, interest in the past has been expanded and transferred into a concern for preservation on an even broader scale. Sometimes termed the "new preservation," this movement focuses upon the desire to preserve the evidence of a region's overall historical development in its proper context and in such a way that it will play an economically viable role in the contemporary scene.

In its broadest sense, this new attitude centers around the need to preserve the remaining physical elements of what have been called historical development patterns, the grouping of structures such as agricultural settlements, industrial complexes, residential neighborhoods, and commercial districts. These historic resources—existing structures as well as archeological sites—are viewed as the tangible remains of past ways of life, rather than as isolated references to an individual or event.

To gain a realistic understanding of the past, it is essential to examine all facets of daily life in the past. Consideration must be given, for example, not only to the decoration of the drawing rooms and sanctuaries, but also to systems used for heating and plumbing, to the function of the outbuildings, and even to the mode and frequency of travel between the houses and the churches. In addition, it is equally necessary to preserve evidence of the total cultural environment remaining in other parts of the community about the ways in which inhabitants earned their livings, carried out financial activities, purchased retail goods, transacted legal and governmental business, communicated with other parts of the world, and spent leisure time. This concern should be directed toward gaining an understanding of all groups that participated in the life of the community, not just the wealthiest or the most famous. Where and how did the other members of society—the shopkeepers, clerks, mill hands, and servants, for example—spend their working hours and their spare moments?

An outgrowth of this attitude toward historic preservation is the increased recognition given to architectural qualities, to urban design features such as open spaces and street patterns, and to elements of landscape architecture and design. Frequently, examples of the work of leading architects, structures that are particularly fine architectural examples of their period, or rare survivors of certain types of buildings or methods of construction, receive well-deserved recognition. But certain structures representative of the conventional approach to building design and construction and those designed by local architects and builders—often called vernacular architecture—should also be preserved for they are frequently even more illustrative of the general historical development than monumental or unusual structures.

Because of its involvement with the total environment and the need to preserve historic resources in their proper physical context, the "new preservation" is particularly concerned with the settings of

*Albany, NY 1972, pp. 7-11.

buildings and with historic districts. The siting and orientation of rural buildings in relation to the land-scape as well as the juxtaposition of urban structures in time and place to each other, to open spaces, and to the street pattern are important factors in an area's character.

The "new preservation" also recognizes the need to analyze the evidence from all eras, from the prehistoric to the most recent. Since its founding, America has been continually growing and developing, and no historian can legitimately assign an arbitrary cut-off date for significant or relevant developments. In fact, as one ardent preservationist has noted, there is no sensible contradiction between wishing to spare good buildings and being a protagonist of contemporary architecture, for both are significant reflections of the culture that created them.

Landmark Preservation*

John S. Pyke, Jr.

Traditionally, landmark preservationists focused their attention on a structure because it was linked with an historic event or person or because it had singular architectural merit. Colonial Williamsburg, the painstakingly restored former capital of England's oldest colony in North America, represents the full flowering of this tradition. Today, however, preservationists are widening their scope to include significant commercial and industrial structures, districts with striking mixtures of design, groups of individually undistinguished buildings which reflect a particular period or style of living, and assorted buildings which, while not important historically or representative of a period, are worth saving for the extravagance, humor or eccentricity that went into their creation.

The Williamsburg approach to landmark preservation is not capable of widespread and general application. In most communities only a few landmarks significant enough to warrant preservation can support themselves as historical museums. Most landmarks must be adapted to other uses than a public exhibition place if they are to be preserved. Architecture critic Walter Muir Whitehill has warned that "we cannot crystallize or pickle the past, nor can we, where there is vigorous life in the community, turn back the clock as it was possible to do, through a combination of hardly-to-be-repeated circumstances, in Williamsburg."

Also, it might be noted that restoring an old village or building in the twentieth century produces the curious result that the village or building is recreated as it never was. Restored Williamsburg is marked by paved automobile roads, endless signs and plaques, a glut of over-elaborate furniture and the Williamsburg Inn, created out of whole cloth to service the tourist trade.

*New York: Citizens Union Research Foundation, 2nd ed., 1972, pp. 1-2.

2.

Why Historic Preservation?

Preamble

As indicated in chapter 1, an active and organized movement for historic preservation is largely a product of the nineteenth and twentieth centuries. Moreover, in the course of these two centuries, there have been several clear-cut changes of perspective on what to preserve, and why. The origin of nineteenth-century concern for such matters is obvious enough: for the first time, the long established physical environment was undergoing rapid change, with frequent demolition of familiar historic buildings and a large amount of new construction that was quite different and often quite unattractive. The early leaders in the active movement for historic preservation were mostly of a type: the standard example is of a group of wealthy old ladies fixing up George Washington's home at Mount Vernon—and creating similar museums from other buildings with similar associations.

The present movement in the late twentieth century is strikingly different. In part, this is the result of a much broader range of interest, with a variety of people taking an active part. In part, it represents a broader view of the scope of historic preservation, essentially as an attempt to understand our cultural background; there has been a concern not only for sites with special historic associations and with special architectural value, but also a concern for social history— how the average person lived. Underlying all this is the clear assumption that the past may be understood more clearly and more vividly in the context of surviving historical buildings and artifacts.

The first few items in this chapter provide summaries of the various reasons for a special interest in historic preservation, seen from varying perspectives. The special problem of the historic "image"—or people's sense of identity with the historic past—comes out clearly in the passage from *A Future from the Past*, in the context of the old New England mills. The reconstruction of Warsaw represents a special and indeed a unique situation—an exception to the usual strict rule against copying previously existing historic buildings that have been destroyed. Since the Germans insisted upon tearing down Warsaw, it became a primary item of Polish national policy to rebuild the city, and to reproduce the pre-war situation as precisely as possible.

A different type of consideration appears in the remaining items. The New York City Landmarks Commission made what was apparently almost an accidental discovery: at least in certain types of situations, the designation of a historic district could play a substantial role in stimulating the revitalization of residential neighborhoods, by giving people a sense of pride in living there and thus providing the long-sought-for key to encouraging indigenous rehabilitation of certain central-city areas. Finally, the later items stress various economic benefits to be derived from historic preservation. In light of current building costs, rehabilitation of historic buildings is often cheaper than building new buildings. Moreover, major historic structures may play a significant role as an "anchor" in central business areas—a point well illustrated by the discussion of the role of Carnegie Hall in midtown Manhattan.

In all these (except the last), the major consideration has been to improve the quality of life. In this respect, historic preservation is simply one example of a broader current trend directed toward that end. Except for the considerations spelled out in the final chapter of this volume, there is no reason to assume that public action on behalf of historic preservation need detract from public concern for the special problems of the poor; yet no one should think that historic preservation has so far made a substantial contribution in dealing with the latter.

The State of Connecticut Historic Preservation Plan: 1970*

Connecticut Historical Commission

The geographical area known as Connecticut, like the larger area that includes it, called New England, in the minds of persons even slightly familiar with it, is something more than a landscape varying from rural to urban, from seashore to mountainous, and from river valley to high upland ridge. Beyond the limits of its large cities and occasionally within their confines, the individuality and quality that confer distinctness as well as distinction upon this state depend in large measure upon the structures of varied type, age, and architecture that stand along the streets of its settlements or within view of roads traversing more sparsely inhabited areas. The village green, which from a town's earliest years provided the center of community life, is often surrounded by buildings that make visible a large segment of its history and, individually or as a group, lend a character to the area unique in nature and attainable in no other way.

Such structures and landmarks are history in tangible, three-dimensional form, preserving the record of man's life and activity, his values and achievements, in more vivid and meaningful terms than any written or pictorial record can possibly offer. If history is people, then in a broad sense the word "historical" will apply to what a people leaves behind that can say something to the present about life in an earlier time. That a large section of the American public in some degree senses and values this fact is evident from the vast numbers, increasing every year, who visit historic sites nationwide and travel to exhibits that recreate a typical or a vanished segment of the past. Contemplation and understanding of such structures and settings reveal much of how the Nation evolved to its present condition, whence it came, and offer some indication as to where it is headed. This is the "sense of orientation" that the Federal Congress in Public Law 89-665 declared dependent on preservation of the country's historical and cultural foundations.

---

*Hartford, Conn., p. 3.

Why Preserve Historic Resources?*

Robert Stipe

It is possible to become so engrossed in legal detail that we run a real risk of losing sight of what it is that we are trying to achieve in the first place. For this reason, a sentence or two on why we seek to conserve historic resources at all is in order. . . .

First, we seek to preserve because our historic resources are all that physically link us to our past. Some portion of that patrimony must be preserved if we are to recognize who we are, how we became so and, most important, how we differ from others of our species. Archives and photographs and books are not sufficient to impart the warmth and life of a physical heritage. The shadow simply does not capture the essence of the object.

Second, we strive to save our historic and architectural heritage simply because we have lived with it and it has become part of us. The presence of our physical past creates expectations and anticipations that are important parts of our daily lives. We tend to replace them only when they no longer have meaning, when other needs are more pressing, and do so with caution, knowing how our environment creates us and how we create our environment.

Third, we save our physical heritage partly because we live in an age of frightening communication and other technological abilities, as well as in an era of increasing cultural homogeneity. In such a situation we subconsciously reach out for any opportunity to maintain difference and uniqueness.

Fourth, we preserve historic sites and structures because of their relation to past events, eras, movements and persons that we feel are important to honor and understand. Preservation of many structures and sites is an outgrowth of our respect for the past, which created our today; in making them accessible we are sometimes able to have the past live for us as it cannot when viewed as a printed page or a piece of celluloid. Nostalgia and patriotism are important human emotions for preservation, and important human emotions must be served. But the important point is that the historic associations inherent in preserved structures and sites should encourage much more than mere nostalgia and patriotism. They are potential sources of imagination and creativity in our attempts to understand and appreciate the past—a past distant from us, but a time that can still offer much to guide us.

Fifth, we seek to preserve the architecture and landscapes of the past simply because of their intrinsic value as art. These structures and areas were designed by some of America's greatest artists. They are as important to our artistic heritage as our decorative arts, our painting and sculpture. If we accept the philosophy of architect Walter Gropius, we should give greater consideration to the preservation of architecture than to that of other artistic objects because, in his view, architecture is a synthesis and culmination of artistic endeavor and the supreme medium of human expression. We cannot prove such an opinion, of course, but the thought does express the importance of architecture to our artistic tradition. If we were to value historic structures as we honor our other works of art, much wanton destruction might be prevented.

Sixth, we seek to preserve our past because we believe in the right of our cities and countryside to be beautiful. Here, with much regret, we must recognize the essential tawdriness of much contemporary design and construction. Much of it is junk; it assaults our senses. We seek to preserve the past, not only because it is unique, exceptional, architecturally significant or historically important,

---

*From *Legal Techniques in Historic Preservation*, National Trust for Historic Preservation, Washington, D.C. 1972, pp. 1-2.

but also because in most cases what replaces it will be inhuman and grotesque. Potentially, of course, many old buildings could be demolished and replaced with contemporary structures of equal functional or aesthetic value. Yet, recent experience has shown that this is not likely, and until it is we shall preserve our past in order to preserve what is left of our pleasing and humane urban and rural landscape.

Finally, and most important of all, we seek to preserve because we have discovered—all too belatedly—that preservation can serve an important human and social purpose in our society. Ancestor workship and aesthetic motivations are no longer enough; our traditional concern with great events, great people and great architects will not serve society in any full measure.

The problem now is to acknowledge that historic conservation is but one aspect of the much larger problem, basically an environmental one, of enhancing, or perhaps providing for the first time, a quality of human life. Especially is this so for that growing number of people who struggle daily to justify an increasingly dismal existence in a rapidly deteriorating urban environment. No one needs to be reminded that our cities are falling apart. If preservation is not to fall into the trap of total irrelevance, we must learn to look beyond our traditional preoccupation with architecture and history, to break out of our traditionally elitist intellectual and aesthetic mold and to turn our preservation energies to a broader and more constructive social purpose. We must look beyond the problems of saving architectural artifacts and begin to think about how we can conserve urban neighborhoods for human purposes. This is particularly urgent at a time when some special interest and ethnic groups, in an effort to discover their own heritages, have begun to isolate themselves even more, rejecting the notion of common heritage for all Americans and substituting a new emphasis on social differences and social conflicts. Success in preservation in this day and age requires that we give as much of our attention to such problems as bathrooms, kitchens, schools, garbage collection, employment and racial conflict as we have traditionally given to architecture and history. The importance of our nostalgic, patriotic and intellectual impulses cannot be denied, but they are no longer a wholly sufficient motivation for what we are about.

Basically, it is the saving of people and lives and cities—not just buildings—that is important to all of us. We have before us an unparalleled opportunity, if we are sufficiently determined, to contribute significantly to the upgrading of the quality of human existence. If we can achieve this, to some extent at least, the architecture and the history will fall into place.

What is Historic Preservation?*

David Poinsett

True historic preservation is objective in its attitude. That is, it regards all periods and styles as inherently equal for learning about our past. We all have our favorite architectural styles, just as we all have our favorite periods of history. Historic preservation, however, admits that it is as important to preserve 20th-century Eclectic and 19th-century neo-Gothic as 18th-century Georgian, or Federal, or Classic Revival. Each relates to a period of our development and each has an intrinsic worth that

*From *Preservation News*, July, 1973, pp. 5-7.

transcends our particular personal choice. A true historic preservationist would no more destroy a particular building because it is not one's favorite style than smash a recording of Stravinsky because one likes Beethoven better.

Historic preservation has existed, in its traditional sense, for three purposes. The first is education. Historic preservation supplements the written word. In a properly interpreted historic house museum, a person gains insight into the life and times of previous individuals and groups. It is, in effect, a three-dimensional learning experience.

Secondly, historic preservation exists for the purpose of recreation. It is fun to visit historic sites, to see the unusual, quaint and often difficult ways in which people lived in an earlier age.

Thirdly, historic preservation exists for inspiration. Patriotism, in its truest sense, is installed and strengthened by gaining a better insight into who we are as a people and nation, whence we came, and where we are headed. Historic preservation can help instill and strengthen these concepts.

There is today a fourth reason for historic preservation. This is the putting of historically and architecturally valuable sites and buildings to economically viable uses. Such uses are often different from, and yet compatible with, the original function of the structure. This is perhaps the greatest challenge and most important work of the historic preservationist. It requires careful planning, creativeness, extra effort and, most important of all, a state of mind that will seek alternatives to the obvious one of demolition.

Historic preservation means building new structures that reflect our time yet blend with the old. In districts of architecturally important buildings, the new should complement the old, not copy it. As Ada Louise Huxtable wrote in the architecture column of *The New York Times* last October, "the best of the past deserves the best of the present, not make-believe muck."

A Future from the Past*

U.S. Department of Housing and Urban Development and Massachusetts Department of Community Affairs

Image

Perhaps the single most important problem facing the New England mill towns is the problem of *image*. The overwhelming decline and collapse of the textile industry in the North has tarnished the image of these cities, not only in the eyes of people from the outside but also in the eyes of the citizens themselves. The discouragement experienced by people as a result of "hard times" has simultaneously destroyed their faith in the future of their communities and paralyzed their belief in the value of their own resources. The loss of confidence is understandable, considering the adversity

---

*Gene Bunnell, ed., Washington, D.C., 1978, pp. 21-22, 67, 75-79.

and the bleak prospects for the future which these communities have faced for the last half century. Nonetheless, the negative outlook can have a debilitating influence on a city's future *economic* prospects. In other words it can be a circular situation with people's attitudes affecting the economic health of a community. Some people tend to forget that economics is in fact a *social* science. . . .

Identity

"How will we know it's us, without our past?"
—John Steinbeck, *The Grapes of Wrath*

The quality of life in a city is more dependent on the need for identity than many people realize. The identity of a community—the sense of place that possesses—is a psychological characteristic, but it can be shown to have a great deal of importance to the economic well-being of the community and its citizens. Gertrude Stein's celebrated comment, "There is no there, there," upon seeing Oakland, California, in 1934, identified what had already become a national problem. In the East, the situation is different in that the existing historic identity which many towns possess is rapidly being lost as important buildings and areas are replaced by standard formula commercial and residential structures which might be found anywhere.

The clearest economic benefit resulting from the positive character and identity of a town is an increase in tourism. This means a great deal, because tourism has become the largest single industry in New England. People don't travel to places which do not have some unique feature, and old buildings constitute the most readily available source for unique character in most New England towns. In Portsmouth, New Hampshire, the attendance at the Strawbery Banke restoration area increased 334 percent in the five years form 1965-70. Translated into dollars, this has meant an increase of 725 percent to Strawbery Banke. . . .

Restoring the Sense of Place

The argument that old industrial buildings and workers' houses must be demolished because they symbolize an unattractive past is often espoused by community leaders, who claim that such buildings would not be used by the citizens who had once worked or lived in them. This argument is hard to oppose because it is so hard to test. It seems logical to many people that the former workers would like to escape the image of the old factories, so the case for conservation is expressed: "I know that people hated working in them and would like to see them go, *but* they are great buildings."

However, as is increasingly being demonstrated, people do not always possess negative associations with their former places of work, at least not in a form which is directed toward the buildings themselves.

When one thinks about the human implications of the claim that people would be antagonistic to the preservation of their old factories, the argument ceases to be as logical as it sounds at first. Factory workers are no more willing than anyone else to reject their life's work, or the places in which they worked for so many years, as being negative or destructive.

The renovation project which has demonstrated the contrast between the expected negative associations of former workers and their actual reactions is the Tannery in Peabody, Massachusetts. The Lawrence Leather Company was once the largest tanning plant in the United States, its acres of buildings filled with steaming caldrons and stinking hides. If ever there was an unattractive working environment, that was it. When a group of developers studied the possibility of turning it into housing, they were warned that people would never live in the place which once housed such a filthy industry. Since the principal market for the new housing was older people, many of whom had once worked in the Lawrence Tannery, the negative associations posed a considerable threat to the viability of the project.

The fears proved to be unfounded. Rather than being a problem, the prior use as a factory proved to be an asset. Residents, including many of those who had worked in the tannery, were attracted to the new housing because, not in spite of, the fact that the apartments had been converted from the former tannery. The developers dropped the original name for their project "Crowninshield Estates," for the more forthright name, "The Tannery," when they realized that the direct reference to the project's prior use had the potential of being an asset. People got a kick out of the fact that the building had once been a smelly tannery, and it proved to be a kind of poetic justice that in its place—not just on the site, but in the same buildings—should now be comfortable and character-filled apartments.

This project stands as a commanding example of the fact that "image" does make a difference, but that, in this case, what by many was thought to be a negative image actually proved to be an essential ingredient of the project's success. Image and identity proved a powerful force for economic development, yet to date they have rarely found a place within a banker's formula. For many towns and cities, especially those beyond a major metropolitan area, the exploitation of a surviving identity and image may provide the best and perhaps the only resource for new economic growth. . . .

Conclusion: A Future from the Past

Why is it important to conserve old buildings? Much of this report has focused on certain economic advantages of preservation, but many people might still say, "Why preserve the old buildings?" All things being equal, why not opt for a new building? Even in those instances where conservation has been proven to be cheaper than new construction, buildings have been destroyed anyway because their owners have sometimes opted for the predictability of new construction over the problems of dealing with the unique features of the older structures.

Phokion Karas

THE TANNERY

AWARDS: 1975 Honor Award of the New England Regional Council of
American Institute of Architects
Henry David Thoreau Grand Award for Excellence in Landscaping

GENERAL CONTRACTOR: Taylor Woodrow Blitman Construction Corp.
ARCHITECT: Anderson Notter Associates, Inc.
OWNER: Crowninshield Apartments Associates

"One of the Tannery Buildings
prior to re-cycling"

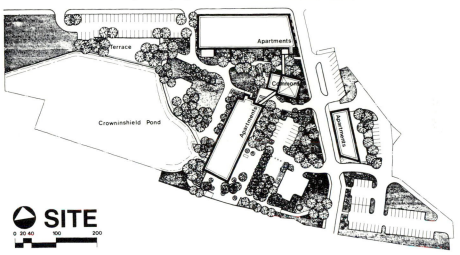

Terrace

Apartments

Commons

Crowninshield Pond

Apartments

Apartments

⬢ SITE

0 20 40   100   200

From the 19th Century until World War II, tanneries abounded in Massachusetts, and the city of Peabody was the "leather capital of the world." Since then, however, escalating regional production costs forced most of the mill operations to relocate in the South, leaving behind abandoned tanning complexes.

Efforts to attract new industries to the largely outdated facilities were unsuccessful. Left unused, those structures became subject to decay, vandalism and, finally, demolition. As eyesores and crime-pockets, they also provoked the decline of the adjoining neighborhoods.

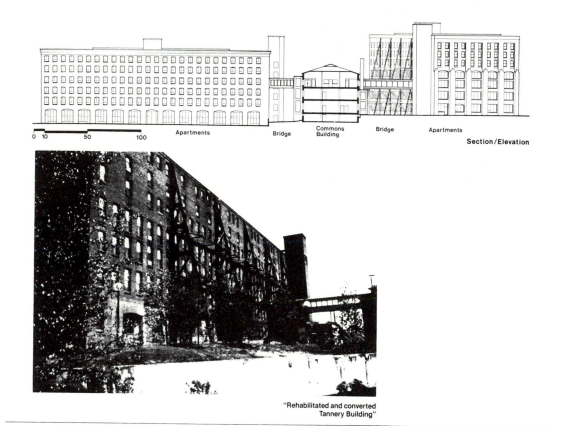

Apartments   Bridge   Commons Building   Bridge   Apartments

0 10   50   100

Section/Elevation

"Rehabilitated and converted Tannery Building"

To counteract this trend, and to help improve the local housing stock, the city government chose several well-located but neglected properties for Massachusetts Housing Finance Agency urban renewal designations. One such site was the former A.C. Lawrence Leather Company mill complex, situated in a residential area only three blocks from the downtown business district and the city hospital. The 8.7 acre plot included five tannery buildings of varying sizes, a power plant, the former Crowninshield family mansion, several minor structures, and a two-acre mill pond.

Recognizing the attributes of the site and the historic importance of the mill structures, Taylor Woodrow Blitman Construction Corp., in its development consulting capacity, helped to formulate a plan to convert three of the factory buildings into apartment houses, rehabilitate and convert the mansion into a community facility, landscape the property with trees, shrubs and tanning artifacts, and restore the neglected pond.

The complicated process of construction included the demolition of extraneous structures, the gutting of the three recyclable factory buildings, the cleaning of exterior walls, the sandblasting of interior wooden beams and ceilings, the dredging of the pond, and the creation of 284 modern apartments. These units, both flats and duplexes, were assembled within two six-story gutted masonry buildings and one three-story reinforced concrete building. Glass enclosed walkways were provided to connect the two large apartment houses to the community facility which now contains laundries, recreational spaces, and the rental office. To facilitate passage through the buildings, the two tannery elevators were refurbished and three additional ones were installed.

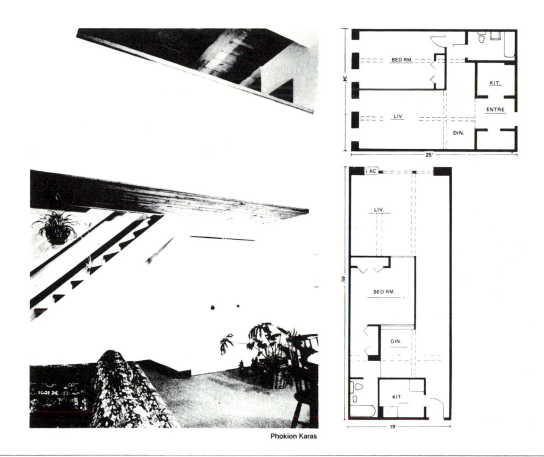

Phokion Karas

Of the total 284 units, 19 are efficiencies, 223 are one-bedroom apartments, and 31 are two-bedroom units. Duplexes comprise 36 of the one-bedroom and 18 of the two-bedroom apartments. Regardless of size, each of the units is furnished with wall to wall carpeting, modern kitchens and bathrooms and also new heating, plumbing, electrical, air-conditioning, and sprinkler systems. Ten percent of the units are specially equipped for handicapped tenants, giving the overall housing complex an orientation for the elderly.

Taylor Woodrow Blitman Construction Corp. completed construction in 1975, nearly six months ahead of schedule. The project was financed by a $6.0 million mortgage from the Massachusetts Housing Finance Agency. It was the first time such funds were applied to "recycled" construction outside the Boston area.

By providing all the conveniences of the city with the visual amenities of the country, Peabody's historic Tannery is again the focal point of community activity and a positive force toward further neighborhood revitalization.

A view of part of the Amoskeag Mills in Manchester, New Hampshire. Despite its stark appearance, it exercises an emotional hold on some of the former mill workers. *Courtesy of Randolph Langenbach.*

Most of this discussion has focused on what are some of the economic advantages of preservation, and what are some of the steps which can be taken to exploit, rather than destroy, old buildings. However, what underlies this discussion is the conviction that building conservation is of more than just practical importance. It is essential to the health and humanity of a community environment. Just as is common during times of war, massive destruction of a community's physical fabric as part of a plan for redevelopment can remove much of what provides a stabilizing influence on people's lives. Stability in the built environment is needed to instill confidence in the future, whereas constant destruction and rebuilding can tear at the very heart of a community. The dislocation and emotional feeling of loss can break down the pride and respect which ordinary citizens may have in their home town. That which they had identified as being their world ceases to be part of them. The civic image can often seem abstract and foreign, as familiar old structures are replaced by glass and steel and concrete—or worse, by dead asphalt.

A community needs to preserve its historic identity, not simply in order to profit from tourists, but to give strength and permanence to its local community. How can a North Adams citizen "say nice things to strangers" if his or her image of the real "North Adams" has been carted away in a wrecker's truck?

This observation appears to be in complete contrast to one of the most commonly held conceptions of what the industrial environment means to the people who spent the greater part of their lives working in it. So often the response by planning officials to the plea that a particular factory building is important and should be saved is, "It should be removed because, to those who worked in it, it is a symbol of hard and degrading work." The success of the tannery project in Peabody demonstrated how wrong this conception might in many cases be. Recently in Manchester, New Hampshire, this was again dramatically revealed during a major museum exhibition of photographs of, and architectural artifacts from, the Amoskeag Mills. Over the six weeks that the exhibit was on display, the gallery was visited by over 11,000 people, the largest crowd in its history. Many of these people were former mill workers. On the final Sunday of the exhibition, over a thousand people came, and, in front of the motion picture cameras of WGBH Channel 2, which documented that historic event, many of these people expressed their excitement at rediscovering their past, and at finding the objects and buildings from it displayed in the museum setting. They expressed a sense of history and relationship to their past place of work with an enthusiasm which was completely unanticipated. The exhibit served as a reunion of former Amoskeag millworkers. Their response to the material demonstrated more significantly a remarkably positive association with their former work environment. For many there was even a genuine affection shown for the place which many planners and city officials had condemned as being associated only with physical degradation and social inferiority. The large majority of workers who came to the exhibit and who have been interviewed as part of an oral history project look upon their past with pride and not with shame. The mills were the setting for a lifetime of work which they are not willing to reject as worthless despite the admittedly low wages and long hours. . . .

Often it is thought that old industrial communities have always been spiritless and drab, but history denies this. A tremendous dynamism and community spirit surrounded and supported the construction of the mills, and the legacy of this spirit was written into the architecture of that same period. It is a thoroughly human document of what these places have meant to people in the past. Today it can become a model for the regeneration of community spirit and faith in the future, and a source of pride and confidence in the present.

Reconstruction of the Old Town Centers of Poland *

Stanislaw Lorentz * *

Protection of Historical Monuments
in Poland, 1918-1959

   The problem of the reconstruction of architectural historical monuments and old town centers on a vast scale appeared for the first time after the First World War. Numerous important historical buildings, as well as entire old town centers, were damaged during the hostilities. The law for the protection of historical monuments, passed in 1918, established the responsibility of the state for architectural monuments and works of art in general. It determined, too, the principles on which the preservation offices were to be organized throughout Poland. A later law in 1928 stipulated the rights and duties of the owners of architectural monuments and works of art regardless of whether they belonged to the state, the municipality, corporations, social organizations, or private individuals. The principles of the preservation of buildings, considered then as the only possible ones, were those resulting from the "anti-scrape" philosophy. We considered it best to preserve and repair only; in case of necessity, to restore; never to reconstruct. Architects and historians who had any tendency to reconstruct historical monuments were severely criticized.

   For a few years after the First World War, the general opinion prevailed that new buildings erected between historic monuments or near them should be absolutely different, in design and in building materials, from the monuments. New buildings were in no way to harmonize with the historic buildings. Soon, however, this view began to evoke strong protests, and ultimately the feeling prevailed that such methods were not justified, especially in such instances as the large modern building in the medieval market place in Kraków. Yet, it was a characteristic of Polish laws for the protection of monuments, passed between the two world wars, that they applied not only to single historic buildings but also to groups of buildings and their disposition. These laws covered the most valuable monuments, but they also protected those of any historical or artistic value at all, thus dealing with a great number of buildings and objects. Behind this great care was the history of losses suffered by Poland both in ancient times and during the period of captivity (1795-1918), when Poland was divided into three parts by Prussia, Russia, and Austria; hence, the patriotic and even sentimental attachment to the monuments of the national past.

---

*From National Trust for Historic Preservation, *Historic Preservation Today*, 1966, pp. 43, 45-47, 49-50.

* *Stanislaw Lorentz is Director of the National Museum, Warsaw, Poland.

Destruction and Damage by the Second World
War. New Principles for the Protection of
Historic Monuments

The change from the traditional attitude toward the methods of preserving architectural monuments came with the Second World War, beginning soon after the great damage to Warsaw during the siege and bombardment of September, 1939. Following the insurrection in Warsaw in 1941, we were faced with the tragic problem of preserving the historic treasures, or at least the remaining traces of them. During the whole month of August, 1944, the heaviest battles took place in the "Old Town" (Stare Miasto) quarter of the city. In the second month of the insurrection, September, 1944, historic monuments were damaged and destroyed in other quarters. The final ruin of the city was completed by the German forces during the three months between the capitulation of the insurgents and the liberation of Warsaw on January 17, 1945. House after house, street after street, was destroyed in obedience to Hitler's order that "the city is to be razed to the ground."

Out of the 1,300,000 prewar inhabitants of Warsaw (and an additional 200,000 who moved to Warsaw during the occupation), 800,000 were killed in the battles for the city, in concentration camps, and in executions. In January, 1945, at the moment of liberation, the center of the city and the adjoining districts were covered with ruins and rubble that totaled 20 million cubic meters. Eighty percent of the buildings and 90 percent of the historic buildings were destroyed. This particularly high percentage of historic buildings is explained by the fact that the center of the city was much more thoroughly destroyed than the outskirts. In such a state the fate of Warsaw as a city hung in the balance. For several weeks it was discussed whether it might be better to move the capital to another town, e.g., Kraków, Lódź, or Poznań; and to leave Warsaw in ruins as a testimony to the atrocities of the war. Moral and economic considerations prevailed against this idea, and in February, 1945, the decision was made to reconstruct the city.

The opinion of professionals, that is, town planners, architects, and historians of art, supported by general opinion, was that the historic quarter and the architectural monuments should be reconstructed in their ancient forms. There were but few voices for the preservation only of those architectural monuments that were not in ruins and for the construction of a completely newly planned modern city in the same place. We realized that the decision to reconstruct Warsaw in its ancient aspect was of great importance to the national culture, but at the same time we fully realized its immense economic consequences and its influence on the daily life of the population. We were fully conscious that we were taking up a great task under exceptionally hard conditions in Poland just after the war and that it would require great sacrifices on our part.

That general opinion, which was uniformly for reconstruction, arose from emotional reasons. The enemy had intended to raze Warsaw, and nearly did it. Therefore it was our duty to resuscitate it. The reconstruction of Warsaw is the last victorious act in the fight with the enemy, which lasted five years, both openly and underground. It is the finishing touch of our unbending resistance against enemy violence. Warsaw was so heroic in its many struggles for freedom and independence that it would be impossible to obliterate its historic aspect. We did not want a new city on the ruins of ancient Warsaw. We wanted the Warsaw of our day and that of the future to continue the ancient tradition. The love of the inhabitants for their town, and their patriotic feelings toward it, governed public

Restoration of the 'Old Town' (Stare Miasto) in Warsaw. The Rynek or Old Town Square was in total ruin when the Germans left, and it was restored by 1953 despite very difficult economic conditions in the country at that time. *Osrodek Dokumentacji Zabytkow*.

opinion. The decision to reconstruct Warsaw was made by the highest authorities, who were confident that they were acting according to the wishes of the people. . . .

It may seem queer that this country should make a decision to bear such heavy charges for protecting so many historic monuments while it was faced with great efforts to complete its general reconstruction and reindustrialization. But it must be emphasized that the attachment to national traditions and the love of monuments of the past are very general in Poland. At a period when architectural expression is very uniform throughout the world (in Poland too, of course), we want, as much as possible, to keep everything that has a specifically Polish expression, from an artistic and cultural point of view—everything that is typical for the Polish landscape, be it a house in a small town or even a folk artist's statue of a saint standing on a country road.

As we traditionally take care of such a great number of authentic historical monuments, real remnants of the past, the question could be raised whether we are justified to reconstruct historic monuments that had been completely destroyed, or nearly so; and this is not only in large towns but all over the country. We must, therefore, state further motives in addition to the emotional and patriotic reasons.

First, it should be remembered that although many historic buildings were completely ruined, most of them were only partly ruined or damaged. For several reasons it is impossible to keep in ruins countless numbers of historic buildings. First, it is difficult to safeguard against further rapid deterioration of buildings made of bricks, especially if these bricks are not very hard or well burned or when the binding cement is not as perfect as that in the ruins of ancient Roman buildings. In Poland we maintain in ruins the walls of medieval castles destroyed long ago, mostly during the wars with Sweden in the seventeenth century. The preservation of these ruins is very hard and requires a lot of work. Thus, buildings destroyed during the last war should either be left to their own fate (which means that in several years or decades they will not exist any more) or they should be dismantled. The latter would be essential in modern active towns, as it would be impossible to leave unhealed war wounds in such living organisms. Therefore the problem involves not only reconstructing but saving those authentic parts still preserved—sometimes just a facade with well-preserved sculptured ornaments. Moreover, it is much better and safer to preserve these authentic details when they are included in a reconstructed building and taken care of by the new user of this building, than when they are left in ruins.

Besides preservation, there are historical reasons that favor reconstruction. If the destruction of historic sections approaches 90 percent, and we should despair of reconstructing them in their previous aspect, the decision would mean that the individuality of the town, its character, and its own historical appearance would be completely obliterated. The great majority of the Polish people would not agree to that. It is not so much a question of national feeling or local patriotism as it is a human need to feel the continuity of our general history and of our personal history which we do not want to see limited to our short life. Before the last war we had in Poland numerous Societies of Friends of different towns. Their activities were concerned with the history of the given town, its historic buildings, and local works of ancient art. It is significant that these societies in general have broadened the scope of their activities. They have added to their statutes amendments providing that, in addition to research on the history of the town and its population, they are obligated to attract the lovers of the town of today, to collaborate in the growth of the town, and to organize discussions on the best ways to develop their town in the future.

The Administrative, Legal and City Planning Role in Historic Preservation*

Harmon H. Goldstone

One of the surprises that has come from seven years' experience with New York City's landmarks law has been the recognition by the city administration that, quite unexpectedly, the law has proven itself to be a most effective device for the stabilization of residential neighborhoods. What started out as the hobby of a handful of architectural antiquarians has turned into a potent tool that city planners envy.

When the landmarks law was first being drafted about ten years ago, everybody thought of a landmark as a beautiful or historic building. Almost as an afterthought, it was suggested that there were certain areas of the city which, while not having the high architectural or historic importance required for an individual landmark, did, nevertheless, have a certain character that set them apart from their surroundings and that this character might well be worth preserving. At the time, it was thought that Greenwich Village, Brooklyn Heights and possibly one or two other areas might be designated as Historic Districts and provision for doing so was written into the statute. No one could have remotely foreseen that New York City would now have 18 officially designated Historic Districts with a total of over 6,000 individual properties under the jurisdiction of the Landmarks Preservation Commission.

The designation of a Historic District seems to give people a new pride in their neighborhood. They suddenly take an intense interest in seeing their surroundings preserved and improved. All sorts of cooperative community activities spring up. Young families—professionals and businessmen—give up their plans of moving to the suburbs. They channel their energies, instead, to the renovation of old row houses. And these are just the sort of actively productive citizens that the city is most anxious to retain.

The designation of individual landmarks, too, has had a social impact far wider than the architectural historians would ever have dared hope. The man in the street has discovered that history and beauty are where you find them—in all sorts of neighborhoods and right on the sidewalk. They are not things that you have to make a trip to a museum to see.

*From North American International Regional Conference, *Preservation and Conservation: Principles and Practices*. Washington, D.C.: Preservation Press, National Trust for Historic Preservation, 1976, p. 51.

The Contribution of Historic Preservation to Urban Revitalization*

U.S. Advisory Council on Historic Preservation.

Summary of Conclusions

Historic preservation activity in urban historic districts has contributed significantly to the revitalization of those districts and, in addition, has contributed economically, socially, physically, and esthetically to the rejuvenation of their cities. The preservation of irreplaceable historic and architecturally important properties, the restoration of exceptional buildings, and the renovation and adaptive reuse of other noteworthy structures have, in fact, encouraged a return-to-the-city movement. . . .

1. Preservation Activities Have Revitalized Urban Historic Districts while Conserving Valuable Older Properties

The revitalization of the four historic districts analyzed (Alexandria, Va., Galveston, Tex., Savannah, Ga., and Seattle, Wash.) is remarkable when the condition of the districts prior to major preservation activity is considered. All were in a less-than-desirable state. Population was either declining both in number and in economic composition or was transient in nature. Housing in residential areas was deteriorating and overcrowded, while that in predominantly commercial areas consisted mainly of flophouses or substandard old hotels. Legitimate business activity declined but illegal activities often flourished. Adjacent land uses were highly incompatible. Land values and the value of the old buildings were falling, as were the tax revenues generated. Crime rates were high—as much as 13 percent of the crime in one city occurred in the 18-block historic district. Fires were frequent; entire buildings were closed for health violations or non-conformity to safety codes; the need for social services was high. A lack of pride in the area was noticeable, both on the part of residents of the area and in the attitudes of the balance of the metropolitan area. . . .

Hundreds of structures in the historic districts have been renovated and returned to their original uses as residences. Some buildings of outstanding merit have been restored as museums and provide strong educational and cultural resources as well as a touch of elegance. Many former commer-

---

*Washington, D.C.: U.S. GPO, 1979, pp. 1, 4-11.

cial structures have been adaptively reused as shops, restaurants, offices, or apartments. Open spaces have been retained or recreated. Architects and developers in all the case study districts maintain that the cost of securing and reusing sound old buildings is far less than building the same amount of space new—and preserves a part of the area's heritage that, once lost, cannot be replaced.

2. Highly Visible Physical Improvements Have Occurred in the Historic Districts

Of all the changes that have occurred in the historic district as a result of the actions stimulated by preservation activity, the most obvious are the physical ones. The renovation of buildings and the resulting generation of activity have focused the attention of the public sector on providing the supplementary infrastructure improvements necessary to upgrade the area.

Although each of the four historic districts is unique, certain common characteristics now are apparent. The changes in scale, signage, color, and space usage have been coordinated due to controls exercised by review boards where ordinances exist or to a carefully conceived redevelopment plan protected by a strong local organization that secures properties privately. . . .

3. Viable Economic Activity Has Been Created in the Historic Districts

The economic base of all the historic districts has been broadened as the result of the stimulus provided by preservation activity. Nearly all of the economic expansion has been sponsored by the private sector, with varying levels of support from local, state, and Federal sources. In each historic district, new businesses have been formed, the housing stock has been upgraded, property values have increased, a major tourist attraction has been created, and the investment of private funds has been stimulated.

(1) New Businesses Have Been Formed

Each historic district has a number of new businesses that have been newly formed or have moved into the district from outside the area. Many have been started in response to the growing market attracted into the area by the renovations. In Alexandria's historic district, for example, there were a total of 26 retail businessess in 1970 in a two-block area surrounded by restorations. By 1978, the number had more than doubled to 53. Others were early risk-takers who were farsighted enough to recognize the future potential that would be generated as has occurred in Galveston's Strand. Here some 25-30 shops have been opened or committed since 1974 where no previous shops or restaurants existed.

A number of the stores, especially initially, have been in fields related to the arts, such as galleries, craft shops, designers, etc. In the more mature historic districts, a wide variety of goods and services is available. Restaurants in the districts range from snack shops to fully recognized gourmet restaurants and serve a dual role. Not only do they provide an additional draw for the retail shops but they increase the nighttime traffic which is essential for a 24-hour living and working environment.

New office centers have been created in all of the historic districts. The Strand and Pioneer Square enjoy a location that adjoins the downtown, and the Central Business District (CBD) is in the middle of Savannah's historic district. Alexandria has its own office concentrations and also is quite close to the Washington, D.C. CBD. Office tenants in the renovated buildings are usually from the general business and professional categories and often have been attracted into the area by the special ambience resulting from the preservation activity. It is important to underscore that many of the shop and office tenants have been newly formed businesses or [come] from out of the city. Most of the businesses located in, or in parts of, the historic districts prior to major revitalization were marginal operations, at best.

(2) The Investment of Private Funds Has Been Stimulated

Prior to the stabilization of each historic district through preservation activity, few traditional sources of financing would make either permanent or construction loans for projects in the district. In Pioneer Square and Galveston, early investors were forced to use personal credit or their homes as collateral. The problem was difficult but not acute in Alexandria due to the strong Washington area housing market and the visionary acumen of the real estate industry.

Once the historic district was so designated, usually after initial private investment and renovation, lenders were more receptive to requests for long-term loans and investors more willing to purchase properties. However, some form of persuasion to lower the risks involved was usually necessary. In Savannah, local commercial banks and a savings and loan firm established a line of credit for the Historic Savannah Foundation's revolving fund of up to $250,000 on 50 percent of the purchase price of important structures. The balance of the revolving fund monies was obtained through a local foundation grant and private contributions. In Galveston, the Galveston Historical Foundation's revolving fund was financed by two local foundations, but long-term financing for individual projects was provided by an agreement with six local lending institutions. Over $1.6 million in long-term loans was committed in a 3-year period. In Pioneer Square, the local financial community would not make any significant loans until after the historic district ordinance and the success of the first major project.

The amount of private investment attracted into the historic districts has been quite large considering the lack of activity prior to the beginning of the revitalization process. The total investment in Alexandria's historic district is not available. Private investment in the other historic districts includes:

• Approximately $80 million in the Savannah Historic District since 1955, including $40 million in restoration costs

• Over $4.2 million in the Strand in Galveston in purchases, rehabilitation and revitalization of Strand buildings from 1972 through 1977

• Approximately $18 million in Pioneer Square in Seattle since 1960, with most investment occurring after 1971

(3) Public Support Has Complemented Private Efforts

Although the major investment in the historic districts was by the private sector, various forms of public funding have added support. The role of the public sector is quite varied in the four historic districts. Involvement includes:

•Over $3.9 million in grants and appropriations for acquisition and restoration of historic properties in Alexandria's historic district and approximately $25 million for the Gadsby Urban Renewal Program
•About $421,000 in Federal and local grants and appropriations in 2-1/2 years for planning studies, infrastructure improvements, etc. in the Strand. A $2.5 million Urban Development Action Grant has been received to create a parking facility, cruise ship terminal and passenger walkway
•Over $36 million in HUD Section 312 rehabilitation loans, the Riverfront and Central Urban Renewal projects, a new County office complex, a new civic center and hospital improvements in the Savannah Historic District plus City funding for infrastructure improvements
•Nearly $2.1 million of Federal and local funds spent in Pioneer Square from 1970 to 1976 for parks, street and lighting improvements, plans and studies, staff, and preservation grants-in-aid.

(4) Increased Tourism Has Resulted from Preservation Activity

Increased tourism has been a major and beneficial impact of preservation activity in the historic district. Based on specific mail inquiries and on volume trends, the interest in visiting historic districts is constantly increasing and attracting both tourists and visitors living in the major metropolitan areas of the historic districts. . . .

(5) Property Values Have Increased Significantly

Significant increases in the real estate value of renovated properties in the historic districts have occurred. . . .Sales figures reflect a direct link between location in a historic district of a rated property and a higher value. Appraisal records in each historic district show the following:

•The average value of a sampling of single-family homes in the Alexandria historic district were as much as 45 percent lower than the Washington metropolitan area average in 1950. By 1970, the value of houses in the sample blocks were from 7 to 95 percent higher than the metropolitan average and by 1977 were from 45 to 100 percent higher
•Property values in the Strand have increased as much as 208 percent in 3 years where renovations have occurred and decreased in value where still in a deteriorating condition or where located away from the major preservation effort
•The value of blocks in the Savannah Historic District has had an annual average increase ranging from 9 percent to 65 percent, depending on the type of property, location and degree of restoration
•The renovation of properties in Pioneer Square had a definite effect on their value. For example, the Grand Central Arcade was valued at $132,880 in 1965 and 1971. After renovation, its value was appraised at $940,160 in 1973 and at $1.27 million in 1977. Similar increases occurred in the value of other renovated properties. The valuation techniques used by assessors in Seattle recognize that preservation activity has a positive impact on the value of adjacent land even when improved with renovated old buildings.

Economic Benefits of Historic Preservation*

Thomas D. Bever

In addition to giving people a sense of time, place, and meaning in terms of where they live, historic preservation has been successful for purely economic reasons—it costs less to rehabilitate a building than to construct a new one, and these preserved buildings compete successfully in the marketplace. Some of the most important benefits from preserving and adapting our built environment are economic: providing jobs, stimulating business activity, revitalizing downtown areas. These are not the only economic benefits that come from historic preservation, nor will such benefits accrue in every preservation or adaptive use project. They have simply been demonstrated to repeatedly occur in the past. These issues—of employment, private sector stimulation, neighborhood revitalization, resource efficiency, and available financing—are considered here as substantive economic benefits from the movement.

Employment

Rehabilitation projects are as high as 75 percent labor intensive, compared to 50 percent for new construction projects, according to an October 1977 report "Conservation of the Urban Environment" by the Office of Archaeology and Historic Preservation, U.S. Department of the Interior. This is important not only in terms of the employment potential of historic preservation, but also in terms of an individual project's multiplier impact on a local economy. Dependent on the size and sophistication of a locality, a higher proportion of construction materials will come from outside the area than will construction labor. For funds that are spent in a local economy, a higher percentage of funds remains as a stimulant in that locality from projects that are labor intensive. Thus, funds utilized in historic preservation projects have greater impact on employment than funds used in the construction of new buildings such as hospitals, schools, and office buildings because of (1) the greater labor intensity of preservation projects, and (2) through this labor intensity the higher multiplier. The Advisory Council on Historic Preservation analyzed projects funded under the Economic Development Act and found that demolition and new construction yielded an average of 70 jobs per one million dollars expended, while renovation including historic preservation created 109 jobs per million dollars. In a separate study the State of Vermont's Division of Historic Preservation found that over 400 new jobs would be created at a cost of approximately 3 million dollars for a recent historic preservation project; that is, a labor intensity approaching 80 percent.

According to testimony of the General Services Administration in support of the Public Buildings Cooperative Use Act (S-865), May 19, 1975, before the U.S. Senate Subcommittee on Buildings

---

*U. S. Dept. of the Interior, Washington, D. C., 1978, p. 9.

and Grounds, rehabilitation creates two to five times as many jobs as new construction for a given expenditure of money. This is enhanced by the fact that the highest concentration of the unemployed tend to reside in those areas with the highest concentration of old structures.

The Downtown Development Corporation of Rutland, Vermont was granted $350,000 from the Department of Commerce's Economic Development Administration for a historic preservation project, which was matched by a $180,000 loan fund created by six local banks. This original $350,000 grant is expected to generate $1.1 million in construction and related activities by the spring of this year. The equivalent of 60 full-time jobs will be created for a period of 18 months; 60 jobs represent approximately 3 percent of the county's unemployed work force. Welfare for 60 people would have cost $360,000. Thus it cost less to provide 60 jobs through a historic preservation project than to provide 60 persons welfare. In this case in Rutland, 24 of the individuals who were actually workmen on the project came from the ranks of the unemployed.

Rehabilitation can be a training ground for a community's unemployed. In Brooklyn's Bedford-Stuyvesant area, one of the largest ghettos in the United States, a community development company titled Bedford-Stuyvesant Restoration Corporation runs a program rehabilitating facades and walkways in the neighborhood. Through this program, welding, masonry, and painting are taught to the neighborhood's unemployed. Thus far, 13,074 houses on 86 blocks have been refurbished and 3,351 men have gone through the training program, at a cost of only $3 million.

Private Sector Stimulation

*   *   *

Rehabilitation costs per square foot are often significantly less than the costs of new construction. Case studies presented at the National Trust for Historic Preservation conference on the "Economic Benefits of Preserving Old Buildings" demonstrated that the cost of rehabilitating old structures generally runs 25–33 percent less than comparable new construction. In those cases where the costs are equivalent, the preservation project provided greater amenities—time saved in construction, more space in either height or volume, or the right location. These amenities frequently produced other economic benefits to a developer through higher occupancy rates and rents. In addition, rehabilitation oftentimes bypasses lengthy development review processes, local neighborhood opposition, and zoning delays.

According to a recent article in the Harvard Business Review:

> A high-rise office building that cost $40 per square foot in 1967 could cost as much as $80 per square foot to replicate today. The average renovation cost now ranges from $15 to $40 per square foot, depending on the quality of the finish. Therefore, if this building can be purchased for less than $40 a square foot, space in the refurbished structure could be offered at a lower cost than comparable space in a new building.

In downtown San Antonio the Alamo National Bank recycled its 23-story 1930s landmark building at a cost of $38 per square foot, whereas similar new construction would have cost $70 million. The job was finished in only 14 months. The cost of rehabilitating the Pioneer Building in

Seattle was less than $19 per square foot, compared to more than $30 for new construction of similar quality. In Maynard, Massachusetts, the Digital Equipment Corporation owned a 19th century textile mill that used to produce blankets for Civil War troops—the company converted it to both corporate offices and modern maufacturing facilities to produce computer hardware. The cost? Fifteen dollars per square foot, about half that of new construction. In Tacoma, Washington, the old City Hall has been adapted to house 30 new businesses on five floors and will eventually add 20 more shops and restaurants; the cost of conversion was $5-$8 less per square foot than new construction. In Baltimore, Maryland, the city's professional theater company Center Stage rehabilitated the old Loyola College and High School into their new auditorium-theater complex. A new theater would have taken 2-3 years to build and cost $2.5 million, whereas recycling the school took less than a year and cost $1.7 million.

The Advisory Council on Historic Preservation states in its report "Adaptive Use: A Survey of Construction Costs" that:

> The Survey indicates that demolition costs inside the buildings being recycled are minimal, normally only 1-4 percent of the total project costs. Structural costs are also low, normally varying from about 5-12 percent of the total project cost, which is less than half the average expenditures for new construction. This reflects the fact that little structural work is normally required when reusing an old building. Architectural costs vary above and below the average for new construction. Generally, in projects where the maximum effort was made to reuse the existing interior and exterior materials, the costs are substantially below those for new construction.

*   *   *

Resource Efficiency

ERDA conducted a study that determined rehabilitation consumes 23 percent less energy than new construction; in 1967, the base year studies, it took 49,000 BTUs per square foot to rehabilitate a structure compared to 65,200 BTUs per square foot to build it new.

Historic preservation is resource efficient, and responds to the contemporary demands of natural resource scarcity. This is the other advantage of rehabilitation's labor intensive nature. That is, since rehabilitation is 75 percent labor intensive, to provide a given amount of usable residential or commercial floor space, fewer natural resources are utilized in the production of physical capital goods (wood, metals, etc.).

*   *   *

Landmark Preservation*

John S. Pyke, Jr.

Economic Benefits of Landmarks

The economic dividends which landmarks bring to a neighborhood are frequently overlooked, often by the very persons who would destroy them in the name of economy. In commercial districts, for example, the benefits may derive from the type of activities housed by the landmarks or the kinds of people they attract. In residential areas, landmarks often set the style and tone of community life which in turn determines property values, assures a solid tax base and prevents the encroachment of urban blight. In historic districts landmarks generate tourism, a profitable industry that requires only moderate investment and maintenance to produce a high return.

One commercial neighborhood which recently came to realize how much it depended upon a local landmark is the Carnegie Hall district in New York City. The City's premier concert hall since 1891, Carnegie Hall has spawned a variety of small shops, restaurants and businesses that cater to its patrons. In addition, it has generated the presence of rehearsal studios and recital rooms and attracted music-loving tenants to nearby apartment buildings. While symbolizing America's finest musical traditions, Carnegie Hall also functions as a lively and vital center of a thriving neighborhood.

The construction of Lincoln Center for the Performing Arts during the late 1950's made the venerable Carnegie Hall expendable and its owners subsequently announced their intention to raze the historic hall and replace it with a modern office tower. A modified Italian Renaissance structure of no surpassing architectural importance (although it does have remarkable acoustical qualities), it had become grimy without and well worn within and desperately needed refurbishing. Given the economics of mid-town Manhattan, Carnegie Hall's owners were undoubtedly correct in asserting that they could realize more income from a commercial building located on the same site. From a broader perspective, however, the destruction of Carnegie Hall was uneconomical for both New York City and the neighborhood, for it would cause the closing of scores of local businesses that depended on the continued presence of the concert hall.

The area's businessmen and landlords joined the chorus of protest and at the last possible moment the landmark was saved when a quasi-public corporation purchased it. Since its rescue and renovation, it has maintained its preeminence as a concert hall, providing New Yorkers and visitors with an alternative to the music programs offered by the newer Lincoln Center. It also continues to be an invigorating influence in a neighborhood of diverse uses. Among the reasons Carnegie Hall won a reprieve from its death sentence was the realization by the owners of businesses and the landlords in the area that its existence safeguarded and promoted the unique economy and substantial property values of the neighborhood.

---

*Citizens Union Research Foundation, 2nd ed., 1972, p. 30.

Practical Advantages of Historic Preservation in the United States

(Editors' Note)

The Advisory Council on Historic Preservation of the U.S. Government sponsored, or carried out, during 1977, 1978, and 1979, several studies on the practical advantages of historic preservation on the basis of experience in the United States. The titles of these studies are:

The Contribution of Historic Preservation to Urban Revitalization (A.C.H.P., 1979, GPO 625-046-1229).

Assessing the Energy Conservation Benefits of Historic Preservation (A.C.H.P., 1979, GPO 625-050/1302-1233).

The Value of Restoring and Rehabilitating Historic Buildings in Terms of the Revitalization of Urban Historic Districts (A.C.H.P., May 1979).

Neighborhood Conservation: Lessons from Three Cities, G. Binder and P. Meyers (The Conservation Foundation, Washington, D.C., 1977).

The conclusions of one of these reports (*The Contribution of Historic Preservation to Urban Revitalization*) include the following:

1. New businesses have been formed.
2. Private investment has been stimulated.
3. Tourism has been stimulated.
4. Property values have been increased.
5. The quality of life and the sense of neighborhood and community pride have been enhanced.
6. New jobs have been created.
7. Land use patterns are compatible.
8. Property and sales taxes have increased.
9. Pockets of deterioration and poverty have been diluted.

As to the comparative advantages of rehabilitation as compared to new construction, the Council printed, in its annual report to the President for 1978, the following table.

Costs per Square Foot

	New Construction	Major Renovation*	Minor Renovation
Property acquisition	$3.00**	$9.00****	$14.00*****
Front end renovation		2.50	1.50
Demolition	.15		
Basic building	38.00	10.00	7.00
Tenant improvements	8.00	8.50	8.05
Subtotal "hard" costs	49.15	30.00	30.55
Interim operating	2.70	.80	1.30
Architect/Engineer/legal fees	2.60	1.60	1.20
Interim cash flow	(negligible)	(1.00)**	(2.00)
Marketing & real estate fees	2.70	2.50	2.80
Developer overhead	1.00	.50	.50
Interim financing	6.60	2.50	3.00
Developer profit	6.00	3.00	3.00
Subtotal "soft" costs	21.60	9.90	9.80
Total:	$70.75	$39.90	$40.35

*No major structural change.
**Site.
***Site and building.
****Net income from existing tenants reduces costs during renovation.

Source: A.C.H.P., *Report to the President and Congress 1978* (1979 GPO Stock No. 052-003-00665-1), p. 13.

As to the advantages of rehabilitation from the standpoint of energy saving, the study *Assessing the Energy Conservation Benefits of Historic Preservation*, p. 6, contains the following conclusion, based on a study of low-cost-housing apartments in Indianapolis, the Grand Central Arcade in Seattle, and a small two-story brick house in Washington, D.C.

Rehabilitation of existing buildings, rather than demolition and new construction, results in a net energy investment "savings" over the expected life of the structures.

•The total energy investment to renovate and operate a rehabilitated Lockefield Garden Apartment will be less than the energy required to construct and operate new facilities for over 50 years—even though new facilities might use less energy annually for operations.

•The Grand Central Arcade will have a net energy investment advantage over an equivalent new structure for the next *two centuries*.

•Over a 30-year period, the rehabilitated Austin House will conserve enough energy to heat and cool an equivalent new apartment building for over 10 years.

3.

Threats to Historic Structures and Sites

Preamble

The factors which, over the long run, have everywhere led to the destruction or deterioration of historic buildings have included wear and tear; changes in fashion; ignorance, indifference and inertia; changes in land use; desire to reuse old materials in new buildings; the invention of new building methods and materials; desire to earn the maximum economic return from every piece of land; political and economic changes in the area (surprisingly the improvement of the local economy has been more destructive of architecture than has economic weakness); population and urban growth and decline; and, more recently, traffic demands and traffic pollution.

In Europe, and particularly in Italy, France, and Britain, a major problem has been the vast number of historical resources of the countries which have been "civilized" for so many centuries that the accumulation of fine buildings, such as castles, churches, and palaces has been increasingly difficult to maintain. Some of these buildings are difficult to adapt to modern conditions, while upkeep costs increase every year.

In the United States, we have faced some particular difficulties. Among these have been:

1. Demolition by neglect, aided by vandalism. The owner of a historic building which is not earning a high return and who has not been given permission to demolish can easily find ways to assist nature in taking its course.
2. Poor, cheap, and bad "modernizations." There are, in every town, builders' supply companies which deal in cheap, factory-made building parts, including aluminum and asphalt siding, aluminum windows, metal awnings, shutters, and doors and other easily applied fixtures which soon spoil the authenticity and beauty of a handsome facade. In applying them, the owner covers and often destroys the original detail. The lack of trained architects and workers has increased this danger.
3. Urban redevelopment and the bulldozer complex. This factor has already resulted in the gutting of the historic downtown areas of many fine old cities. Portsmouth, New Hampshire, is alleged to have lost a third of its 18th-century houses in an initial blitz paid for by urban redevelopment. The development of the interstate highway system has added to this threat.
4. The attitude of nonprofit organizations, that any destruction they may commit is justified by their public purpose, has been disastrous, as anyone living near a university, hospital, or church is apt to discover.

89

5. Fire, especially, in the United States, where a large proportion of early buildings have been of wood construction, has been a serious threat.

6. Poor planning and zoning, which, in the United States, has resulted in our ignoring the historical assets of a community and has frustrated efforts to preserve many important buildings. The lack of cooperation and ignorance of government officials, many of whom are out of sympathy with preservation efforts, have contributed to these unfortunate results.

Landmark Preservation*

John S. Pyke, Jr.

The Challenge

The heedless and rapid eradication of old buildings in our cities boggles the imagination. Landmarks such as Carnegie Hall continually face the threat of destruction as the American city, like some great organism constantly renewing itself, replaces its older, less efficient and less profitable buildings with newer structures. This process was summed up several years ago in a *Saturday Review* cartoon which pictured two helmeted workmen who, in the course of demolishing an office building, have just broken open the cornerstone bearing the date "1952." One workman is reading a scroll taken from the cornerstone: "To you children of history, who on some far distant day down the dim dark corridors of time, may breach this stone. . . ."

A Historical Guide to Florence**

John W. Higson, Jr.

Little more than a century ago, the weary traveler making his slow approach to Florence by carriage or horseback over dusty and difficult roads, and at last catching sight ahead of that legendary city nestled in its green valley, must surely have experienced a deep, soul-tingling thrill. There in the distance loomed the familiar shape of the Cathedral's great dome, while around it crowded the

*New York: Citizens Union Research Foundation, 2nd ed., 1972, p. 60.

**New York: Universe Books, 1973, pp. 17-26.

jumbled, irregular rooflines of the city, still confined within the orderly limits of its ancient wall. From every direction, a countryside of spectacular beauty, unmarred by industrial suburbs, extended to the great stone gates themselves.

Here on the banks of the river Arno lay a city with a unique character, its general appearance almost unchanged since the 16th century. Bell towers, cupolas, and the rugged battlements crowning its more imposing structures still dominated the surrounding mass of the town. Dun-colored stones and terracotta tiles blended serenely with the encircling hills. No jarring contrasts unsettled the eye. A hazy atmosphere, diffused with the golden light peculiar to Tuscany, enveloped the scene—a happy collaboration of man and nature.

Florence attained this essential form during the twilight of the Middle Ages and in the glorious period of the Renaissance that followed. In those years it played a prominent part in the European drama, profoundly influencing the course of events in Italy and across the continent. But in the 16th century, the conquest of the peninsula by foreign powers extinguished the city's independence and creativity, and Florence gradually slipped from the mainstream of history, no longer to shape or be affected by the great movements of the times. The extravagances of the Baroque era, which so altered Rome, left scant trace in Florence. The age of exploration and discovery provided no new opportunities for the city but in fact accelerated its decline. Even during the turbulent period of the industrial revolution, Florence remained quiescent. The population continued relatively static* and little new building took place. Maps dated around 1850 show a city scarcely altered from the time of Michelangelo. Considerable areas still devoted to agriculture remained within the walls. The medieval heart of the city survived intact, and the beautiful Tuscan countryside reached out on all sides, undisturbed. To have rounded a bend in the road and beheld ahead that famous city, towered and domed, girded by its wall and set like a jewel amid the green of field and vineyard, must have etched on the mind of many a traveler a vivid and unforgettable picture.

But in many respects this peaceful scene was not to last, and today the traveler to the valley of the Arno experiences a less romantic introduction. The approaches to Florence itself have been drastically changed by the inevitability of progress. The old Via Bolognese from the north and the Via Senese from the south happily still retain something of their ancient appearance, but there is little to admire along the other principal roads, including the connections to that main artery of travel in Italy, the Autostrada del Sole. These follow the plain of the Arno on almost flat land and pass through acres of commonplace suburban development, the hallmark of our 20th-century civilization. Here, where a rich soil once supported an abundant agriculture, factories, apartment blocks, gasoline stations, and all their attendant phenomena have steadily encroached, and the sprawling suburbs have progressively insulated the city from the surrounding countryside, which no longer provides a complementary and nourishing influence to Florentine life.

One's first impressions, therefore, on entering the city are somewhat disappointing, but past the suburbs, the relatively unspoiled character of old Florence becomes increasingly apparent, until reaching the core area we discover that, in spite of much rebuilding, there still remains a significant part of the ancient city yet undisturbed. In fact, it is an interesting paradox and a measure of the inherent quality of the city that, even after the unfortunate changes that have taken place, Florence still somehow remains more closely linked to its past—less violently wrenched into the 20th century, and hence more truly its historical self—than most other important European cities. That being said, it is nevertheless worthwhile, for a better appreciation of the things that make Florence famous, to identify and distinguish those alterations to the city for which our modern age must be held accountable.

The beginning of major change in Florence may be traced to the middle of the 19th century, at a time when profound new forces disrupted the stability of Europe. The consequences of the industrial

---

*Around 100,000. Today it is more than 500,000.

The Piazza Dei Signoria, the Governmental Center of old Florence, is an example of the comparatively unspoiled character of the old city. *Courtesy of Italian Government Tourist Office.*

revolution had altered social and economic relationships of long standing, creating problems that taxed the resourcefulness of every government and threatened the very existence of many. Radical new doctrines challenged the existing political order and demands for reform echoed across the continent.

Italy, on the fringe of these developments and long split into a number of separate kingdoms and principalities, responded in its own unique way. An impetus was given to the old but languishing idea of national union—the welding together of the diverse states of the peninsula, the overthrow of the various regimes and tyrannies, including the temporal rule of the Catholic Church, and the achievement of a national purpose and a national government. At last this became not only a dream but a possibility. Known as the Risorgimento (literally, Resurrection), this dramatic and turbulent phase of Italian history culminated in 1861 with the effective unification of most of the peninsula under the benevolent rule of the House of Savoy.

Florence, selected as the provisional capital of the new Italy, partly for its central position and partly for its favorable political climate, experienced an influx of court and government officials, soldiers, and businessmen, all impatient to refashion the life of the nation. Thus began the process of destruction and rebuilding which, uninterrupted by the removal of the central government to Rome (when the Papal State was incorporated into the new kingdom in 1870) and continuing down to our own day, has in some respects forever altered the city's traditional character.

Looking back to the years immediately following the unification, it is not difficult to understand why so little concern was given to the preservation of the old appearance of the city. Strong feelings, long pent up, had been released by the Risorgimento, sweeping aside the forces of conservatism. With the Pope in retreat and the Tuscan grand duke deposed, the new politics required a break with the past and the removal of the apparatus of tyranny and the symbols of the old order. Villas and *palazzi* were taken over by the royal court and by the various ministries to serve the needs of the new regime. In the space of a few years, scores of beautiful buildings were cut up and disfigured. Monasteries and convents, seized from the church, were hurriedly converted to offices, barracks, schools, or hospitals—more often than not failing to serve adequately their new purposes.

In like spirit, to permit the anticipated expansion of the city and indeed to encourage it, the encircling historic walls north of the river were pulled down in the 1860s and a broad boulevard was laid out on their perimeter. Housing developments and an increasing population continued the transformation, and the suburbs spread out in every direction. At first, these extensions were not unattractive, but subsequent additions have been progressively more commonplace, until today's huge cubical apartment blocks, repetitive imitations of each other, appear devoid of any architectural merit.

Equally irreparable and less justified, a misconceived project, rigorously carried out in the 1880s, sought to modernize a large section of the heart of the city centering on what had been for centuries the Mercato Vecchio (Old Market). Around this piazza since medieval times had grown up a jumble of ancient towers, churches, *loggie*, tabernacles, and other historic structures amid a tangled maze of narrow streets. All this was indiscriminately swept away to make room for construction of the present prosaic Piazza della Republica and its adjoining blocks of uninteresting buildings.

The motive for this is clearly set forth in an inscription on an archway over one of the streets leading into the piazza: *L'antico centro della citta da secolare squallore a vita nuova restituita* (The ancient center of the city from centuries of squalor restored to a new life). Although the area doubtless needed cleaning up, it was not necessary to level it. The very buildings that seemed to be such obstacles to progress in the 19th century comprised much of the essential heart and soul of the old center. Those on the perimeter of the project that were allowed to remain are proof of that. Unfortunately, the possibilities of judicious restoration succumbed to a stronger desire to wipe away reminders of the past and to rebuild in accordance with the mood and tastes of that day.

Each century had witnessed a few changes in Florence's general appearance, but not until after the Risorgimento were alterations on such a large scale attempted. Many of these were inspired by the intellectuals and romanticists of the Victorian period, who had recently "rediscovered" the Italian Gothic style and the artists of the duecento and trecento (particularly Giotto and his followers). Not the least influential of these arbiters of public taste were the members of the foreign colony in and around Florence, mostly British and American. To them and to local opinion in general, which they greatly influenced, it was inconceivable that churches and public buildings should be left in an unfinished state. The fact that the greatest artists of the Renaissance had apparently felt unequal to the tasks of final completion (the most difficult part was often put off indefinitely) did not give them pause. And so, to the many changes made in the name of hygiene or progress, others were made in the name of art. The great rough stone frontal walls of the Duomo and the church of Santa Croce, for example, were "improved" at tremendous cost by the addition of elaborate facades. Castles and other buildings, including the so-called Casa di Dante, were "restored" in an exaggerated and artificial way, according to the then imperfect understanding of medieval architecture. Landmarks were removed and statues in the eclectic style of the times placed about the city. Frescoes, which had long been left to molder and decay, were inexpertly patched up and repainted, with unfortunate results. Looking back today, we see more of the attitudes of the 19th century in these works than was perhaps intended.

But on an even larger and less restricted scale, and at a progressively faster tempo, the compelling realities of our own era have everywhere left their mark. These are especially apparent if we enter the city through the ever widening sprawl of the eastern and western suburbs which have grown so rapidly since World War II. Zoning here, according to occupancy and use, is unheard of, and few districts are set aside exclusively for residential purposes. Instead, Italians customarily live in congested and diverse surroundings so as to maximize social contacts at all times. The newer sections therefore include shops, offices, factories, apartments, markets, bars, and restaurants all mixed up together. Here all of the paraphernalia of postwar prosperity seem to have mushroomed in superabundance. New buildings rise up everywhere. New businesses manufacture and display their products. Neons and advertisements crowd upon one another. Traffic becomes increasingly congested despite the devices employed to control it—signals, painted lines, signs of all kinds.

The consequences of progress, however, are even less acceptable in the older parts of Florence, but the urgent quest for modern conveniences and for a higher standard of living have dictated the course of civic development. An attractive inner courtyard of an old Renaissance palazzo, once filled with the sight and sound of a splashing fountain, is now marred by the creaking mechanism of an elevator. A noble facade or roofline is disfigured by the electric wires and television antennas that grow thicker daily. A little vegetable stand, which has displayed its profusion of color in front of an old, stone building since beyond memory, must surrender its place so that a few more automobiles may park; a weathered shrine to the Madonna, with its devotional image set up centuries ago, must accommodate itself to a "no left turn" sign; ancient piazzas, formerly reserved for human activity, now are packed tight with motor vehicles of all kinds, their pavements marred by oil and grease.

What Time Is This Place?*

Kevin Lynch

The city of Bath, built as an aristocratic health resort within a span of seventy years in the eighteenth century, is still a miraculous whole—our best remaining example of a Georgian town. Images of it appear in every standard text on city design; it attracts 300,000 tourists every year. Its unique visual qualities, its architectural importance, its representation of a particular period in British social history, its romantic associations, all make it a special legacy.

Its problems today are equally special, reminiscent of those in many other historic areas, though in Bath inflated. There are 3,818 buildings officially listed for preservation in the city, or one for every twenty-eight inhabitants. The homogeneous building stock is homogeneously obsolete. Forty percent of the floor space in the central area is vacant, and much more of the remainder above the ground floor is in only nominal use. Interiors are ill suited for contemporary activities. Speculators built Bath, and their principle was ostentation. The thin stone walls and light frames are in poor condition, exaggerated by deferred maintenance. The handsome Georgian plaster ceilings offer no resistance to fire. Were ordinary legal standards strictly applied, Bath would have to be rebuilt.

While the predicted growth of the city will create severe demands for land for expansion, the residential use of the center has been declining, and its substandard dwelling units are occupied by old, poor tenants. Remodeling would drive these tenants out and would probably require substantial subsidies in any case. And who would be attracted to live in the remodeled apartments? Hotels, large shops, and new offices are sorely needed, and they now tend to locate in areas not subject to architectural control. There is some danger that commercial enterprises not oriented to the tourist may move out of the city altogether. Yet it is the lively, colorful center, even more than the impressive but rather lifeless Georgian terraces, which is the principal tourist attraction. Access and parking are difficult, and adequate provision for the new traffic will require two tunnels and a network of primary roads at a cost well beyond ordinary national yardsticks for such improvements.

Bath could be allowed to continue its slow physical decline, paradoxically squeezed by its steady population growth, until some more violent readjustment took place. Or massive renewal could be undertaken to serve the new needs, though it would be sure to damage Bath's unique character. Or large subsidies might preserve the city as a national treasure, a policy that could only be expected to accelerate its transition to an elegant tourist encampment. No other use has yet been found for the center that can be accommodated without destruction of the existing landscape.

For tourists or visiting professionals the scene is magnificent on a fine day: the green setting, the harmonious stone terraces, a leisurely air, the sense of a place long inhabited. Popular postcard views fix the importance of particular visual memories: the Abbey through the Stall Street colonnade; the green hills from the city center, seen over the Orange Grove and the Avon. But the town, like a stage set, lacks the historic depth and living presence that is felt in an active, complex city.

What does this unique place mean to its visitor: the Roman baths underground, the bright shops, some famous views, and the house where Nelson dallied with Lady Hamilton? With affection? With frustration? With a cool economic eye? What should they be willing to sacrifice to preserve it? In-

*Cambridge, Mass.: MIT Press, 1972, pp. 9-12.

Royal Crescent at Bath, a city which is suffering from an "embarras de richesse" as a result of having so many historic buildings. *Courtesy of British Tourist Authority.*

deed, what *should* it mean to them, for Bath was built by the rents wrung from an exploited peasantry and out of the profits of the mills?

Why Buildings Wear Out*

Harmon H. Goldstone

Why Landmarks Are Lost

The question of why landmarks are lost should be asked at the outset. Why are fine old buildings torn down? Why are they allowed to decay so that they have to be torn down? Or why, as often happens, are they "modernized" in such a fashion that one wishes they had been torn down?

These are hard questions that cannot be dismissed lightly. It may be comforting to imagine that some malign fate, some diabolical plot, is working against efforts to preserve our architectural heritage. But such comforting fancies do not save buildings. The facts are real and, if buildings are to be saved, the facts must be squarely faced.

First, preservationists must accept certain inexorable realities. Buildings, like people, grow old. The repair or deferred maintenance of an old building is usually expensive. The uses for which a structure was originally designed can become obsolete. The people who originally used a building may die or move away. Fashions change. Urgent new needs compete for limited amounts of land. And most people like to make money; in particular, they expect a fair return on their investments. There is nothing inherently evil about any of these facts. They are simply the inescapable elements of a very real problem. No amount of hopeful thinking can wish them away.

In addition, there are the factors of ignorance, indifference and inertia to be faced. Many people know little about architecture or history; of those who do know something, most are preoccupied with other concerns. Of the few who both know and are concerned, a great number, unfortunately, feel that circumstances are so unfavorable for preservation that the loss of old buildings is inevitable.

*From North American International Regional Conference, *Preservation and Conservation: Principles and Practices*. Washington, D.C.: Preservation Press, National Trust for Historic Preservation, 1976, pp. 46–47.

Preservation of Historic Adobe Buildings*

U.S. Department of the Interior

Whether built in the 17th century or in the 20th century, adobe buildings share common problems of maintenance and deterioration. This brief discusses the traditional materials and construction of adobe buildings and the causes of adobe deterioration. It also makes recommendations for preserving historic adobe buildings. By its composition, adobe construction is inclined to deteriorate; however, the buildings can be made durable and renewable when properly maintained.

What is Adobe?

The adobe, or sun-dried brick, is one of the oldest and most common building materials known to man. Traditionally, adobe bricks were never kiln fired. Unbaked adobe bricks consisted of sand, sometimes gravel, clay, water, and often straw or grass mixed together by hand, formed in wooden molds, and dried by the sun. Today some commercially available adobe-like bricks are fired. These are similar in size to unbaked bricks, but have a different texture, color, and strength. Similarly some adobe bricks have been stabilized, containing cement, asphalt, and/or bituminous materials, but these also differ from traditional adobe in their appearance and strength.

Traditional adobe construction techniques in North America have not varied widely for over 3-½ centuries. Adobe building methods employed in the Southwest in the 16th century are still used today. Because adobe bricks are not fired in a kiln as are clay bricks, they do not permanently harden, but remain unstable—they shrink and swell constantly with their changing water content. Their strength also fluctuates with their water content: the higher the water content, the lower the strength.

Adobe will not permanently bond with metal, wood, or stone because it exhibits much greater movement than these other materials, either separating, cracking, or twisting where they interface. Yet, many of these more stable building materials such as fired brick, wood, and lime and cement mortars are nonetheless used in adobe construction. For example, stone may be used for a building's foundation, and wood may be used for its roof or its lintels and doorways. In the adobe building, these materials are generally held in place by their own weight or by the compressive weight of the wall above them. Adobe construction possibilities and variations in design have therefore been somewhat limited by the physical constraints of the material.

Preserving and rehabilitating a deteriorated adobe building is most successful when the techniques and methods used for restoration and repairs are as similar as possible to the techniques used in the original construction. . . .

Preservation Briefs: No. 5. Washington, D. C., 1978, pp. 1, 4-6

Sources of Deterioration

There are many tell-tale signs of structural problems in adobe buildings, the most common being cracks in walls, foundations, and roofs. In adobe, cracks are generally quite visible, but their causes may be difficult to diagnose. Some cracking is normal, such as the short hairline cracks that are caused as the adobe shrinks and continues to dry out. More extensive cracking, however, usually indicates serious structural problems. In any case, cracks, like all structural problems, should be examined by a professional who can make recommendations for their repair.

Water-related problems: Generally, adobe buildings deteriorate because of moisture, either excessive rainwater or ground water. Successful stabilization, restoration, and the ultimate survival of an adobe building depends upon how effectively a structure sheds water. The importance in keeping an adobe building free from excessive moisture cannot be overestimated. The erosive action of rainwater and the subsequent drying out of adobe roofs, parapet walls, and wall surfaces can cause furrows, cracks, deep fissures, and pitted surfaces to form. Rain saturated adobe loses its cohesive strength and sloughs off forming rounded corners and parapets. If left unattended, rainwater damage can eventually destroy adobe walls and roofs, causing their continued deterioration and ultimate collapse. Standing rainwater that accumulates at foundation level and rain splash may cause "coving" (the hollowing out of the wall just above grade level). . . .

As the moisture content of the adobe increases, there is a point at which the adobe will become soft like putty. When the wall becomes totally saturated, the adobe mud will flow as a liquid. This varies with the sand, clay, and salt content of the adobe.

If the adobe becomes so wet that the clay reaches its plastic limit, or if the adobe is exposed to a freeze-thaw action, serious damage can result. Under the weight of the roof, the wet adobe may deform or bulge. Since the deterioration is hidden from view by the cement stucco, damage may go undetected for some time. Traditional adobe construction techniques and materials should, therefore, be used to repair or rebuild parts of the walls. . . .

Wind Erosion: Wind-blown sand has often been cited as a factor in adobe fabric erosion. Evidence of wind erosion is often difficult to isolate because the results are similar to water erosion; however, furrowing caused by wind is usually more obvious at the upper half of the wall and at the corners, while coving from rainsplash and ground water is usually at the lower third of the wall. . . .

Vegetation, insects, and vermin: Vegetation and pests are natural phenomena that can accelerate adobe deterioration. Seeds deposited by the wind or by animals may germinate in adobe walls or roofs as they would in any soil. The action of roots may break down adobe bricks or cause moisture retention which will harm the structure. Animals, birds, and insects often live in adobe structures, burrowing and nesting in walls or in foundations. These pests undermine and destroy the structural soundness of the adobe building. The possibility of termite infestation should not be overlooked since termites can travel through adobe walls as they do through natural soil. Wood members (lintels, floors, window and door shutters, and roof members) are all vulnerable to termite attack and destruction. . . .

Material incompatibilities: As adobe buildings are continually swelling and shrinking, it is likely that repair work has already been carried out sometime during the life of the building. Philosophies regarding adobe preservation have changed, and so have restoration and rehabilitation techniques. Techniques acceptable only 10 years ago are no longer considered appropriate. Until recently, adobe bricks have been repointed with portland cement; deteriorated wooden lintel and doors have been replaced with steel ones; and adobe walls have been sprayed with plastic or latex surface coatings. The hygroscopic nature of adobe has rendered these techniques ineffective and, most important, destructive. The high strength of portland cement mortar and stucco has caused the weaker adobe brick to crack and crumble during the differential expansion of these incompatible materials.

Opportunities for Historic Preservation *

*Southeastern Connecticut Regional
Planning Agency*

What causes this rapid disappearance of these relics from the past? The following are some of the causes:

1. *Fire*. A large percentage of old buildings have undoubtedly fallen victim to the flames. Large, open fireplaces, dry wood, and crumbling chimney stacks are not the safest combinations in the world.
2. *Demolition by neglect*. A building must be maintained if it is to survive. This is especially true for those structures that have withstood use and abuse for more than 150 years. Once abandoned, an old house deteriorates rapidly.
3. *Poor alterations*. Without preservation controls, the style of a historic house can be easily destroyed by a tasteless owner. Dormers, bay windows, asbestos siding, large porches and other structural additions are all features that can seriously harm the character of an old house if improperly and thoughtlessly used. Furthermore, an old building that has been altered to the extent that it can no longer be identified with a particular period or style is not likely to generate the interest and action needed to preserve it.
4. *Changes in use*. The way a structure is used on the inside frequently is reflected in its outward appearance. Converting a Colonial house to a grocery store, for example, is usually accompanied by enlarging the windows and extending a multi-colored sign out from the front of the building. However, such transitions can be effected without destroying the integrity of the style. . . .
5. *Urban renewal*. In the past the procedure in renewal project areas has been to wipe out the old and replace it with the new. Many fine old buildings have been accordingly destroyed in New London and others are likely to meet this fate in other parts of the region. Virtually every historic structure in the core area of a city is in danger of being demolished to make way for an industry or business producing a higher economic return to the municipality or the property owner. . . .
6. *Highway construction*. Over the years some of the region's finest homes have been destroyed in favor of "good highway design." However, in recent years the Connecticut Highway

---

*Norwich, Conn., 1968, p. 36

The H. H. Richardson-designed railway station in New London was saved from destruction under the urban renewal program only in the nick of time as the result of strenuous efforts on the part of a handful of concerned citizens. *Courtesy of the National Trust.*

Department has aided historic preservation by identifying historic structures in the paths of new highways and then seeking out preservation minded individuals or groups to remove them for preservation. In some instances outstanding historical structures have been moved by the Highway Department and given to local groups for preservation.

7. *Incompatible zoning*. A historic structure is only as valuable as its setting and surroundings. An old dwelling in a commercial or industrial zone is not likely to be maintained very well by its owner, especially if obnoxious non-residential uses move onto adjoining properties. Appropriate zoning can be an incentive for keeping an old building in good repair.

Preservation and Rehabilitation of a Historic Commercial Area *

New Bedford Redevelopment Authority

Q. How do contemporary transportation and communication systems affect the character and function of a historic commercial area?

A. The space requirement and by-products of contemporary transportation and communication systems are generally destructive of historic and architectural values when such systems are superimposed on a historic area.

As a general rule, busy roads, freeways, and rail systems should be separated from a historic area and properly landscaped, buffered, and treated to minimize such by-products as noise, air pollution, and visual blight. Such an area should be relieved of heavy volumes of vehicular traffic. Furthermore, rules of the road, circulation systems and provisions for loading and off-street parking should be designed in such a manner as to give priority to pedestrian use of the area, and to provide the convenience of the automobile without its being allowed to impinge upon historic and architectural values.

Similarly, other types of communication systems can also destroy the qualities of a historic environment. Overhead electrical distribution systems and cables, television aerials, and light and power poles detract from the visual unity of a historic area and materially affect its economic and esthetic potential. Solution of the design problems created by the existing transportation and communication systems must be a prime concern in planning the rehabilitation of historic areas.

---

*New Bedford, Mass., 1973, p. 45.

The Distinctive Architecture of Willemstad*

J. Stanton Robbins and Lachlin F. Blair

What does the typical cruise passenger see in Curaçao, architecturally speaking? When he sees the Punda from a distance, it will seem a picturesque and colorful grouping of buildings, generally pleasant in aspect, but with no dramatic focus or exciting form. The refinery area has such form, particularly at night, but many cruise passengers will not see it at all.

On the streets of the Punda, however, there is much fascinating architectural form and color which carries appeal for both the uncultured tourist and the sophisticated esthete. The playfulness of detail in pudgy columns, profuse arches, and diversely curved pediments creates an effect suggestive of a fairyland. But this is primarily an upper-story effect within the business district. The blending of old Dutch, baroque, and tropical elements of architecture is happily evident in the upper facades of many of the older buildings, but the street level in almost every case has been "modernized" to the point where it has no style. The cruise passenger could just as well be home in Brooklyn unless he lifts his eyes above the ground floor shop fronts.

Cobble Hill Historic District Designation Report**

New York City Landmarks Preservation Commission

Cobble Hill is currently undergoing a renaissance as young couples acquire and renovate the attractive, moderate sized houses on its tree-lined streets. Like Brooklyn Heights, it is emerging from a rather long period of quiescence. This period actually protected it from the rapid pace of rebuilding and alteration, so typical of much of the City. Most of the fine old houses were preserved with little change. Apartment houses appeared in the area in the 1880s but they are not very high and few were built there after the 1920s. The fact that apartment houses did not invade the streets in recent years is responsible for the charming, low lying quality of this neighborhood where the skyline is punctuated occasionally only by church spires.

The real cause for alarm today is the "modernization" of houses by the application of spurious veneers. In these remodelings, handsome wood window sash is often replaced by aluminum windows with screens or storm sash set flush with the wall surface. This gives the houses a flat, card-

---

*New York: Stanton Robbins & Co., Inc.; Blair Assoc., 1961, p. 2.

**New York, December 30, 1969.

Willemstad in Curaçao is a charming mini-Amsterdam in the Caribbean, just off the Venezuelan coast. Most of the buildings are done in brilliant pastel shades. *Courtesy of Tromson Monroe Public Relations.*

board appearance, where once they had interestingly revealed window openings set in walls of brick or stone—honest expressions of the actual structure.

The addition of an upper story or a roof parapet has almost invariably resulted in the loss of a fine cornice. Stoops have sometimes been removed to provide basement entrances. The partial imbedding of ironwork in concrete—an expedient method of repair—results in loss of considerable beauty. All these changes and "improvements" create jarring notes in otherwise harmonious rows of houses. These renovations, intended to increase property values, tend to have the opposite effect in Historic Districts, where the very thing that attracts buyers is wantonly destroyed.

Revitalizing Older Houses in Charlestown *

Boston Redevelopment Authority, Historic Preservation Planning Program

Before discussing ways of treating individual details, however, let us look more closely at two representative types of these later 19th-century Charlestown houses.

On the following page are two sketches of a brick row house typical of many in the area. The first sketch shows the front as originally designed and—fortunately—as it still exists in many cases; the second sketch by contrast shows how the good qualities of the original design can be completely destroyed by the use of bad details in the process of remodeling.

In Figure 1 it will be seen that much of the simple and harmonious quality of the original design is due to the use of consistently vertical—or upright—proportions in both the window openings (the holes in the walls), and the subdivisions of the glass (the panes)—this also being echoed in the glazed parts of the doors. In Figure 2 the simplicity and harmony of the original front have been replaced by a hodgepodge of openings and panes of all shapes and sizes—both horizontal and vertical—the end result being rendered neither "charming and old" by the use of small Colonial-type panes, nor genuinely modern by the use of large picture windows and the offset entrance door. One of the chief factors in the deterioration of the design quality in the second facade is the tampering with the original proportions of the window openings—or the "holes" in the brick wall. This has been done not only by the opening up of the ground floor to form a large horizontal hole for the picture window, but also by the blocking down of the window heads on the second floor. (The latter has become a common practice for adapting window openings to fit smaller standard sashes, or for concealing the edges of ceilings that have been lowered beneath the heads of the existing window openings.) Other details which have contributed to the design deterioration shown in Figure 2 are the "streamlining" of

---

*Boston, 1973, pp. 10-13.

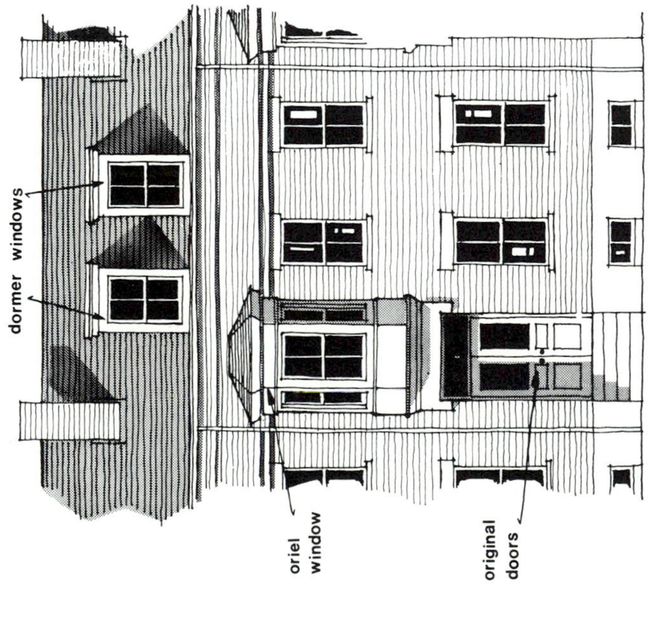

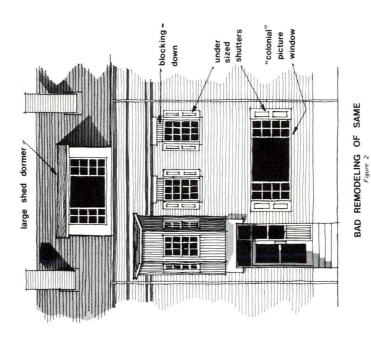

BAD REMODELING OF SAME
Figure 2

large shed dormer

blocking-down

under sized shutters

"colonial" picture window

THE ORIGINAL FRONT
Figure 1

dormer windows

oriel window

original doors

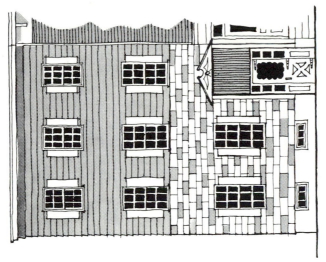

wide
window
trim

architrave

pilaster

original
door

cornice

brackets

blinds or
shutters
optional

corner
board

THE ORIGINAL FRONT
Figure 1

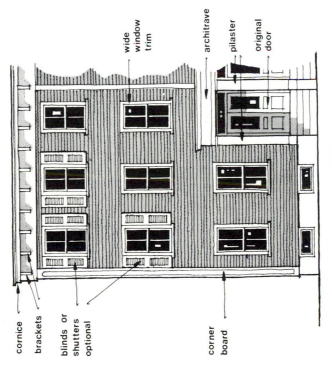

BAD "RESTORATION" OF SAME
Figure 2

the oriel window, which deprives it of most of its former character, and the use of undersized shutters or blinds at the windows.

A large "shed" dormer such as shown in the roof of Figure 2 does not usually improve the appearance of the front of the house, but is sometimes used in order to get more headroom in the rooms inside the roof. In such cases, whenever possible, it should be located facing the rear of the building rather than the front. Similarly, "picture" windows or large windows are also best located to the rear of the building—not just for esthetic purposes, but because they work better there and in many cases can be arranged to open onto a patio or pleasant, well-planted space, however small. It should never be forgotten that picture windows can be looked through from both sides and, when facing a street, usually lose their point by having to be heavily draped for privacy.

[Also presented here] are two drawings of a wood frame house typical of many to be found in Charlestown. The first shows the original design with all the details that give it its distinct character: the narrow-gauge clapboards, the corner boards, the flat trim around the windows, the "two-over-two" panes in the windows, the recessed doorway with flat columns (or pilasters) and molded architrave above, and, crowning the whole facade, the deep bracketed cornice. The shutters or blinds which have been shown on some of the windows only are optional.

The second sketch, by contrast, shows the unhappy results when all the original detail is removed and replaced by certain standard current lumberyard items. An attempt has also been made to make the building look older than its real period by using details that are supposed to be of Colonial design, but which are actually only unconvincing imitations of the real thing. (It must be added, however, that even if the details were genuine, the result would still be unsatisfactory as it is really almost impossible to make a building look older than it was when first built. The end result is always different from that of genuine restoration.) In this example, as is often the case, the fake historical items appear mainly at the doors and windows: the stamped metal "barn" door with frills which do not belong to any known historical style, the sad imitation of a genuine Colonial pediment over the door in the form of a triangular-shaped piece of wood, the undersized shutters or blinds that don't even *look* as if they could work and, lastly, the "six-over-six" paned windows which belong properly to the eighteenth century or to earlier nineteenth century houses in the Greek Revival style.

The design of the front has been further weakened in the second sketch by the removal of the corner boards and the deep cornice which framed the clapboards. Also, the upper part of the wall is now covered with wide gauge synthetic siding, and the lower part with artificial stone, with the line of demarcation up at second floor sill level, giving an indecisive half-and-half appearance to the whole front.

The Historic Preservation Program for New Mexico. Vol. 1, The Historical Background*

New Mexico State Planning Office

Major Preservation Problems and Suggested Solutions

By far the greatest problems confronting preservation forces are those generated by man. Of these, vandalism must be placed high on the list. Ranging from deliberate destruction to commercial pot hunting enterprises, which are probably considered by those engaged in such activities as legitimate economic pursuits, vandalism accounts for more destruction in New Mexico today than all other man-made causes combined.

Confined specifically to the field of historic preservation the artifact hunter tops the list of destroyers. Armed with detectors, trowels, picks, shovels, whiskbrooms, and even backhoes, these unrestrained agents of destruction have riddled scores of New Mexico sites, ranging from early-man hunting camps to 19th century ghost towns and military installations, and have almost eliminated any possibility of a thorough archaeological investigation of the Mimbres branch of the Mogollon Culture. The principal stimulus is, of course, financial gain. Mimbres pottery, for example, brings exorbitant prices on the market, and it is possible to derive a handsome income from the sale of this ware.

Hunters of bottles, buttons, spent bullets, and other trivia, gouging at the foundations of old buildings, forts and walls have taken their toll, as have the treasure hunters, encouraged by recurring wild tales of buried wealth periodically published in sensational journals or in certain magazines whose primary reason for existence is to supply advertising media for the manufacturers of detectors and other treasure hunting paraphernalia. In past years organized caravans, [comprising] club members representing a variety of destructive interests, have descended upon the state and spent several days engaged in their favorite forms of looting.

Irresponsible bearers of firearms present a serious problem. Their attention is most commonly directed to signs and windows and to the priceless examples of Indian rock art which are found throughout the state. After a big game rifle has been targeted in on a particularly tempting petroglyph, the question of its preservation becomes irrelevant, and the state has lost another ancient treasure of inestimable value.

In recent years, theft from churches, chapels and moradas has threatened almost complete loss of historic religious materials dating from the early 18th century. Again, the motive has been profit. The "discovery" by some art dealers and private collectors of the "folk art" values to be found in the statues and paintings created by local santeros during the Spanish and Mexican periods and the unique character of objects used in the rites of Penitente confraternities has created a ready market for the sale of these items. The looting of church buildings, particularly in remote areas, reached such proportions that on August 8, 1972 Governor Bruce King issued an executive order declaring that a

---

*Santa Fe, N.M.: State Planning Office, 1973, pp.61-62.

state of emergency existed "with respect to the preservation and security of New Mexico religious art" and called on all citizens to assist law enforcement agencies in the prevention of further thefts as well as in the location of stolen objects and the apprehension of those responsible. Action taken by the Chief of the New Mexico State Police in coordinating the efforts of law enforcement agencies and particularly the skillful investigation conducted by a dedicated two-man team consisting of one state police [officer] and one City of Santa Fe detective has resulted in the recovery of many of the stolen statues and furnishings.

Comprehensive Land Use Plan for the Plantations and Unorganized Townships of the State of Maine*

Maine Land Use Regulation Commission

Development of Maine's "wildlands" has over time produced a variety of historic, archaeological, architectural, and cultural resources in the jurisdiction.

Most of the known historic resources are related to the timber industry. They include a canal (the Telos cut), dams, narrow and standard gauge railroads, sluiceways, and logging settlements. Other historic resources include archaeological sites and Indian trails, architectural sites, military fortifications and objects (such as the Arnold Trail and old fortifications), and historic commercial and industrial sites (such as Katahdin Iron Works).

Historic resources are directly or indirectly threatened by the following:

•Improperly conducted timber harvesting, and development, which can destroy the character of historic trails, sites and objects
•Increased use of historic resources, which increases the likelihood of their being damaged or destroyed by abuse, overuse, and vandalism
•The legal and fiscal inability of the Maine Historic Preservation Commission to implement effective preservation programs
•The lack of effective preservation programs at the state level involving tax relief and historic trust instruments
•The lack of clear statements of policy concerning historic resources
•The lack of coordination among the agencies of the State of Maine relative to their policies concerning historic resources

The protection of historic resources by the commission is made extremely difficult by the fact that no comprehensive inventory of historic resources in the commission's jurisdiction exists.

*Augusta, Maine, 1976, p. 59.

"For God, for Country and . . . ." *

Michael F. Leccese

Connecticut preservationists seem to have succeeded in educating Yale University to the need for preserving one of the state's foremost 19th-century mansions.

Yale acquired Henry Austin's 1868 Davies mansion, considered one of the state's finest examples of a Second Empire style house, in 1972. The university sought the site primarily for its land: seven wooded acres overlooking the campus and crowded central New Haven.

Although it was not immediately evident, Yale had no plans to save either the mansion or its landscaped environs. No immediate development plans were in motion, but the university was definitely seeking "a cleared site," to expand onto at some point, according to Peter Halsey of Yale's Community Relations Office.

Boards went up on the house and maintenance ceased. Peeling paint, looting of fine detail work, roof leaks and other structural problems soon developed.

Preservationists were perplexed by Yale's apathy, particularly since the university has a fine architecture school and has commissioned works by many noteworthy architects (including Edward Larabee Barnes, who adapted another Austin mansion nearby).

Finally in 1978 Yale spent $5,000 to subsidize a reuse study, which concluded that the mansion's restoration was feasible only if the seven acres were heavily developed with highrise apartments and clustered townhouses in front of the mansion. However the report did not consider possible tax breaks for preservation. In addition, Yale wanted preservation groups, including the Connecticut Trust for Historic Preservation and the National Trust to bear most of the estimated $750,000 cost of renovating the Davies mansion. (The preservationists declined on the grounds that their money would subsidize a private developer.)

In 1978 the Connecticut Trust, the State Historic Preservation Office and the New Haven Preservation Trust countered with a $2,000 study of its own and a list of 34 interested developers.

Yale answered in the summer of 1979 by setting a March 31, 1980, demolition date for the house, which the university deemed unsafe. "That was an arbitrary deadline," Halsey of Yale told *Preservation News*. "It was our way of saying, you guys (preservationists) have to help out or the thing will come down."

Some preservationists didn't take it that way. "University officials seem to believe that it is beside the point that it was the university's own neglect that contributed largely to the house's condition," wrote *New York Times* architecture critic and Yale alumnus Paul Goldberger, adding it was "sad" that Yale—"a center of cultural artifacts as well as a forum of ideas"—needed to be persuaded to save a fine old building.

Students and faculty members joined in the dissent—their motto "For God, For Country and For the Davies Mansion" emblazoned on a Yale blue bumper sticker.

Although it claims preservationists have not been influential, Yale now seems headed toward leasing the land for "40, 50 or even 99 years," Halsey said, to one of two developers. One would create a conference center, the other an inn. Either would completely restore the mansion at an estimated cost of $50 a foot and preserve the land.

Preservation News, June, 1980, p. 1.

The Davies Mansion, located at the top of Prospect Hill in New Haven, Connecticut. Long used by the Culinary Institute of America (compare 143 Conn. 257, 121 A. 2d 637 (1956)), the building was acquired in 1972 by Yale University, whose interest was obviously primarily in acquiring the seven acres of land, right near the northern edge of the campus. *Courtesy of the National Trust, The Connecticut Trust and Mr. and Mrs. Thomas Wallace IV.*

With the March 31 deadline ignored, and Yale near selecting a developer, it would seem the mansion is secure. Unless, Halsey added, "the developers find that renovation would cost $75 a foot instead of $50. Grant money would have to compensate, or the house still could come down."

Local preservationists nonetheless feel they have made important points here.

"People are realizing that preservationists are no longer going in with only an emotional appeal," said Nancy Campbell of the Connecticut Trust, "but are willing to consider economics and work with institutions to resolve these pressures."

"This project will launch the Connecticut Trust into other projects with nonprofit institutions," she concluded. "There's a lot of educating to be done."

State University Threatens Church[*]

Carleton Knight

Richmond, Va.—A preservation battle among several state agencies is brewing over a landmark church owned by the state here.

The Medical College of Virginia, part of the state's Virginia Commonwealth University, wants to demolish the old First Baptist Church (1838-41), designed by Thomas U. Walter, and replace it with a new $18 million health education building. . . .

The university contends that the new building must be on the church site because so much money has been spent on planning to date and because the new structure will save money by sharing some facilities with Sanger Hall, an undistinguished contemporary structure adjacent to the church. In a letter to the National Trust, the university's Lauren Woods wrote, "If we were to select a new site at this time, the university, the state, and therefore the taxpayers, would lose nearly $800,000." That figure is the amount spent to date on architectural and engineering fees.

Edwin Slipek, Jr., writing in the university newspaper, *Commonwealth Times*, noted that the money spent already is but 4 percent of the total cost of the new building and added, "Some would argue that it is better to admit a $750,000 mistake than to commit an $18 million act of urban vandalism."

. . . but changing minds will be difficult. As Calder Loth, senior architectural historian with the state landmarks commission, has said, "Arguing with doctors is like arguing with God. They're saying, 'We're saving lives and need the space.' "

Right now, the only thing going for preservationists is the as-yet-unenforced executive order and the fact that there is no construction money.

---

[*]*Preservation News,* May 1977, p.1.

The First Baptist Church in Richmond, Virginia, a National Register building, threatened by Virginia Commonwealth University's expansion program. *Courtesy of the National Trust*.

A Fire in Galveston Ends Dispute on the Fate of Historic Building*

New York Times

Galveston, Tex., Feb. 11—Six months of controversy in this island city ended last week when the 118-year-old Ufford Building was destroyed by fire.

It was the third historic structure in the Strand area, once known as the "Wall Street of the Southwest," to go up in flames within five days.

"It's all over," said Peter Brink, of the Galveston Historical Foundation, which had fought to save the Greek Revival, pre-Civil-War Building.

One of the city's largest banks acquired it in 1975, intending to raze it to make room for a parking lot. The Historical Foundation, in negotiations with the bank, was trying to find an alternative site for the parking lot.

But in July, to the surprise of the foundation, a wrecking crew showed up to level the Ufford Building. More than a dozen irate Galvestonians staged a sit-in on the third floor as the demolition crew stood by. The protesters occupied the building until, in an emergency City Council meeting, the bank's demolition permit was revoked.

A Federal judge later issued a preliminary injunction requiring the bank to delay demolition work until a Federal historical survey of the Ufford Building was completed. The bank appealed and sought damages in excess of $10,000 from the Historical Foundation.

Many of the foundation members who occupied the building last year were in tears as they watched it collapse in flames a week ago.

Editors' Note: The Ufford Building Case

In the case of *Brink v. First Hutchings-Sealy National Bank*. (U.S. District Court for the Southern District of Texas, July 25, 1977), the court found that the Ufford Building had "historical and cultural value" and that its "immediate destruction without careful analysis and evaluation would cause irreparable injury."

Demolition by Neglect**

There is one threat to buildings that has nothing to do with demolition crews, urban renewal schemes or bulldozer-style development. That is the seldom discussed threat of neglect. Ignore any building long enough and time will take its toll, eventually rendering the wrecking ball unnecessary. If historic structures are left untended and unprotected against the ravage of man and nature, there is, finally, nothing left worth preserving.

---

*February 12, 1978, p. 52
**Editorial, *Preservation News*, March 1978, p. 4.

Three tragic fires in Galveston, Tex., during a single week in early February point up this problem dramatically. The most devastating of these blazes destroyed the Ufford Building, an 1860 commercial structure that had been at the center of a six-month controversy between local preservationists and its owner, the First Hutchings-Sealy Bank (*PN*, November 1977). The fire was apparently started by transients trying to keep warm in the abandoned building, which is located in the Strand National Historic Landmark District. At least one other of the recent fires seems to have arisen from similar accessibility of an unoccupied structure.

Peter Brink, executive director of the Galveston Historical Foundation, said the fires have resulted in "tremendous efforts to get owners to seal their buildings." Galveston city manager Tom Muehlenbeck told a group of townspeople that he had asked for inspection to insure that fire, safety, electrical and plumbing requirements were being met. In Galveston, at least, there is now growing concern for the condition of abandoned buildings.

The U.S. Department of the Interior has requested the opportunity to comment on the Ufford fire, since the building's owner was under a court injunction not to demolish the building. An Interior Department spokesman said the case raised important legal issues concerning interim protection of historic properties.

Though blame has yet to be fixed for destruction of the Ufford Building, there are other instances in which benign neglect has been a major factor in the loss of a structure. If a developer wants to avoid public criticism of demolition, he can simply allow a building to deteriorate until it either falls down or is condemned as a public hazard.

Fire Department Burns Down Historic House in Jersey County*

Washington Post

Paramus, N.J., Dec. 17 (AP)—History buffs are fuming because an 18th-century house was burned to the ground this week in a practice drill by the fire department. But fire officials said the owner planned to raze the house anyway to build three new homes on the site.

The Van Saun house—named for Cornelius Van Saun, an early Dutch settler—was built in 1750, and may have been the oldest pre-Revolutionary frame house in the county, said officials of the Bergen County Historical Society.

"It's a shame," said Claire Tholl, the society's vice president, as she picked up metal door hinges and nails from the charred ruins.

The house, which overlooked a mill pond and was occupied until about a month ago, was used to store blocks of ice cut from the pond by early Dutch settlers.

---

*December 18, 1977, p. 14.

The fire department said the owner of the house, who was not identified, invited the department to burn it to the ground.

"I appreciate nostalgia, but the training the men received was invaluable," said Fire Assistant Chief Thomas Carman.

The simple farm house was marked for preservation by the Bergen County Freeholders' Historical Sites Advisory Committee, and was included in the U.S. Historic American Building Survey in the Library of Congress, said Tholl.

"The owner can do what he wants, though," she said, adding that the Society learned about the fire practice drill too late to try to stop it.

Don't Tear It Down, Inc., v. General Services Administration *

United States District Court, District of Columbia

Memorandum-Order

GASCH, District Judge.

This case is before the Court on defendants' motion to dismiss on grounds of mootness. The Court thinks it well to set forth the facts and circumstances giving rise to the present posture of the case.

I. Legal Background

The National Historic Preservation Act of 1966[1] provides that any Federal project shall be begun only after taking into account the effect of such project on any property, site, structure or object which is listed on the National Register of Historic Places. The statute also provides that the Advisory Council on Historic Preservation shall be afforded the opportunity of commenting on such projects.[2] Executive Order No. 11593[3] also provides that the Advisory Council shall have an opportunity to comment on such a project.[4]

The Advisory Council on Historic Preservation ("Council") has promulgated regulations setting forth the procedures for obtaining its comments. In general these regulations provide that the agency in charge of a proposed project must determine whether the project will affect a Register property. If such agency finds that the project adversely affects a Register property (or if the Director of the Council timely objects to a determination of no adverse effect), an elaborate consultation process must be complied with. This process includes an on-site inspection by agency head and Council

---

*401 F. Supp. 1194 (1975).

Director, a meeting on the matter open to the public, and an opportunity for the Council to suggest alternative plans.

II. Facts

This case began, ironically enough, on Constitution Day of 1973.[5] On that day the General Services Administration (GSA) advised the Council that it intended to construct a new building for the Federal Home Loan Bank Board (FHLBB) in the 1700 block of G Street, N.W., in Washington, D.C.

The buildings in question here are four. The first of these is the Winder Building, built in 1857,[6] which was the site of part of the War Department during the Civil War and from which the search for the Lincoln conspirators was directed. The Winder Building was listed on the Register. The second was the Winder Annex which was, as its name implies, an integral part of the Winder Building. Third was the Riggs Bank Building, erected in the 1920's, whose imposing facade was regarded as an excellent example of the architecture of those days. Finally, there was the building occupied by the Nichols Cafe, a fine Federal townhouse from the early 19th Century (one of the few specimens of that style in the downtown area). In its letter of September 17, 1973, GSA stated that it would "determine the relationship" of the new building to the old ones.[7] Since it is a well-known physical law that two objects cannot occupy a given space simultaneously, the "relationship" in question would appear to have been clearly adversary.

On January 7, 1974, another communication issued from GSA to the Council. GSA found that the new building would have something of a detrimental effect on the Riggs Bank Building (total demolition) but that the Winder Building would be positively affected. The "positive effect" would be encirclement of the Winder Building by the FHLBB edifice. On January 31, 1974, it entered a contract for the demolition of the various buildings concerned.[8]

On February 5, 1974, the Council wrote GSA concerning the Riggs Bank Building, the Winder Annex and the Nichols Cafe, pointing out that all three buildings might be eligible for inclusion on the Register (and thus bringing into play the provisions of Executive Order No. 11593, *supra*). GSA adopted the useful expedient of ignoring this letter. On February 8, 1974, therefore, the Council sent a telecon message to GSA which reiterated the views expressed in the letter of February 5. The telecon also pointed out that the contract of January 31, 1974, appeared to be a clear violation of the law. GSA ignored this message also.

Undeterred, the Council then communicated the entire problem to an appropriate official of the Department of the Interior and itself requested Interior to determine the eligibility of the three buildings for inclusion on the Register. On the next day (February 14, 1974) the Council informed GSA of its action—again without response. On February 20, 1974, Interior determined that the buildings were eligible for the Register and so informed GSA and the Council. On February 22, 1974, the Council itself informed GSA of the decision by Interior and stated that the Council looked forward to the undertaking of the legally required procedures of consultation.

On February 27, 1974, GSA did respond. By letter of that date it advised that it had reevaluated its proposal in light of the determination by Interior and that it had decided to demolish the three buildings. This judgment was accomplished only seven days after notification of Interior's decision, thus showing how expeditiously the "Government's Housekeeping Agency" can weigh the most delicate of artistic and historical factors. GSA did, however, indicate its willingness to continue in the consultation process (leading to a decision which it had apparently already made). On the same day, GSA representatives met with those of the Council.

At that meeting, the Council informed GSA that there had been no acceptable agreement regarding minimization of adverse impact on the buildings in question. GSA apparently agreed that it would undertake no demolition of the buildings until after submission of the matter to a full Council meeting on May 1-2, 1974. This agreement was set forth in a letter from the Council to GSA, dated March 1, 1974

Meanwhile, on February 26, 1974, an attorney for plaintiffs herein contacted GSA and expressed plaintiffs' concern over the matter. Plaintiffs, through counsel, stated that they would file a law suit against GSA if the agency intended to continue demolition before completion of the consultation procedures. An official of GSA advised plaintiffs' counsel that GSA would not demolish the buildings until completion of the consultation procedures. Ominously, however, a news release on March 1, 1974, from GSA, stated that the agency would continue to clear the site in question.

On March 1, 1974, then, there was some confusion regarding the position of GSA. On Sunday, March 3, 1974, uncertainty terminated. GSA clarified the issue by execution of a classic Sunday sneak attack. It sent in the wreckers.[9] Before any action could be taken, the Nichols Cafe was obliterated, the Riggs Bank demolished (save only for its facade) and the Annex roof pierced. On Monday, March 4, 1974, this Court granted a temporary restraining order to halt demolition until the Court could act on the question of a preliminary injunction.[10]

There followed a number of orders,[11] the intent of which was to give the parties an opportunity to comply with the relevant consultation procedures. The result was that a special meeting of the Advisory Council was set for April 2 and 3, 1974. The first day's meeting was to be a public session while the second day's was to be an executive session, closed to the public. This scheme, of course, would seem to violate the requirement that the meetings be public. 36 C. F. R. § 800 (5) (c).

The first day's meeting went off without difficulty. On April 3, 1974, Mr. Sampson expressed his view that the Council staff members were misleading and misusing the Council to gain their own objectives.[12] Sampson warned that these machinations by the staff were undermining the Council's credibility and "clout."[13] He stated that he had previously consulted with persons (on various official bodies) who had far more expertise than the Council staff and these persons had agreed with the GSA decision.[14] Sampson then continued:

At this point you may wonder why I did not attempt to call a meeting of the Council, or meet with Council staff, or Secretary Morton, or somebody—before ordering demolition.[15]

Indeed, the Court itself has often so wondered. It need not have done so. The answer, said Mr. Sampson, was "simple." It was the staff again. The staff, according to Sampson, was intransigent, inflexible and had "the power to control and/or influence the Council."[16] Further consultation, thought Sampson, would be futile. The legal requirements were thus not deemed necessary and demolition began. The "simple" explanation, then, reduced itself to a statement that Sampson believed that the Council (of which he was a member) was under the misguided tutelage of its own staff and the staff would never agree with Sampson's views. Therefore, further consultation was vain and would not be carried on despite the legal mandates. In other words, Mr. Sampson was the dealer and the game was dealer's choice.

While perhaps not expressed with the purity of a classical syllogism, this logic was probably not without effect. In any event, the Council issued its comments on the next day, April 4, 1974.[17] To the astonishment of all defendants, the plaintiffs were not happy with this exercise of participatory decision making. On April 9, 1974, plaintiffs returned to Court seeking leave to amend their complaint. On April 11, 1974, they sought another temporary restraining order and a preliminary injunction, pointing out the fact that the Council meeting was not in accord with law.[18] The defendants serenely filed a motion to dismiss on the ground that they had now done all that was required. Despite this eloquent argument, the Court granted the restraining order (April 11, 1974).

Also on April 11, 1974, the Court ordered the defendants to produce any tapes or transcripts which might exist of the April 3, l974, Council meeting. Concerned that the Court had departed the path of right reason and was unduly concerned over trivial matters, defendants (on April 16, 1974) moved the Court to reconsider. The Court denied this on the same day. This led to the revelation of Sampson's speech to the Council.

The Court then extended the restraining order by subsequent order (April 23, 1974) and by approved stipulation (April 26, 1974). Except for two orders permitting some necessary work to be done on the site, matters remained at rest until July 19, 1974, at which time the Court dissolved the restraining order but enjoined any work which would affect the integrity of the Riggs building until such time as the removal thereof had been agreed to by the Joint Committee on Landmarks, the Commission on Fine Arts and the National Capital Planning Commission.

The matter is now again before the Court on motion to dismiss. The agencies concerned have gone to great pains to revise the construction plans to save, where possible, the remaining buildings. The record now reflects GSA's regret for the precipitousness of its prior actions and acknowledges GSA's responsibilities, under the Historic Preservation Act, to consult with the Advisory Council. It notes the recent efforts of defendants to comply with the law. The case, say defendants, is moot.

Conclusions

A nation is an entity in many senses beside the political. Shared beliefs and experiences provide the flesh and sinew which cover and unite the bones of political organization. These common beliefs and experiences are nourished, sustained and, indeed, sometimes created by history. Historical knowledge, then, is the life's blood of a people. To cut it off is to assure the eventual disintegration of the political entity. Congress has wisely recognized this and has provided, in the statutes here involved, for a careful consideration of historical values before a project which may destroy those values is begun.

This is not to say, of course, that contemporary needs should be utterly subordinated to the remnants of the past. That would indeed be to crush the present under the detritus of antiquity. All that is required is that the Government agency concerned take into consideration the historical values which may be affected by any planned project. The Congress has provided a procedure whereby this may be done. The situation is not dissimilar to that existing under the National Environmental Policy Act of 1969, except that the values protected here are less tangible, if no less valuable, than environmental values.

It seems clear to the Court that the actions of GSA through April 3, 1974, were in contravention of the policies and procedures mandated by Congress. Since that time, GSA has conformed to the law, although such conformity may well have been dictated more by concern for this Court's coercive powers than by any general respect for law. It is not, therefore, without some hesitation—and even trepidation—that the Court concludes that this case is moot and must be dismissed.

The plaintiffs sought an injunction prohibiting work until compliance with the consultation process, an injunction prohibiting Mr. Sampson from sitting on the Council on this matter, a declaratory judgment that GSA acted unlawfully herein and an injunction ordering GSA to comply, in the future, with the National Historic Preservation Act. All requisite permissions were obtained. It is undisputed that Mr. Sampson played no significant part in the Council's deliberations. There is no further need for a declaratory judgment. So far as the Court is aware, the conduct of GSA, although redolent of the "age of absolutism," has not been duplicated in any other instance relating to historic preservation. That it will be duplicated must be deemed speculative. GSA does not dispute the impropriety of its conduct, and, indeed, apologizes for it. The case is moot. *See O'Shea v. Littleton*, 414 U.S. 488, 94 S.Ct. 69, 38 L.Ed.2d 674 (1974); *Laird v. Tatum*, 408 U.S.1, 92 S.Ct. 2318, 33 L.Ed.2d 154 (1974); *United States v. W. T. Grant Co.*, 345 U.S. 629, 73 S.Ct. 894, 97 L.Ed. 1303 (1953); *Hinton v. Udall*, 124 U.S. App. D.C. 283, 364 F.2d 676 (1966); *Brandenfels v. Day*, 114 U.S. App. D.C. 374, 316 F.2d 375 (1963).

Accordingly, it is by the Court this 23rd day of April, 1975, ordered that the motion of defendants to dismiss this action be, and the same hereby is granted and the said action is dismissed.

Editors' Note: Later Events in the GSA Controversy

After the decision, GSA constructed the new building that the Federal Home Loan Bank Board wanted. An effort was made to maintain the cornice line of the Winder Building and to minimize the new building's mass.

A successful historic preservation effort might have led the government to locate this building in an area needing revitalization. During the controversy, Wolf Von Eckardt, the architectural critic of the *Washington Post*, observed: "I am sure the Federal Home Loan Bank Board is a most worthy institution. But if I understand the purposes of federal home loans correctly they are to help people obtain decent, safe, and sanitary homes in a suitable living environment. This coincides with the worthy purposes of the federal urban renewal program. You would therefore think that the board would be glad to help the cause and take its building and its 1,500 employees to the downtown urban renewal area, which badly needs some evidence that our federal government has some confidence in its own programs."

It is worth noting how different Federal laws may be involved in a single project. The Public Building Cooperative Use Act, which establishes a preference for GSA use of historic buildings, also encourages the location of commercial activities within Federal buildings. The Federal Home Loan Bank Board building contains shops on its first floor and was the first mixed-use building completed after the passage of the law.

Notes

1. 80 Stat. 915, 16 U.S.C. § 470f(1970).
2. *Id*.
3. 36 Fed. Reg. 8921 (May 13, 1971).
4. The Executive Order also requires an agency head to refer any questionable actions to the Secretary of Interior for an opinion regarding the property's eligibility for inclusion on the Register. *Id*. Where the Secretary of the Interior determines that the property should go on the Register, the referring agency must reconsider the entire project in light of this classification. *Id*.
5. September 17, 1973.
6. It is one of the few pre-Civil War office buildings left here.
7. The letter, however, made no mention of the Winder Annex or the Nichols Cafe.
8. This appears to have been a clear violation of 16 U.S.C. § 470f, since the Council had had no reasonable opportunity to comment on the project before approval of the expenditure of funds.
9. Mr. Sampson, Administrator of GSA, has stated elsewhere that demolition actually began on Friday, March 1, 1974. See Statement by Mr. A. F. Sampson before the Advisory Council on Historic Preservation on April 3, 1974 (copy on file in this case). It is a well-known principle, however, that a plaintiff's allegations must be taken as true for purposes of a motion to dismiss.
10. The temporary restraining order halted demolition until the case could be heard on March 12, 1974. It was later extended to March 13. On March 14, 1974, pursuant to the consent of all parties, the Court entered an order terminating all work (other than clearing rubble and the like) on the site until a hearing on the motion for a preliminary injunction which was set for March 23, 1974. On March 20, 1974, a similar consent order was entered providing that GSA would undertake no further work (with some exceptions) without giving five days notice thereof.
11. *See supra*, note 10.
12. *See supra*, note 9.
13. *Id*.
14. *Id*.
15. *Id*.
16. *Id*.
17. The Council thus bettered GSA's own reaction time in the delicate judgmental task involved here. It may be that this was due to the Council's greater experience and expertise herein. It may be also that the Council's ability to call on one of its members, Mr. Sampson, who had also figured largely in GSA's decisions, speeded its deliberations.
18. GSA had given notice that it intended to resume demolition.

Education of Architectural Preservation Specialists in the United States*

Stephen W. Jacobs

The last generation of architects to be trained in the traditional way established in the schools of architecture a century ago is now dying out. These practitioners were exposed to historical archetypes as models, and were expected to be able to produce reasonable imitations of the more admired features of archaic structures. Many of them were sufficiently scholarly and sympathetic to original materials, or sufficiently imbued with ingenuity and a flair for the picturesque, to make memorable contributions to the preservation scene. Others had a limited repertoire and little sympathy for the off-beat or atypical relic, replacing or "colonializing" buildings of all eras that came their way. In any event, they have few direct heirs, although some will be succeeded by younger men trained in their offices.

Until recently, the architecture schools provided relatively little help. Since 1945 training available in the regular professional curricula has been inadequate to qualify architects for historical work. From 1945 to 1960 the emphasis was on "modernity" and "progress," with little sympathy displayed by most practitioners or educators for evidences of the past which might inhibit new schemes. Historic structures were thought to be technically and socially obsolete, and to represent planning obstacles and financial opportunity losses rather than important environmental resources. The design religion of the Old Masters from Europe—Le Corbusier, Gropius, Mies van der Rohe—even though clearly based on knowledge and analysis of the achievements of the past, was regarded as requiring a rejection of all existing values and forms, in order to avoid the hazard of imitation or the drag of quotation. Cubist esthetic and machine age dynamism, new building technologies and new transport patterns, seemed to put a brave new world within reach, but one which had no desire to appear rooted. Even today an expendable, unstable environment is regarded by some as a desirable design objective.

*From North American International Regional Conference, *Preservation and Conservation: Principles and Practices*, Washington, D.C., Preservation Press, National Trust for Historic Preservation, 1976, pp. 458-59.

Part II

What to Preserve

4.

Criteria for Decisions on Preservation—Historic Aesthetic, and Practical

Preamble

This chapter is concerned with the choices to be encountered in making specific decisions as to what buildings we should preserve. Normally there will be more candidates for preservation than can in fact be taken care of. To a considerable extent, such choices are necessarily based on the criteria spelled out in chapter 2, with varying degrees of emphasis in different countries; for example, historic preservation in this country has been (or, at least, was at first) concerned primarily with the historic associations of certain buildings, whereas in England primary emphasis was placed on visual considerations and on preserving amenity in the physical environment. However, in many instances practical considerations will also play a substantial role. For example, how authentic is the existing building? How much is left of the original building and its context? What are the realistic possibilities for its reuse, perhaps for a different purpose? Again, a historic building that is in immediate danger will naturally receive priority in consideration over others not so threatened.

The various items in this chapter set forth specific examples on all of these considerations. The criteria for listing in the National Register should provide a summary of the relevant considerations. This chapter also provides an indication of the criteria used by the Landmarks Commission in New York City.

Historic Structures Report, Part I *

Norman Souder

This area, like so many other areas of the United States, produced styles and building practices which became characteristic of the locality. While they may not be as outstanding as the famous buildings designed by early well-known architects in the metropolitan areas, they are, nevertheless, unique to the area and as such should be preserved as regional examples.

The basis of selection, therefore, was first, architectural merit; second, historic association; third, selection for preservation as most representative of a local style or type.

Historic Districts: Identification, Social Aspects and Preservation * *

William G. Murtagh and G. C. Argan

It is interesting to observe in the context of associative values that the United States has developed a priority of preservation value judgments diametrically opposed to the priority that developed in Europe. In writing about conservation areas or town centers, Europeans usually refer to the two basic criteria as, first, aesthetics and, second, association (or architecture and history). In the United States the order of reference is reversed. One is therefore drawn to the conclusion that in the United States consideration traditionally has been given to historical association first, with artistic endeavor as a secondary consideration.

Editors' Note: Alexandria Historic District Ordinance

The City of Alexandria Historic District Ordinance was amended to provide protection to structures over 100 years old lying outside the district. The ordinance sets forth the following criteria to be used in selecting these structures:

---

*For Delaware Water Gap National Recreation Area, National Park Service, pp. ii–iii.
* *Washington, D.C.: Preservation Press, 1975, p. 12.

Sec. 42-98.2. Criteria.

In considering whether or not to include a building or structure over one hundred years old on the list for preservation, at least two of the following criteria shall be met:

(a) Is it entered upon the National Register of Historic Places as called for by the United States Congress in the Historic Sites Act of 1935 and the Historic Preservation Act of 1966?

(b) Is it entered upon the Virginia Landmarks Register pursuant to Section 10-138 of the Code of Virginia?

(c) Does it exemplify or reflect the architectural, cultural, political, economic, social or military history of the nation, state or community?

(d) Is it associated with persons of national, state, or local prominence or with events of national, state, or local historical significance?

(e) Is it a good example of local or regional architectural design or exemplify local craftsmanship, making it valuable for a study of a period, style or method of construction?

(f) Is it the work of a nationally recognized architect or can it be attributed to a local architect or builder of local prominence?

(g) Does it foster civic pride in the city's past or enchance the city's attractiveness to visitors?

Conservation of Historic and Cultural Resources *

Ralph W. Miner

Checklist of Criteria for Evaluation

Historic Considerations

Is the structure associated with the life or activities of a major historic person (more than the "slept here" type of association)?

---

*A.S.P.O. (American Society of Planning Officials) Planning Advisory Service, Report no. 244, 1969, pp. 19-20.

Is it associated with a major group or organization in the history of the nation, state, or community (including significant ethnic groups)?

Is it associated with a major historic event (whether cultural, economic, military, social, or political)?

Is the building associated with a major recurring event in the history of the community (such as an annual celebration)?

Is it associated with a past or continuing institution which has contributed substantially to the life of the city?

Architectural Considerations

Is the structure one of few of its age remaining in the city?

Is it a unique example in the city of a particular architectural style or period?

Is it one of a few remaining examples in the city of a particular architectural style or period?

Is it one of many good examples in the city of a particular architectural style or period?

Is the building the work of a nationally famous architect?

Is it a notable work of a major local architect or master builder?

Is it an architectural curiosity or picturesque work of particular artistic merit?

Does it evidence original materials and/or workmanship which can be valued in themselves?

Has the integrity of the original design been retained or has it been altered?

Setting Considerations

Is the structure generally visible to the public?

Is it, or could it be, an important element in the character of the city?

Is it, or could it be, an important element in the character of the neighborhood (either alone or in conjunction with similar structures in the vicinity)?

Does it contribute to the architectural continuity of the street?

Is the building on its original site?

Is its present setting (yards, trees, fences, walls, paving treatment, outbuildings, and so forth) appropriate?

Are the structure and site subject to the encroachment of detrimental influences?

Use Considerations

Is the building threatened with demolition by public or private action?

Can it be retained in its original or its present use?

Does it have sufficient educational value to warrant consideration of museum use?

Is it adaptable to productive reuse?

Are the building and site accessible, served by utilities, capable of providing parking space, covered by fire and police protection, and so forth, so that they can feasibly be adapted to contemporary use?

Can the structure be adapted to a new use without harm to those architectural elements which contribute to its significance?

Cost Considerations

Is preservation or restoration economically feasible?

Is continued maintenance after restoration economically feasible?

The State of Connecticut Historic Preservation Plan *

Connecticut Historical Commission

Criteria or Standards Applicable to Choice of Sites

1. Buildings by great architects or master builders, and important works of minor ones.
2. Noteworthy examples of various architectural styles, periods, or methods of construction.
3. Any building, though perhaps undistinguished in itself, that is the sole or very rare survivor of its style or period.
4. Architectural curiosities, one-of-a-kind buildings.
5. Village greens, by themselves or including adjacent structures that enhance the appearance; old militia training grounds.
6. Areas or groups of typical or related buildings in original setting, preserving enough of historical surroundings to maintain the atmosphere of an earlier time.
7. Sites of events significant in cultural, political, economic, military, or social history of town, state, or nation.
8. Homes of notable persons during their active years.
9. Sites and groupings representing historic community development patterns: seaports, county seats, concentrations around transportation facilities.
10. Old commercial structures and sites.
11. Early or abandoned transport facilities and adjuncts.
12. Structures related to the civic life of a community.
13. Indian remains or sites.
14. Churches recorded when:
    a. Outstanding for age or architecture, or both.
    b. Scene of historic events.
15. Cemeteries recorded when:
    a. Outstanding for age, length of use.
    b. Burial place of outstanding historic personages.
16. Integrity of a site or structure requires:
    a. No doubt that it is authentic and the original.
    b. Material and workmanship mostly original.
    c. Structure preferably on original site.
    d. Favorable surroundings, probability of continuing so; or possibility of replacing unfavorable surroundings through such activity as urban renewal.

---

*Hartford, Conn., 1970, pp. 8-9.

National Register of Historic Places*

Part 60, sec. 60.4 (1981)

The criteria applied to evaluate properties for possible inclusion in the National Register are listed below. These criteria are worded in a manner to provide for a wide diversity of resources. The following criteria shall be used in evaluating properties for nomination to the National Register, by the National Park Service in reviewing nominations, and for evaluating National Register eligibility of properties. . . .

National Register criteria for evaluation. The quality of significance in American history, architecture, archaeology, engineering, and culture is present in districts, sites, buildings, structures, and objects that possess integrity of location, design, setting, materials, workmanship, feeling, and association, and:

(a) That are associated with events that have made a significant contribution to the broad patterns of our history; or

(b) That are associated with the lives of persons significant in our past; or

(c) That embody the distinctive characteristics of a type, period, or method of construction, or that represent the work of a master, or that possess high artistic values, or that represent a significant and distinguishable entity whose components may lack individual distinction; or

(d) That have yielded, or may be likely to yield, information important in prehistory or history.

Criteria considerations. Ordinarily cemeteries, birthplaces, or graves of historical figures, properties owned by religious institutions or used for religious purposes, structures that have been moved from their original locations, reconstructed historic buildings, properties primarily commemorative in nature, and properties that have achieved significance within the past 50 years shall not be considered eligible for the National Register. However, such properties will qualify if they are integral parts of districts that do meet the criteria or if they fall within the following categories:

(a) A religious property deriving primary significance from architectural or artistic distinction or historical importance.

(b) A building or structure removed from its original location but which is significant primarily for architectural value, or which is the surviving structure most importantly associated with a historic person or event.

(c) A birthplace or grave of a historical figure of outstanding importance if there is no appropriate site or building directly associated with his productive life.

(d) A cemetery which derives its primary significance from graves of persons of transcendent importance, from age, from distinctive design features, or from association with historic events.

(e) A reconstructed building, when accurately executed in a suitable environment and presented in a dignified manner as part of a restoration master plan, and when no other building or structure with the same association has survived.

(f) A property primarily commemorative in intent if design, age, tradition, or symbolic value has invested it with its own exceptional significance.

(g) A property achieving significance within the past 50 years if it is of exceptional importance.

---

*Criteria for Eligibility for Listing in the National Register, 36 C.F.R., part 60, sec. 60.4 (1981).

Landmark Preservation *

John S. Pyke, Jr.

Since 1965 the [New York City] Landmarks Preservation Commission has designated over 360 structures as landmarks and 18 areas as historic districts.

The Landmarks Preservation Law defines a "landmark" as:

> Any improvement, any part of which is 30 years old or older, which has a special character or special historical or aesthetic interest or value as part of the development, heritage or cultural characteristics of the city, state or nation and which has been designated as a landmark pursuant to the provisions of [*the Landmarks Preservation Law*].

The Commission's "Guide for the Preparation and Presentation of Testimony at Public Hearings of the Landmarks Preservation Commission" suggests additional bases upon which nominated landmarks will be evaluated. These include architectural significance, whether national, regional or local; uniqueness of design; status as the work of a noted architect; its place in the continuity of architectural development in New York City; and special historical associations with individuals or events.

In actuality, once the Commission began to select and designate New York's landmarks, it settled without difficulty on the designation of one hundred or so old structures and sites of high quality which were universally recognized as landmarks. For instance, any 18th century building not in an advanced state of decay was an immediate candidate for designation. As a criterion for preservation, mere antiquity is important if all the other buildings of that era have perished.

Other structures had definite historical associations, such as the Edgar Allan Poe cottage in the Bronx and the Hamilton Grange, the home built by Alexander Hamilton and from which he left for his fatal meeting with Aaron Burr on the duelling field at Weehawken, New Jersey. Still other buildings had clear architectural importance or were identified with distinguished architects; examples of this type were the cast iron buildings, City Hall (described by Burnham in *New York Landmarks* as "an architectural treasure without peer"), and the one building in the City designed by Louis Sullivan. Finally, some structures, such as the New York Public Library on Fifth Avenue at 42nd Street and Columbia University's Low Memorial Library, had been built more or less as public monuments and deserved official recognition as such.

In selecting landmarks, however, the Commission has looked beyond those buildings popularly regarded as landmarks to buildings highly valued by special interest groups, such as historical architects or history buffs. In these cases the building's place in the community's preservation program also figured in the decision-making process.

Following the principle that landmarks are assets to their respective communities, buildings have been designated in each borough on the ground that they were the best existing examples of a particular architectural style or method of construction in that borough or area. In proceeding from borough to borough, however, the Commission has endeavored to apply one set of standards even though some boroughs had a rich heritage of old structures while others had relatively few.

---

*New York: Citizens Union Research Foundation, 2nd ed., 1972, pp. 17-18.

Part III

How to Preserve

5.

Criteria on Conformity with Architectural Styles in the Area

Preamble

Awell-thought-out historic preservation program is likely to cover a wide variety of activities, but normally a major part of such a program is based on historic districts and accordingly is concerned with maintaining the historical character of these districts. In such areas new construction normally plays a relatively minor role, although it is of course important when it occurs; the routine administration of such a program is usually concerned primarily with monitoring minor changes in the exterior of historic buildings, to be sure that these do not introduce a jarring element in the overall situation. To do this requires a clear definition of the basic characteristics of such an area—i.e., the main elements of the design vocabulary. Almost all experts in the field are in agreement that what is *not* needed is a requirement of conformity to a single architectural style. The definition of what constitutes conformity therefore presents real problems. Some districts are distinctive, with an unusual and well defined architectural vocabulary; others, much less distinctive, involve varied types of building, but with certain elements in common.

The problem is to define what these basic common elements are, for there is no other way (beyond mere whim and caprice) to decide whether a proposed new element conforms with them. Moreover, to do this is important not only as a matter of practical administration, but for legal reasons. With a recent strong run of favorable decisions, a historic preservation program may be confident of considerable support in the courts, *provided* it is possible to give assurances that the program will be carried out with substantially uniform treatment to everybody concerned. What is needed, then, is the development of realistic standards.

A different, although somewhat analogous, problem occurs in the case of historic landmarks. Such landmarks may be historic because of their association with important personages, or because they represent particularly good examples of a given style of architecture. To determine the latter requires real acquaintance with (a) architectural history, and (b) standards of good design.

The items in this chapter represent a broad range of experience. Some are concerned with really distinctive historic districts, as in New Orleans, Nantucket, and Santa Fe, where the problem of defining standards is relatively simple: the standards are inherent in the prevailing architectural style.

Others are involved with historic districts with a much broader range of building types, as in New York City, Newport, and New Bedford. The passage from the Springfield historic district regulations focuses attention on important details that may otherwise be overlooked. Finally, the passage from Boston's Beacon Hill handbook elaborates in detail the importance of certain details—for example, color, signs, and the precise treatment of doors.

The most penetrating analyses of criteria for conformity have come from historic district studies in Savannah, and the even more elaborate study made in Tucson, Arizona. Moreover, the sections on the historic town of Woodstock, Vermont (actually prepared for a seminar in historic preservation law at the Vermont Law School) provide an unusual sensitivity to the considerable variations, street by street, within a relatively homogeneous Vermont village.

In order to understand the problem of developing workable standards, it is necessary to know something about the history of architecture—for example, what are the distinctive features of the various successive styles? Considerations of space preclude including a large amount of relevant material in the present volume. However, in addition to the many standard histories of architecture, there are three heavily illustrated pictorial guides to American architecture that would be useful to any student using the present volume—and particularly to a student not well versed in the history of American architecture. These volumes are as follows:

1. Blumenson, *Identifying American Architecture: A Pictorial Guide to Styles and Terms, 1600-1945* (Nashville, Tenn.: American Association for State and Local History, 1977.

2. Poppeliers, Chambers, and Schwartz, *What Style Is It?* (Washington, D.C.: National Trust for Historic Preservation, 1977).

3. Whiffen, *American Architecture Since 1780: A Guide to the Styles* (Cambridge, Mass.: MIT Press, 1969).

Two other particularly useful volumes, dealing with specific local areas and also with extensive illustrations, are:

1. Southeastern Connecticut Regional Planning Agency, *Opportunities for Historic Preservation* (1968).

2. Historic Annapolis, Inc., *A Guide to Domestic and Commercial Architectural Styles in Annapolis* (1975).

Conservation of Historic and Cultural Resources*

Ralph W. Miner

Guidelines for Architectural Review

Virtually all historic zoning ordinances require that new construction in the district (whether totally new buildings or additions or alterations to old ones) be architecturally "compatible" or "harmonious" with the character of existing structures. Compatibility and harmony are not defined. It is left to the architectural review board to determine this when the sponsor of new construction applies for a certificate of appropriateness. Some ordinances cite a few vague generalities about what should be considered in determining appropriateness: the general design, arrangement, texture, material, color, and fenestration of the proposal must be similar to these same characteristics of existing structures in the district. Except for the case of College Hill in Providence, where appropriate contemporary design is encouraged by ordinance, the result of such provisions has tended to perpetuate imitations of earlier architectural styles. Even in districts which contain numerous styles, one particular style seems to emerge as the favorite of the review board, and virtually all new construction appears in imitations of that style.

Established formal criteria by which to judge new construction proposals are probably rare if not nonexistent. Yet this is one of the most crucial aspects of the architectural control provisions. Without some established standards, the character of a district can gradually move toward the stylistic preference of the review board members. Admittedly it is difficult to develop precise criteria for judging which wholly retain their objectivity and which permit adequate review of new designs in a variety of styles, from the traditional to the contemporary. In fairness to the architects whose plans are reviewed and to the board itself, whose membership may change, it would appear desirable to have some general public guidelines as a basis for reviewing projects for certificates of appropriateness. What follows is a preliminary attempt to outline such general guidelines, with the full understanding that they must be refined to be applied to particular historic districts in particular localities.

Framework for Architectural Review

The architectural review framework outlined here is [composed] of several premises:

1. Guidelines for determining appropriateness must be as objective as possible so as not to favor one particular architectural style over another. A well-designed contemporary structure should have just as much chance to "pass the test" as, for example, an equally well-designed Georgian structure.

---

*A.S.P.O. Planning Advisory Service Report no. 244, 1969, pp. 46–48.

2. The existing structures in any historic district have certain basic visual elements and relationships in common which can be considered as the unique "design vocabulary" of that district.

3. This essential design vocabulary can be identified for any district and can be abstracted and documented as a basis for judging the appropriateness of new construction proposals without reference to architectural style.

4. The question of whether a new proposal will be compatible can be viewed in terms of fit or misfit with the basic design vocabulary of the district. A proposal incorporating the same essential vocabulary, regardless of style, will fit and should be judged appropriate. On the other hand, a proposal reflecting a different design vocabulary (even if it offers some stylistic similarities to other structures in the district) would be considered a misfit which would not be appropriate within the district.

The discussion here is oriented toward the case of a separate new structure being judged in terms of its appropriateness for construction in the historic district. Similar focus could be placed on alterations or additions to existing structures.

Guidelines

The design of the new structure can be tested against the established design vocabulary of the district on at least three levels (though there are some overlapping concerns). Failure of the design to fit reasonably well at any one level could provide the basis for denying the certificate of appropriateness.

The first level incorporates many of the basic regulations in the zoning ordinance which affect appearance either directly or indirectly. (Misfit here would automatically mean denial because of conflict with established legal provisions.) If the proposal passes this first test, considerable design latitude would remain to be tested at the other levels. Here the guidelines would ask: Does the new design fit with respect to:

> building spacing?
> lot coverage?
> yard limits?
> setbacks?
> density of use?
> bulk?
> height?

At this and the other levels the specific list would be developed by the local architectural review board to reflect the existing regulations and the perceived design vocabulary of the particular district.

The second level reflects specific elements in the district's design vocabulary related to detailed architectural design. The guidelines would ask: Does the new design fit with respect to:

> materials?
> surface textures?
> colors?
> fenestration pattern?
> utilization of characteristic local forms
> (such as stoops and front porches)?
> roof form and pitch?
> simplicity?

elements of composition?
symmetrical or asymmetrical appearance?
basic shape or form?
expression of detailing?

The third level draws upon elements in the district's design vocabulary related to environmental relationships. The guidelines would ask: Does the new design fit with respect to:

scale?
rhythm of the block face?
orientation?
proportion?
general spirit of the area?

This framework and set of guidelines attempts to provide a more objective method of evaluating the appropriateness of new construction proposals in historic areas. It is preliminary and suggestive only. Details of the guidelines at each level must be drawn from the perceived design vocabulary of the particular historic district in which the approach is to be tested.

Guidebook for the Old and Historic Districts of Nantucket and Siasconset*

Nantucket, Mass. Historic Districts Commission

The beauty of an area derives from the order and harmony of the components, not from the aesthetic qualities of the individual structures alone. A modern house and an old fashioned house both may be beautiful, but placed adjacent to each other the two houses can create a discord, and neither may properly display its virtues. The discord can be even worse when a modern "improvement" is grafted onto an old structure. Many older cities in the East contain hundreds and even thousands of historic and beautiful structures yet the whole environment remains so ugly and discordant that it repels the visitor. Beauty is balance, order, and harmony; ugliness is disproportion, confusion, and discord. The ugliness of so many communities that have succumbed to "progress" lies in the disorder and lack of harmony created by the hot dog stand next to the cemetery, the gas station alongside the home, the used car lot abutting the park, and the development houses scattered without design among the traditional.

---

*1967, p. 4.

The order and harmony of this row of mansions on the main street óf Nantucket adds to the beauty of the individual buildings. *Courtesy of the National Trust.*

Aesthetics in Historic Districts*

Harmon H. Goldstone * *

It was a lawyer, the late Albert S. Bard, who first introduced the word *aesthetic* into the laws of the State of New York. His amendment to the General City Law, adopted on April 2, 1956, has since been widely cited as the Bard Law.[1] The word *aesthetic* had, until the Bard Law was enacted, been carefully avoided in proper legislative circles. This attitude is quite understandable for the word opens a Pandora's box of ill-defined, if not essentially undefinable concepts which are capable of stirring people to strong passions. From Socrates to Santayana some very ugly arguments have taken place over the question of what is beautiful and what is not. Even the meaning of the word has never been resolved to everyone's satisfaction.

Yet, eleven independent-minded individuals, as the officially appointed members of New York City's Landmarks Preservation Commission, have the responsibility of making aesthetic judgments every day. These aesthetic judgments are made in connection with the Commission's power to grant or deny requests to construct, alter, or demolish a landmark or portion of a historic district. Their authority for doing so stems directly from the New York City's Landmarks Preservation Law of 1965 which lists the consideration of aesthetic values and significance as one of the factors governing the determination of such a request.[2] This mandate and the declaration of public policy in the preamble[3] to the statute involve the Landmarks Preservation Commission in making not only aesthetic judgments, but also in considering cultural, historical, social, economic, political, architectural, utilitarian, recreational, promotional, and educational questions, as well as in the cultivation of civic pride and general welfare. It is not surprising that at times this multiplicity of responsibilities makes decisions on individual cases difficult—particularly difficult when they hinge primarily on so subjective a criterion as an aesthetic judgment. The following suggestions are presented as guidelines which may be helpful in making such decisions.

The criteria that are appropriate to the design of an entirely new building within one of New York City's historic districts are quite different from those that are appropriate to the replacing of a missing part of an existing old building. Within a historic district there is also a third situation in which, from one point of view, the criteria applicable to the district as a whole seem appropriate while, from another point of view, the situation should be treated as if an isolated building were being restored. Each of these three problems will be considered in turn.

1. *New Buildings in Old Districts.* The City of New York has thus far designated as historic districts eighteen areas containing over 6,000 properties. The popularity of this part of the landmarks preservation program has exceeded all expectations. More people than anyone had ever imagined really enjoy living and working in neighborhoods that are characterized by the harmonious qualities of good urban design and by a sense of continuity with the past. The joint effort to preserve such qualities has raised community morale, and the designation of historic districts has, in fact, proven to be a surprisingly potent force for social stabilization.

---

*From *Law and Contemporary Problems,* Vol. 36, 1971, pp. 378-85.

* *Harmon Goldstone, F.A.I.A., A.N.A., was Chairman, New York City Landmarks Preservation Commission.

A typical street in Greenwich Village (Waverly Place, just east of the Avenue of the Americas) provides an illustration of an underlying unity, which yet embodies several architectural styles. *Courtesy of New York City Landmarks Commission.*

It is important, however, to understand the difference between New York City's historic districts and the various "museum towns" that have been preserved, restored, and reconstructed around the country. The museum towns can equally well be justified, but for quite different reasons. Williamsburg freezes a moment of history—the climax of British colonial culture in Virginia. Plymouth Plantation shows how the earliest New England settlers lived, dressed, and worked. Cooperstown demonstrates the forthright qualities of nineteenth century rural crafts. Richmondtown shows how a country town, a county seat, grew and developed for over two centuries. These history lessons—in three dimension—are valuable and deservedly popular. Since they are, in the full sense of the word, "museums," a curatorial approach is quite properly applied not only to every detail of each building but also to every aspect of the surroundings. The streets, the street lighting, the gardens, the walls—even the costumes of the guides and the horse-drawn carriages—must all be as exactly consistent with the period represented as it is possible to achieve. It is quite appropriate, therefore, in these museum towns to insist that, insofar as possible, every aspect of the work be carried out by means of the same handicraft techniques that were originally used. Although these demonstrations are fascinating and instructive, they are not, and are not intended to be, integral and vital parts of a dynamic metropolis in which twentieth century people live and earn a living.

If a New York City historic district is not a museum piece in the sense of a Williamsburg or a Plymouth Plantation, then what, exactly, are the qualities that set it apart from its surroundings? What is there about it that is worth preserving? And how can these worthwhile qualities be preserved?

The statutory definition of a New York City historic district requires that "special character or special historical or aesthetic interest . . . cause such area . . . to constitute a distinct section of the city,"[4] and yet the same statute specifically provides that it may "represent one or more periods or styles of architecture typical of one or more eras in the history of the city. . . . "[5] In fact, most of the historic districts contain a wide variety of styles. Despite this heterogeneity, there are attributes which unify these distinct sections.

A high, general level of architectural quality in the majority of their buildings is a first criterion, but of equal significance is the fact that despite a mixture of styles, a historic district conveys an agreeable feeling of harmony that is in strong contrast with the surrounding areas of the city. This sense of harmony does not depend upon uniformity of style; rather, it is based on the qualities of good urban design. That these have developed naturally, spontaneously, and even accidentally, in certain isolated areas of the city is our good fortune. Now that these areas have been identified and officially designated, it is the responsibility of the Landmarks Preservation Commission to insure that future growth and change within a historic district be guided along the lines that gave it, in the first place, the qualities we appreciate. These qualities are, in descending order of importance, mass, color, scale, and style.

In specific terms the most important factor to be maintained is uniformity of the roof line and the setback line; next, compatibility of color, texture, and type of materials; third, the scale of the openings; and, finally, the details of a particular architectural style or fashion. It is a sensitive variation of individual designs within the limits of these criteria that gives our historic districts so much of their appeal. It is particularly important to note that, insofar as the attractive character of the street scene is concerned, adherence to the details of a particular architectural style is the least important factor. In fact, when there is complete conformity in each of the four criteria a deadly monotony can result.

When an entirely new structure is proposed to be built on an existing empty lot in a historic district, the significant criterion that should control its design is compatibility with its neighbors in mass, color, and scale. Every age in history has produced an architecture expressive of its economics, aspirations, techniques, materials, and aesthetics. It is the harmonious juxtaposition of these evolutionary changes that gives our historic districts so much of their interest.

A pressing question concerns the desirability of demanding that new buildings conform to the architecture of the period represented in the district. There are those who would discriminate against introduction of the architectural expression of our own era. Proponents of this view bear the burden of showing the appropriate historical cutoff point. The difficulty encountered in this task provides an answer to their own arguments about the inappropriateness of expressions. An actual example makes the point. Brooklyn Heights began to emerge in its present form after the opening of the Fulton Street Ferry in 1814. In a recent census, the district contained 60 Federal style houses, 405 Greek Revival houses, 201 Anglo-Italianate houses, and 216 in miscellaneous, eclectic styles dating from after the Civil War. If a Landmarks Preservation Commission had been established around 1830 and if it had supported the point of view that nothing could be added to a historic district that did not follow the style of what was already there, then 93 percent of what most of us at present enjoy would not exist today. If such a commission had not been established until 1860, we would still miss almost half of the best buildings that now survive on the Heights.

Growth and change must occur in New York City's historic districts if they are to remain vital parts of a dynamic organism. When a new building is proposed for an empty lot which may have existed at the time the district was designated or which may, for whatever reason, have become subsequently available, then the aesthetic criteria appropriate to its design are exactly the same as those that unconsciously guided its predecessors through their various periods and styles—compatibility of mass, color, and scale with its surroundings. The new building should also be as good an expression of the architecture of our own period as the best of its predecessors were of theirs.

This standard admits of one exception. In the few historic districts that are completely homogeneous in style, new buildings—in order to preserve the entirely uniform character of their surroundings—should also conform in style. These are, however, rare and exceptional situations.

2. *New Parts for Old Buildings.* A different question is presented by a suggested replacement of a damaged or missing part of an old building in a historic district or the correction of inappropriate changes which earlier owners may have made without appreciation of the architectural qualities of their building. It is the responsibility of the Landmarks Preservation Commission not only to insist on the retention of every good building that has survived in a historic district but also to encourage its appropriate restoration. The protection of such architecture is inherent in the very fact of the district's designation.

If the building in question is entirely of one period and style and has come to the Commission complete, except for the missing part, then to replace that part with anything which did not closely match the original would impair the integrity of the original design. It is a rare occasion when the part can be replaced with something that was made at the same time and in the same manner as the original. If such a part is not obtainable a handcrafted imitation is preferable to a machine-made copy, particularly when it will be located at eye level. If the hand skills are no longer available, or if the owner cannot afford to pay for them, a good machine-made reproduction is better than either omitting the part or inserting something obviously different in style from the rest of the facade.

The argument is sometimes made that any new work added to an old building should be so immediately distinguishable that no one will be deceived by what is "original" and what is not. This is the archaeologist's attitude, and he is quite justified when he is reconstructing some great monument of antiquity. He is anxious, on the one hand, to recreate the original overall appearance of the structure and, on the other, not to pretend that his contemporary restoration is part of the original work. To apply this sort of scholarly conscientiousness to the replacing of a missing brownstone baluster or a section of a simple Greek Revival cornice misses the point of preservation of such works. Even the best of buildings in any of New York City's historic districts are simply good examples of honest workmanship in a variety of once-popular styles. The names of a few of the architects who designed them are known, but hundreds of the buildings that give the historic districts their appreciated quality were erected by anonymous builders who worked from stock plans. Their value is their overall effect. To insist, for the sake of archaeological purity, on distinguishing new work from old could destroy the very values sought to be preserved.

3. *Mixed Situations*. While clear and valid distinctions can thus be made between the criteria appropriate for the restoration of a single building in a single style and for the erection of an entirely new building on an empty lot within a historic district, there remain two types of mixed situations for which appropriate aesthetic criteria are more difficult to fix. To restore a building of mixed styles or to add an entirely new wing, with new functions, onto an old building is a more subtle and complex problem. In such cases, the Commission must also consider the relative visual "weights" of one part to another, their historic associations, and the visual relationship of the parts in question to their surroundings. An attempt may be made to carry over the color and some of the materials and characteristic details from one part of a structure to another, as in Edgar Tafel's 1960 addition to Joseph C. Well's Gothic Revival First Presbyterian Church on the corner of Fifth Avenue and 12th Street in New York City. Or only the gross scale of the adjoining row houses may be carried over—in contrasting materials and with starkly contrasting detail—as in James Stewart Polschek Associates' remarkably interesting new headquarters for the New York State Bar Association in Albany, New York.[6]

An actual example of the second sort of mixed situation recently came before the Commission for decision.[7] The problem concerned the design of an entirely new building on an empty lot in the middle of a row of similar houses. The question raised was whether a row of houses, built at the same time, should be considered as a single architectural composition or simply as a series of individual buildings that happen to bear a closer resemblance one to another than to the others around them. Is the problem of filling a gap in such a row the same as restoring a missing part to an individual building, or is it, rather, like erecting a new building on any other vacant lot within an historic district? There seems to be no single, simple, and universally applicable answer. It depends on the nature of the row and its surroundings. It is necessary to determine whether the row was originally conceived as a unified composition, as the Royal Crescent in Bath; or whether it fills an entire block front as does the row on Washington Square North (with one intrusion) between Fifth Avenue and University Place; or whether it defines a distinctive geometric form, as does the so-called "Renwick Triangle" in the St. Marks Historic District. It may be that a row merely starts where the original developer's property began and stops where his money ran out. Other considerations are the present condition of the other houses of the row and the nature of their surroundings. In short, the Commission seeks to identify the elements that give a particular section of a historic district its qualities and then asks whether a specific proposal to fill a gap in the row would enhance or harm these qualities.

If this discussion of aesthetics in historic districts seems to have proposed more questions than answers, it is because the problem is a complex and subtle one. The Commission is frequently urged to supply a simple set of guidelines so that the owner of a property in a historic district would merely have to ascertain the style of his building in order to learn exactly how to carry out appropriate repairs and replacements. While there would be no particular difficulty in preparing an illustrated collection of typical and "correct" details for every one of the many styles that occur in New York City's several historic districts, the compendium would have limited applicability. Such an encyclopedia would provide no answers to the broader questions that have been raised here. It would supply no clue as to whether in a specific case it is more appropriate to be archaeologically pure or to provide a visually acceptable imitation, what style should be followed in buildings of mixed character, how to add a compatible new wing onto an old building, or when a row is an architectural entity in itself or merely a fairly uniform stretch in an otherwise heterogeneous neighborhood. A mere catalogue of period details would give no consideration to the fundamental questions of to what a given set of aesthetic criteria are being applied and why they should be so applied.

It was to decide such matters as these that the New York City Landmarks Preservation Commission was intentionally set up to be as widely representative as possible. It is not a committee of historians, or of designers, or of architectural historians, or of professional politicians, or of popular community leaders. It consists of eleven members, serving three year overlapping terms, and the Commission must at all times contain three architects, one city planner or landscape architect, one realtor, one historian specializing in New York City history, and concomitantly, one resident from each of the City's five boroughs. By prudent tradition it has also included one or two lawyers, preferably with experience in municipal government, and several laymen with no specialized qualifications other than their concern for the City's good. The drafters of the Landmarks Preservation Law felt that such a Commission of devoted and experienced nonspecialists would be best equipped to reach just decisions on the complex aesthetic problems it must resolve.

Notes

1. N.Y. Gen. City Law §20(25-2) (McKinney 1968), as amended, N.Y. Gen. Munic. Law §96-a (McKinney Supp. 1970).
2. N.Y.C. Admin. Code ch. 8-A, 207-6.c(b) (2) (Supp. 1970).
3. "b. It is hereby declared as a matter of public policy that the protection, enhancement, perpetuation and use of improvements of special character or special historical or aesthetic interest or value is a public necessity and is required in the interest of the health, prosperity, safety and welfare of the people. The purpose of this chapter is to (a) effect and accomplish the protection, enhancement and perpetuation of such improvements and of districts which represent or reflect elements of the city's cultural, social, economic, political and architectural history; (b) safeguard the city's historic, aesthetic and cultural heritage, as embodied and reflected in such improvements and districts; (c) stabilize and improve property values in such districts; (d) foster civic pride in the beauty and noble accomplishments of the past; (e) protect and enhance the city's attractions to tourists and visitors and the support and stimulus to business and industry thereby provided; (f) strengthen the economy of the city; and (g) promote the use of historic districts and landmarks for the education, pleasure and welfare of the people of the city." *Id.* §205-1.0.
4. *Id.* §207-1.0(h) (a)-(c).
5. *Id.* §207-1.0(h) (b).
6. For illustrations of these and similar examples, see Goldstone, "*The Marriage of New Buildings with Old*," *Historic Preservation*, Jan.-Mar. 1971, pp. 19-23.
7. See New York City Landmarks Preservation Commission LPC-70239 Certificate of Appropriateness 186, 18 West 11th Street, Greenwich Village Historic District, Block 574, Lot 35, Manhattan, May 18, 1971, with attached reports in favor of and in opposition to the granting of the Certificate. Because this case was before the Commission at the same time that the present article on aesthetics in historic districts was being written, much of the material in the favorable report, with which a majority of the Commission concurred, is similar to the argument which is given here in more general terms.

Administrative and Procedural Matters before Boards of Review*

*Joseph H. McGee, Jr.***

In presenting the case, the argument of style should be minimized and the case built on the general latitudes that appear in the code and those that relate to mass, scale, height, set-back, building interior, textures and the like. The building's complete conformation in architectural style is not really the aim of historic preservation and is not as likely to be enforced by the courts as [are] the other standards.

There is, of course, no precise mathematical formula. One method, using 16 criteria and suggesting that a building should meet at least six was discussed in *Historic Preservation* (Vol. 23, no. 1, January-March 1971). This is not necessarily the answer. It does not weigh the relative merits of these scales, and it is entirely possible that a perfectly awful building could be designed that would meet six of the 16 tests. But it is an interesting thought that an aesthetic approach can be reduced to a series of numbered items.

The Distinctive Architecture of Willemstad Its Conservation and Enhancement†

J. Stanton Robbins and Lachlin F. Blair

The real problem, however, arises in the judgment of contemporary styles when compared to the old. As a general policy in drafting regulations, it is suggested that the important examples of architectural styles of the past be scrupulously protected from change. On the other hand, it is recommended that new buildings or renovations of unimportant older buildings be encouraged to be designed in contemporary style, but with materials, proportions, textures and colors that complement rather than conflict with the neighboring structures. In this way, the character of the community can be preserved, yet the growth and life of the island of today and of future generations can be reflected in architecture which will take its place side by side with that reflecting the life and times of the past.

---

*From National Trust for Historic Preservation, *Legal Techniques in Historic Preservation*, 1972, pp. 26-27.
**Mr. McGee was involved in the expansion of the Charleston, S. C. preservation ordinance.
†New York: Stanton Robbins & Co., Inc.; Blair Assoc., 1961, p. 28.

View of Willemstad showing narrow entrance to harbor. *Courtesy of Tromson Monroe Public Relations.*

We have given consideration to the desirability of a specific listing of materials, design elements and proportions for new structures in the historic district, but we are fearful that strict application of such a list of rules might result in sterile and uninspired facades which catch the letter but not the spirit of the rules. As guides, however, new structures should retain the stucco, wood trim and tile roof color combination which is characteristic of all of the present styles in the historic district. Cornice heights should be set comparable to the principal existing ones for each street facade, but the administrative official or board should be authorized to vary these when necessary to permit the introduction of a major new bold form into the area.

Preservation and Rehabilitation of a Historic Commercial Area*

New Bedford, Mass. Redevelopment Authority

The aesthetic quality of the area as a whole is a direct consequence of the unity of building types, design traditions, spatial configurations and materials produced in a preautomotive, preelevator age. Streets and roadways are relatively narrow, blocks are short, and distances from point-to-point are limited. Building heights do not exceed four stories, even in late nineteenth-century buildings, and the bulk and massing of individual structures is essentially that of a rectangular solid. Building materials are largely indigenous wood, granite, brick or brownstone.

The scale of the area as a whole was determined by limited distances, restrained building height and bulk, and the combinations and proportions of building parts and materials. Scale, the relationship of parts to the whole, was conditioned by the proximity and position of the observer.

In the historic district the observer was intended to move at pedestrian speed. Consequently the details of architectural ornament, textural effects, and combinations of materials were important design elements. Seen from a moving vehicle, these elements blur into an apparent hodgepodge. Perceived at a pedestrian pace they become interesting, varied, picturesque, intimate parts of the urban scene.

---

*1973, p.31-32.

A typical Charleston, South Carolina house in that city's historic district. Note the two-level porch which (in most cases) faces south to catch the harbor breezes. *Courtesy of the National Trust.*

The Urban Design Plan: Historic Hill, Newport, Rhode Island *

Providence Partnership and Wright

The form and visual image of Historic Hill can be described in terms of its major physical components, topography, focal points, paths and edges, and associative landmarks. The topography of Historic Hill . . . begins at grade 0 at the water's edge and rises in a gentle sloping pattern to the east, until, at the intersection of Bellevue Avenue and Memorial Boulevard, it reaches 80 feet. Narrow plateaus exist in the waterfront area, along Thames and Spring Streets and at Bellevue Avenue, while the remainder of the area is a continuous incline, creating a clear visual panorama toward Narragansett Bay.

Focal points are concentrations or nodes of a definite and easily indentifiable use pattern. Focal points, similar to the five land use areas previously described, occur in the waterfront area, Eisenhower Park, the antique shop area along Franklin Street, and the CBD shopping area along the first block of Thames, to Mary Street. These are areas of distinctive visual character, negative or positive, and should be recognized in the design phase of the study.

Paths and edges are two distinctive components of the physical structure of Historic Hill. Paths are corridors of movement through or within the area, and include Thames and Spring Streets as well as the major east-west channels linking them—Mary, Church, Mill, Pelham, Prospect Hill and Franklin streets. Edges are either physical, visual or psychological boundary lines which create a district. The present day edges of Historic Hill as a district are Eisenhower Park, the easterly side of Spring Street, Memorial Boulevard and the westerly side of Thames.

Since these edges do not coincide with the boundaries of the renewal project, which includes parts of four other districts (School Street-Division Street residential area, Golden Hill, the residential area south of Fair Street, and the waterfront), a determination will have to be made as to the extent of desirable integration of the districts into a whole and how best to achieve this goal.

Associative landmarks are well known reference points easily singled out and located by residents and visitors alike. Associative features are usually the more important for residents of the area—schools, churches, the post office and the YMCA, while tourists relate to well advertised attractions—the Brick Market, Trinity, Colony House and restaurants like Christie's. Associative landmarks are potential destinations within a district (or group of districts) defined by edges and are linked by paths or corridors of pedestrian or internal vehicular movement. Each of these three are considered as design resources in Historic Hill and are utilized in the design plan.

A vista can best be described as an impressive view directed at either an unusual scene or an interesting building. Because of the sloping topography of the Hill area and the height of parts of the landscape structures, both types of vistas occur within the project area . . . Important vistas of buildings are directed at Trinity Church and St. Mary's from almost any point within Historic Hill. Perry Mill terminates excellent vistas along Thames Street and especially down the Memorial Boulevard Extension, while the Brick Market closes vistas at Eisenhower Park and along Thames

---

*1971, pp. 14-16.

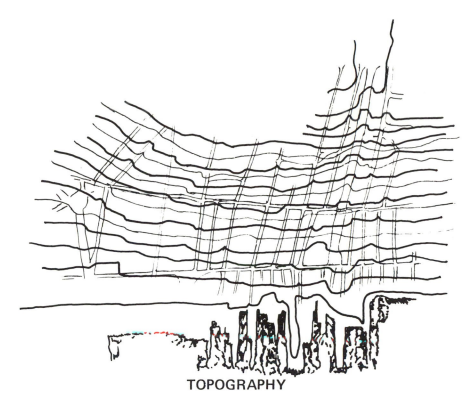

TOPOGRAPHY

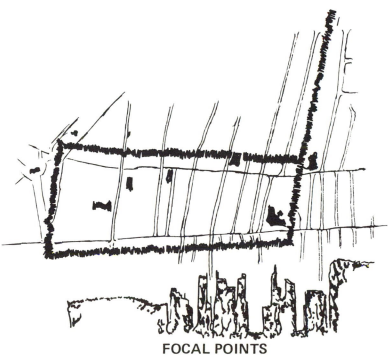

FOCAL POINTS

Street. Vistas are important, although often neglected, visual design determinants, and should be recognized and respected in all site planning and building location plans.

Building heights are limited to three stories, with the exception of an apartment house on Spring Street and church towers or steeples. This height restriction is a carry-over from the eighteenth and nineteenth centuries, when construction techniques, the availability of land, and the threat of fires kept buildings to a modest height. The Stiles Map of 1758 shows the height of 156 residential structures within the study area. Only three of those identified were three stories, with 21 one story and 132, or 85 percent, two stories in height. Two or two-and-one-half stories remains the predominant building height today. One-story buildings, with the exception of garages and other accessory stuctures, are almost all twentieth-century retail or industrial uses along Thames, Mill and William streets and in the waterfront area. Virtually all of the existing three-story buildings date from the latter quarter of the nineteenth century, with a scattering of mid-nineteenth and early twentieth century buildings. Most of these three-story buildings are located along Thames Street.

Façade materials play an important part in establishing the character of an area. In most instances, the visual quality of individual structures is recognized at the pedestrian level and is determined to a large degree by the use of materials—finely detailed beaded clapboards, Flemish bond brick work, patterned shingle work, or in a negative sense, asbestos, asphalt or metal sidings. All of these materials and textures, with others, occur in Historic Hill, in direct relation to the land use areas discussed previously. The predominant materials in the residential area east of Spring Street are clapboard and shingle with a number of frame structures unfortunately "remodeled" with artificial siding materials. Spring Street is characterized by clapboard and shingle with a few later brick structures and two stone churches. The mixed use area between Spring and Thames Street contains virtually every facade material in use in Newport, from clapboard and shingle to flush siding, brick and stone, to concrete block, asbestos, asphalt, aluminum, porcelain panels and glass. The predominant material in use along Thames Street is brick, with some stone, clapboard, shingle and stucco. The waterfront area is distinguished by the widespread use of shingles, with some brick and artificial siding also present.

Building coverage and massing follow the original building and street patterns laid out in the early eighteenth century. With very few exceptions, buildings are placed on the front lot line, perpendicular to the steet, which because of the street pattern gives a distinct north-south emphasis to the area. This occurs along School, Division, Spring, Clarke and Thames streets, and is broken only by Prospect Hill and John Street, east of Spring, and the east-west streets south of Memorial Boulevard. Mill, Pelham, Green and Franklin streets are developed in an east-west pattern, but this is made less apparent by the slope of these streets, breaking the visual continuity of the building rows. The waterfront area, however, shows an east-west axis, reflecting the original finger-like development patterns stretching from the mansion houses on Thames to the dock buildings and finally the docks themselves. Most of the pre-twentieth century buildings in Historic Hill are either rectangular or ell shaped, reflecting the simple building forms of the pre-Victorian period. Projecting bays, semioctagonal and round forms appear in the late-nineteenth-century buildings, a number of which were attached to existing, simpler building forms. It was not until the twentieth century that this pattern of simple massing and small scale was violated, notable examples being the U.S. Post Office and the YMCA.

The relationship of building coverage to open space divides the project area into two visual districts at the rear building lines of the structures fronting on the east side of Thames Street. To the east of this imaginary line, very few buildings are attached to others, resulting in a streetscape composed of solids and voids—buildings and open spaces. The existing buildings fronting on Thames Street,

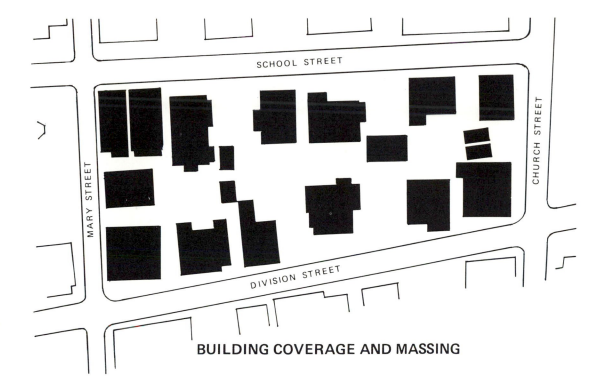

BUILDING COVERAGE AND MASSING

however, are built so close together as to resemble a solid wall of construction and with the height of the structures relative to the narrow width of the street, a tunnel-like effect is created.

Any sense of directional emphasis of building coverage is weakened in the waterfront area, because of the vast amount of open land area, but the original form of the area can be determined, as evidenced by the Bowen's Wharf project.

Roof forms vary considerably in the project area, but are directly related to the architectural style or period of the structure. Virtually all of the pre-Revolutionary, Federal and Greek Revival structures have either hip, gambrel or simple gable roofs, sometimes in combinations, notably the Cotton House. Additions to these early buildings have gable, hip or shed roofs. Later buildings, constructed in the various styles popular in the Victorian period, introduced the mansard, turreted, conical and various combination roof forms to Historic Hill, while most of the twentieth-century buildings have flat or shallow hipped roofs . . .

The almost exclusive use of gable or hip roofs for new construction must be selected on the basis of block-long street facade studies, comparing new forms to surrounding buildings.

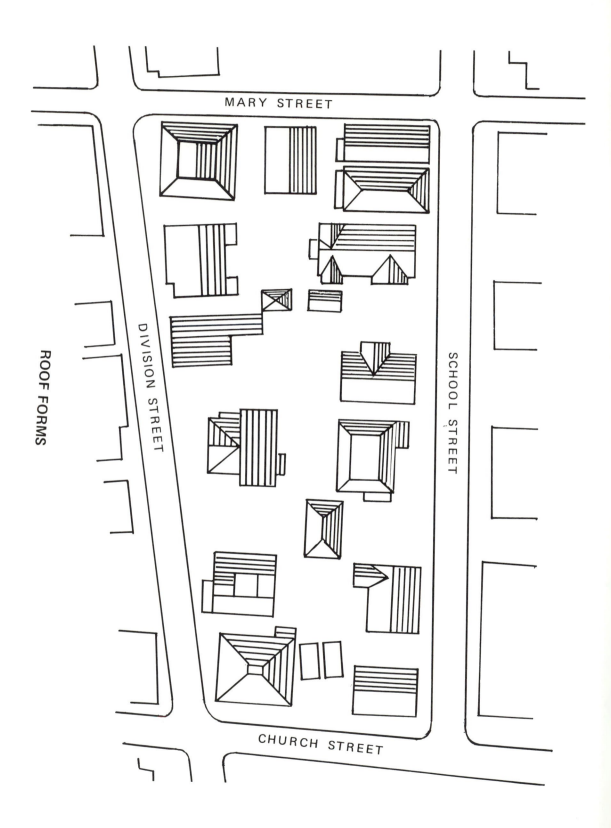

ROOF FORMS

Final Report on the Proposed McKnight Historic District*

Springfield Historical Commission

Exterior Architectural Guidelines for McKnight
Historic District

Note: These controls apply only to the *exterior* of a property which can be viewed from a public street. Any part of the property which cannot be seen from the street is not subject to control. Also, any normal maintenance undertaken by a property owner, in which no changes are to take place, is permissible. In each case below, controls have been proposed so that the individual character of each house will be respected and that the integrity and visual cohesiveness of the neighborhood is retained.

Feature	Guidelines
Driveway	No control.
Walkway	No control.
Gutters and Downspouts	No control.
Foundation Planting	No control.
Light Fixtures	No control.
Fencing/Screen Planting	To protect street vistas, the yard between the street and foundation line, or an extension thereof, should be kept open. Only under unusual circumstances on a case-by-case basis will fencing or screen planting be allowed. Screen plantings should not exceed a height of three feet at maturity.
Steps	Replacement shall be in the shape and design of the original; change in material, e.g., wood to concrete, is permissible.
Roof	Change of shape of roof shall require approval.
Building Additions	Design to be approved on a case-by-case basis.
Grillwork (on roofs and porches)	Shall be retained unless it can be demonstrated to the Commission that retention would result in a safety hazard or an economic hardship.
Siding (also see Trim)	Original wood, clapboard, or shingle siding should be maintained whenever possible. A change in type or material of siding shall require approval on a case-by-case basis. Any change should not affect trim or other decorative features.
Trim (cornerboards, window detail, cornices, etc.)	Color not subject to control; removal of or a change in design is subject to control.

*Springfield, Mass., 1975, pp. 5-6.

Feature	Guidelines	(Continued)
Windows	Size or design change shall require approval.	
Doors	All doors shall require approval for changes in size, location or design.	
Porches (including railings)	Any change in shape, location or design, including enclosure, shall require approval.	
Chimney	Any change in shape, location or design shall require approval.	
Awnings	Rigid permanent awnings are not allowed. Canvas or other fabric is recommended. Rollable aluminum awnings will be considered.	
Signs	Size, shape and designs of signs larger than one square foot shall require approval.	
Garages	Changes in shape or design subject to approval feature by feature as listed above.	
Paint	Color of paint is not controlled; however, approval must be sought prior to painting any previously unpainted masonry.	

Beacon Hill Architectural Handbook*

Beacon Hill Civic Association

C. Notes on sign design (Excerpted from the Boston Sign Code)

This sense of history and feeling of architectural unity is one of Boston's unique characteristics; it is attractive to both tourists and residents alike. And although nothing in the long run can replace the quality and character of a business concern's services or merchandise in drawing and keeping customers, the architecture of an individual building—and the combined impact of groups of adjoining buildings—can be part of the attraction of a shopping district.

Ideally, then, to maximize the effectiveness of signs and building architecture, every sign should be an integral—but of course, noticeable—part of its building, and each building should be a good neighbor within its block of buildings. As a result, the building and its sign become part of an overall image, each supporting the other and helping to draw customers.

This leads to a simple but vital point: a sign on a building should always be thought of as part of the building and not as an unrelated object attached to it.

Design criteria established by the Architectural Commission are as follows:

1. Graphics shall be limited to a single sign, excluding the introduction of a projecting symbol.

*Boston, Mass., 1975, pp. 12, 22-23.

2. Overhanging signs are generally discouraged except in the case where a flat sign cannot be appropriately mounted.

3. Trademarks shall be limited to 25 percent of sign area.

4. Paper signs attached to windows (announcing sales, etc.) are discouraged and under no circumstances are to be allowed beyond 15 days.

5. Lighting: back-lit signs are not allowed and shielded indirect lighting should be encouraged.

6. Location: should be integrated architecturally with the building, or on an awning in accordance with the zoning code limitations. In no case should a sign applied to the building obscure architectural detailing on the building face.

7. Restoration of free-standing signs is discouraged.

In closing, something should be said about two of the most important aspects of sign design—the choice of colors and the choice of lettering. A few basic rules may help to simplify the task of choosing from the almost unlimited range of colors and letter styles available.

1. Do not use too many colors on a sign. Too many colors can work against each other and detract from the strength of a sign's visual image. A simple combination of black and/or white and a single well-chosen color is often the most striking and effective.

2. Try to relate the general color effect of the sign to the building to which it belongs.

3. Choose a style of letter that is appropriate to the business and building. (Preferably no more than one style per sign).

4. Make sure that the letters are clearly legible, whatever style is chosen, or they will not be doing their job. It should be emphasized that the greatest legibility is not necessarily the result of the largest size letters.

5. Choose the size of the letters carefully. Just as the sign should be in proportion to its building, the size of the letters should be in proportion—both to the sign and the building.

D. A note on existing signs. (Excerpted from the Boston Sign Code)

If there is an old, existing sign on the building that is still appropriate to the business, make sure that it is not of historic interest or esthetic merit before replacing it. Many signs dating from around the turn of the century still exist and, when restored, can contribute character and distinction to the business, building and the street.

Architectural Features

Color

Colors on the Hill were, when new, considerably brighter than today. A century of dirt dulls brick walls considerably. Then, too, today's painters, in an effort to be authentic and reproduce the "original" colors they found under layers of paint, forget that the linseed oil paint base darkens with

Louisburg Square typifies the successful preservation work carried out on Beacon Hill in Boston. *Courtesy of National Trust.*

age and they repaint with a darker color. The original pigments—carbon black, white lead, yellow ochre, Prussian blue, and chrome green were broadened in later Victorian years.

Repainting existing exterior woodwork with the same color does not require approval of the Architectural Commission and is encouraged if the present color is appropriate. When selecting new colors for this work, choose from the range of colors in the immediate neighborhood. Common courtesy suggests that you consult with your neighbors about the proposed change before seeking approval of the Architectural Commission. A good color scheme will enhance the neighborhood as well as the individual building. A list of selected paint colors is available at the office of the BHCA and the Secretary of the Architectural Commission as reference.

Note: Raw aluminum storm windows and screens if unpainted are not appropriate and are not allowed.

Doorways

The style of windows and doorways is critical to the character of Beacon Hill. Most houses have the main door facing the street, with a short flight of steps running up to it beginning directly on the sidewalk line, making a recessed entrance. The recesses are very much a part of the street design and add interest to what might otherwise be a flat frontage. Nothing looks better than the original door, or doors, and every effort should be made to save them, together with the sidelights and glass transom which light the staircase.

Good weatherstripping will assist in keeping out the cold. Additions of a storm door on the sidewalk line should be avoided or removed, as the new door would be required to swing outward onto the street, making a hazard to pedestrians. Proper lighting at the entry is not only attractive but helps to illuminate what might otherwise be a dark, concealed lurking place.

Burglars find most Beacon Hill homes likely targets because of inadequate security. Be sure that the door frame is firm and strong. Use a lock which cannot be opened with a credit card, such as a dead lock. A double cylinder (inside and outside) deadbolt lock will prevent the burglar from leaving by the front door if he has entered through the window. All apartment buildings are required to have a self-closing front door with an automatic locking device.

Windows

Historically, windows were the chief source of interior light. The openings are long and large, repeating at regular intervals. The facades are punctuated by bays and oriels. The windows were nearly always constructed as double-hung sash.

Replacement windows should be the same size and have the same pane divisions as the originals. In all cases the long dimension of the pane and window is vertical. Large picture windows which are visible from a public way are not appropriate. One of the great charms of Beacon Hill is the rhythm of uniform window openings from building to building.

Leaded glass windows use preformed lead strips, called cames, soldered between the panes. Broken panes can be replaced, although not so easily as in other windows.

Blinds (or shutters) were installed on windows both front and rear, except for dormers and oriels, of all the older buildings. Replacement blinds should appear as if they could close and just cover the entire window. Sources for purchases of blinds/shutters and the necessary hardware are available by calling the BHCA office.

Storm windows and screens should match the window frame in both color and size. Window frames often become loose and drafty with age, wasting a great deal of heat in winter. This condition may be corrected by installing a special weather-stripping track for the original sash to slide in.

Window Boxes

Our streets are enlivened by natural beauty through the efforts of many residents who maintain window boxes through the summer.

The Beacon Hill Garden Club and the Beacon Hill Civic Association started annual window-box contests in 1958 and award prizes for a number of categories.

Volunteers are willing to assist individuals in the planning of their boxes and in any beautification effort in the community. An excellent pamphlet, *City Window Box Planting,* is available at the Beacon Hill Civic Association office. Boxes are available at cost from the BHCA and at street fairs in the spring.

Put your plants in pots and the pots in the boxes—that saves weight and makes them easy to bring into the house in the fall. The weight of the soil and water must be adequately supported and the box securely fastened to the window frame.

Trees and Paving

There have been trees on the Hill for many years and recent efforts have brought many new trees. Young trees especially must be protected from damage by automobiles and dogs. A sturdy pipe at least three inches in diameter, driven well into the ground at curb line and filled with concrete, will help protect the tree and reduce the damage. A low fence keeps the dogs off.

Young trees need a couple of buckets of water every week in the spring and summer. Loosen the soil and build a dam to hold the water and allow it to percolate to the roots. If a lower limb is broken, saw off the stump close to the trunk. If a tree is badly damaged, call the Park Department, Maintenance Division (524-0610). . . .

The sidewalk can easily be washed frequently—a blessing to all who walk on the Hill—if a frost-free faucet is installed on the front of the building and fitted with a quick-release hose fitting. Installation is simple because the City water line generally enters the basement at the front of the building. The sidewalk paving should drain rainwater away from the basement entry and windows. The sidewalk paving itself is the responsibility of the City Public Works Department, Highway Yard (536-7150).

Utilities

Utilities equipment should be restricted to underground entry or kept to the rear of the building wherever possible. This includes TV antennas and cables as well as air conditioners, which should be installed in rear windows. When window air conditioners must appear in streetfront windows, they must not project beyond the building face and should be painted to match the window trim. Heating oil filler pipes and vents should be kept short and the area around them kept clean.

Savannah, Georgia Zoning Ordinance*

Sec. 38-122.4, Historic District

Section 4. *Classification of Buildings and Structures*: Within the Historic District, all buildings and structures shall be classified and designated on the Historic Building Map adopted and approved by the Mayor and Aldermen and made a part of the zoning map. Such buildings and structures shall be divided into two (2) classes:

Criteria

(1)   *Historic*. Those buildings classified as Historic shall possess identified historical or architectural merit of a degree warranting their preservation. They shall be further classified as:
  A. Exceptional
  B. Excellent
  C. Notable
  D. Of Value as part of the scene
(2)   *Contemporary*. Those buildings and structures not classified on the Historic Building Map as Exceptional, Excellent, Notable, or Of Value as part of the scene.

Section 5. *Certificate of Appropriateness Required.* A certificate of appropriateness issued by the Zoning Administrator after approval by the Board of Review shall be required before a permit is issued for any of the following:
(1)   Within all zones of the Historic District:
  A. Demolition of a historic building.
  B. Moving a historic building.
  C. Material change in the exterior appearance of existing buildings classified as Historic by additions, reconstruction, alteration, or maintenance involving exterior color change; and
(2)   Within Historic Zone I:
  A. Any new construction of a principal building or accessory building or structure subject to view from a public street.
  B. Change in existing walls and fences, or construction of new walls and fences, if along public street rights-of-way, excluding lanes.
  C. Material change in the exterior appearance of existing contemporary buildings by additions, reconstruction, alteration, or maintenance involving exterior color change, if subject to view from a public street. . . .

Section 9. *Development Standards:*
(1)   *Preservation of Historic Buildings within All Zones in the Historic District.* A building or structure classified as Historic or any part thereof, or any appurtenance related thereto including but not

---

*Sec. 38-122.4, § § 4, 5, 9.

These Savannah facades demonstrate the entrance rhythm criterion on which Savannah places importance. *Courtesy of National Trust.*

limited to stone walls, fences, light fixtures, steps, paving and signs shall only be moved, reconstructed, altered or maintained in a manner that will preserve the historical and architectural character of the building, structure or appurtenance thereto.

(2)   *Demolition of Historic Buildings.* Whenever a property owner shows that a building classified as Historic is incapable of earning an economic return on its value, as appraised by a qualified real estate appraiser, and the Board of Review fails to approve the issuance of a certificate of appropriateness, such building may be demolished, provided, however, that before a demolition permit is issued, notice of proposed demolition shall be given as follows:

1. For buildings rated Exceptional: twelve (12) months
2. For buildings rated Excellent: six (6) months
3. For buildings rated Notable: four (4) months
4. For buildings Of Value as part of the scene: two (2) months

Notice shall be posted on the premises of the building or structure proposed for demolition in a location clearly visible from the street. In addition, notice shall be published in a newspaper of general local circulation at least three (3) times prior to demolition, the final notice of which shall be not less than fifteen (15) days prior to the date of the permit, and the first notice of which shall be published not more than fifteen (15) days after the application for a permit to demolish is filed. The purpose of this section is to further the purposes of this ordinance by preserving historic buildings which are important to the education, culture, traditions and the economic values of the City, and to afford the City, interested persons, historical societies or organizations the opportunity to acquire or to arrange for the preservation of such buildings. The Board of Review may at any time during such stay approve a certificate of appropriateness in which event a permit shall be issued without further delay.

(3) *Relocation of Historic Buildings.* A historic building shall not be relocated on another site unless it is shown that the preservation on its existing site is not consistent with the purposes of such building on such site.

(4) *Protective Maintenance of Historic Buildings.* Historic buildings shall be maintained to meet the requirements of the Minimum Housing Code and the Building Code. Provided, however, that notice to the owners as required by the building code for unsafe buildings shall further provide in the case of historic buildings that this ordinance will require a permit after approval of the Board of Review before demolition and in the meantime the owner shall make such repairs as will secure the building and upon failure to do so the building official shall cause such building or structure or portion thereof to be secured in which event the cost thereof shall be charged to the owner of the premises and collected in the manner provided by law.

(5) *Contemporary Buildings, Zone I.* The construction of a new building, or structure, and the moving, reconstruction, alteration, major maintenance or repair involving a color change materially affecting the external appearance of any existing contemporary building, structure, or appurtenance thereof within Zone I shall be generally of such design, form, proportion, mass, configuration, building material, texture, color and location on a lot as will be compatible with other buildings in the Historic Area, and particularly with buildings designated as Historic and with squares and places to which it is visually related.

(6) *Visual Compatibility Factors.* Within said Zone I, new construction and existing buildings and structures and appurtenances thereof which are moved, reconstructed, materially altered, repaired or changed in color shall be visually compatible with buildings, squares and places to which they are visually related generally in terms of the following factors:

A. *Height*. The height of proposed building shall be visually compatible with adjacent buildings.

B. *Proportion of Building's Front Facade*. The relationship of the width of building to the height of the front elevation shall be visually compatible to buildings, squares and places to which it is visually related.

C. *Proportion of Openings Within the Facility*. The relationship of the width of the windows to height of windows in a building shall be visually compatible with buildings, squares and places to which the building is visually related.

D. *Rhythm of Solids to Voids in Front Facades*. The relationship of solids to voids in the front facade of a building shall be visually compatible with buildings, squares and places to which it is visually related.

E. *Rhythm of Spacing of Buildings on Streets*. The relationship of building to open space between it and adjoining buildings shall be visually compatible to the buildings, squares and places to which it is visually related.

F. *Rhythm of Entrance and/or Porch Projection*. The relationship of entrances and porch projections to sidewalks of a building shall be visually compatible to the buildings, squares and places to which it is visually related.

G. *Relationship of Materials, Texture and Color*. The relationship of the materials, texture and color of the facade of a building shall be visually compatible with the predominant materials used in the buildings to which it is visually related.

H. *Roof Shapes*. The roof shape of a building shall be visually compatible with the buildings to which it is visually related.

I. *Walls of Continuity*. Appurtenances of a building such as walls, wrought iron, fences, evergreen landscape masses, building facades, shall, if necessary, form cohesive walls of enclosure along a street, to insure visual compatibility of the building to the buildings, squares and places to which it is visually related.

J. *Scale of a Building*. The size of a building, the mass of a building in relation to open spaces, the windows, door openings, porches and balconies shall be visually compatible with the buildings, squares and places to which it is visually related.

K. *Directional Expression of Front Elevation*. A building shall be visually compatible with the buildings, squares and places to which it is visually related in its directional character, whether this be vertical character, horizontal character or nondirectional character.

Design Criteria for New Buildings in Historic Savannah*

Criteria

1. *Height*—This is a mandatory criteria that new buildings be constructed to a height within ten percent of the average height of existing adjacent buildings.

RATIO PROPORTION 1-1½

2. *Proportion of buildings' front facades*—The relationship between the width and height of the front elevation of the building.

*Historic Preservation Plan for the Central Area General Neighborhood Renewal Area, Savannah, Georgia, 1968, pp. 12-17. Reprinted by permission of the City of Savannah from a report prepared for the Housing Authority of Savannah, Georgia, by Eric Hill and Associates in collaboration with Muldower & Patterson Associates, Inc., A.I.A.

WINDOW PROPORTION 2-1

3. Proportion of openings within the facade—The relationship of width to height of windows and doors.

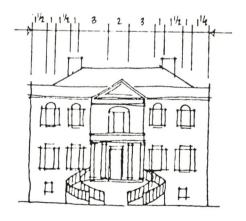

RHYTHM 1½-1-1½-1-3

4. *Rhythm of solids to voids in front facade*—Rhythm being an ordered recurrent alternation of strong and weak elements. Moving by an individual building, one experiences a rhythm of masses to openings.

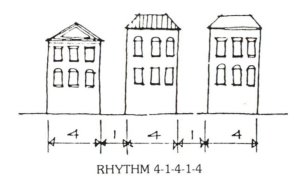

RHYTHM 4-1-4-1-4

5. *Rhythm of spacing of buildings on streets*—Moving past a sequence of buildings, one experiences a rhythm of recurrent building masses to spaces between them.

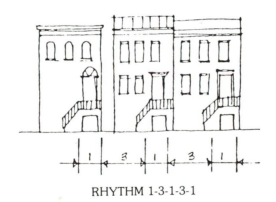

RHYTHM 1-3-1-3-1

6. *Rhythm of entrance and/or porch projections*—The relationships of entrances to sidewalks. Moving past a sequence of structures, one experiences a rhythm of entrances or porch projections at an intimate scale.

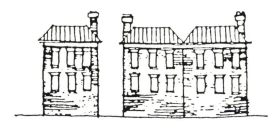

MATERIAL/BRICK
TEXTURE/RAKED JOINT
COLOR/RED BK., GREY TRIM

7. *Relationship of materials*—Within an area, the predominant material may be brick, stone, stucco, wood siding, or other material.

8. *Relationship of textures*—The predominant texture may be smooth (stucco) or rough (brick with tooled joints) or horizontal wood siding, or other textures.

9. *Relationship of color*—The predominant color may be that of a natural material or a painted one, or a patina colored by time. Accent of blending colors of trim is also a factor.

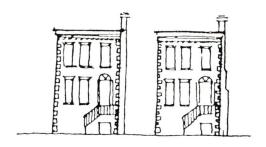

10. *Relationship of architectural details*—Details may include cornices, lintel, arches, quoins, balustrades, wrought iron work, chimneys, etc.

11. *Relationship of roof shapes*—The majority of buildings may have gable, mansard, hip, flat roofs, or others.

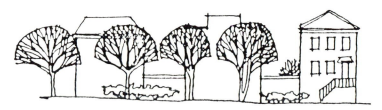

WALLS & LANDSCAPING CONTINUOUS

12. *Walls of continuity*—Physical ingredients such as brick walls, wrought iron fences, evergreen landscape masses, building facades, or combinations of these, form continuous, cohesive walls of enclosure along the street.

13. *Relationship of landscaping*—There may be a predominance of a particular quality and quantity of landscaping. The concern here is more with mass and continuity.

GROUND COVERING

14. *Ground cover*—There may be a predominance in the use of brick pavers, cobble stones, granite blocks, tabby, or other materials.

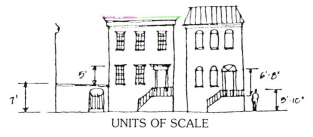

UNITS OF SCALE

15. *Scale*—Scale is created by the size of construction and architectural detail which relate to the size of man. Scale is also determined by building mass and how it relates to open space. The predominant element of scale may be brick or stone units, windows or door openings, porches and balconies, etc.

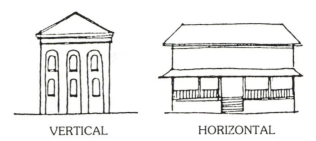

VERTICAL   HORIZONTAL

16. *Directional expression of front elevation*—Structural shape, placement of openings, and architectural details may give a predominantly vertical, horizontal, or a non-directional character to the building's front facade.

Tucson's Historic Districts: Criteria for Preservation and Development*

City of Tucson, Department of Community Development, Planning Division

Criteria for Development

To provide for proper development within a historic district, a balance that permits future progress within an existing historic framework must be achieved. In order to establish this balance the construction of new buildings, as well as the renovation of the existing buildings, located within a historic area should be encouraged. The continued construction and remodeling of buildings located within historic areas is a necessity in order for the area to remain active and contribute to the vitality of the entire community.

New buildings must not be designed in such a manner as to ignore the character of the existing historic buildings. If the design of the new building or remodeling does not harmonize with the surrounding buildings, the visual image of the entire area is diluted and eventually lost. Contemporary buildings have been constructed within historic areas without destroying the existing character of the area. However, there are all too many examples of buildings which were designed without regard to their location within historic areas.

To prevent this situation from arising in Tucson, a series of design and development criteria was

---

*Tucson, Ariz., 1972, pp. 26-34.

established to provide workable standards which can be used to compare and evaluate the relatedness of new or rehabilitated buildings to adjacent historic buildings. These criteria are the basis for the Historic District ordinance.

Since Tucson does not have a predominant architectural style, comparisons between buildings should be based on shared design components—building height and setback, for example. This approach has been used successfully in a number of communities, particularly in the City of Savannah, Georgia. Where applicable the development policies utilized in Savannah, as presented in the publication *Historic Preservation Plan for the Central Area General Neighborhood Renewal Area*, were investigated and modified to embody the architectural characteristics unique to Tucson.

The criteria are designed for use within any area which might be given historic designation—now, or in the near or distant future. Since the character of each area could be expected to differ from that of the others, it is not possible to establish rigid design standards which could regulate future development within these areas. Rather, the guidelines will require that any new building or remodeling take into account the collective character of the buildings in its immediate vicinity.

Before the individual qualities which collectively constitute the general character of an area can be identified, a determination as to which of the surrounding adjacent structures would relate most directly to any new construction or remodeling, must be undertaken. The "immediate vicinity" of any such building, as defined below, will constitute its *development zone*.

- *Development zone for an interior lot.* The development zone of any lot located on an interior lot (as defined by the Tucson Zoning Code, Sec. 23-17) shall include any lot fronting on the same street as the lot in question and within the same block, as well as those lots located on the opposite side of the street, except such portions of the zone which fall outside the boundary of the historic district.
- *Development zone for a corner lot.* The development zone of any lot located on a corner lot (as defined by the Tucson Zoning Code, Sec. 23-16) shall include any lot fronting on the same streets as the lot in question and within the same block, as well as those lots located on the opposite side of the streets, including the opposite corner, except such portions of the zone which fall outside the boundary of the historic district.
- *Development zone for a boundary lot.* The development zone of any lot located adjacent to a historic district boundary shall include all lots located in the same block plus those lots located on the opposite side of any street adjoining that block, as well as those lots located on the opposite corners, except such portions of the zone which fall outside the boundary of the historic district.

With the establishment of standards for delineating the extent of the development zone, an investigation of the physical elements which define the character of a building and provides the continuity between all structures was undertaken. Within each historic district there exist similarities in the design and construction of each building that provide a basis for determining the general character of a historic district.

The similarities which exist between buildings are expressed by a number of basic design components, including:

1. Building height
2. Setback
3. Proportions
4. Pattern and rhythm
5. Roof types

6. Surface texture
7. Color
8. Site utilization
9. Projections
10. Architectural details

These design components or "development criteria" comprise the tools with which the desired relationships between historic and modern structures can be attained. Thoughtful application of the development criteria would assure the retention of those qualities which make historic areas unique and identifiable, while encouraging creativity, inventiveness and flexibility in the design of modern buildings.

Application of Development Criteria

In order to obtain approval for the construction of a new building, or for the remodeling of an existing building, the proposed design must satisfy the requirements of the ten development critieria detailed on the following pages. If the proposed plans do not adequately reflect the architectural character of the district, suggestions would be made for modification in the design which would assure compliance with the conditions of the ordinance. Thus, if approved, the design of any new or remodeled building would be compatible with the majority of structures located within its development zone.

application of development criteria

In order to obtain approval for the construction of a new building, or for the remodeling of an existing building, the proposed design must satisfy the requirements of the ten development criteria detailed on the following pages. If the proposed plans do not adequately reflect the architectural character of the district, suggestions would be made for modifications in the design which would assure compliance with the conditions of the ordinance. Thus, if approved, the design of any new or remodeled building would be compatible with the majority of structures located within its Development Zone.

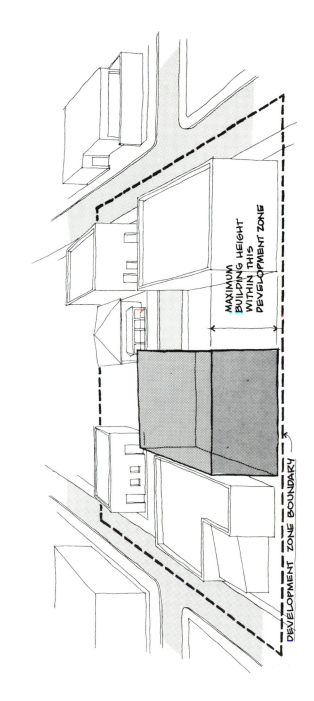

MAXIMUM BUILDING HEIGHT WITHIN THIS DEVELOPMENT ZONE

DEVELOPMENT ZONE BOUNDARY

Development Criteria

1 Height

New structures must be constructed no higher than the tallest building located within the development zone.

2 Setback

New structures must maintain the prevailing setback existing within the development zone.

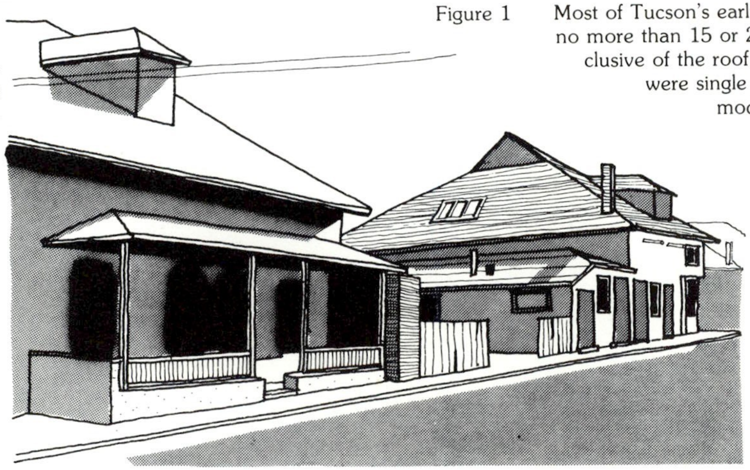

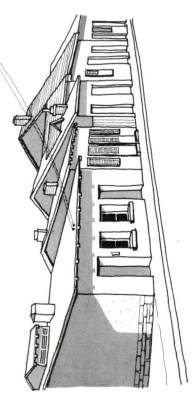

Figure 1   Most of Tucson's early buildings were no more than 15 or 20 feet high, exclusive of the roof. Although most were single story structures, modern buildings of that height can accommodate 2 stories

Figure 2   These buildings on North Meyer Street have no front setback at all—their front facades are all located on their front property lines. This effect could be achieved in a number of ways—a high wall, a fence, or a dense hedge might be located on the property line, allowing the building, itself, to be set farther back.

3 Proportion

The idea of proportion refers to the relationship between the height and width of the front elevation of a building. The buildings shown in figures 3 and 4 are about twice as wide as they are high—a proportion of 2 to 1. This proportion holds true for many of the buildings in the el presidio and barrio libre areas. When most of the buildings in a development zone have similar proportions, whatever they may be, it would be destructive of the character of the zone for a new building to be constructed which had very different proportions.

Figure 3

Figure 4

Figure 5

Figure 5 shows a group of five buildings which have different heights, but which have the same proportions, and one which has different proportions. The odd building represents a new structure which does not relate well to the others because of its markedly different proportions.

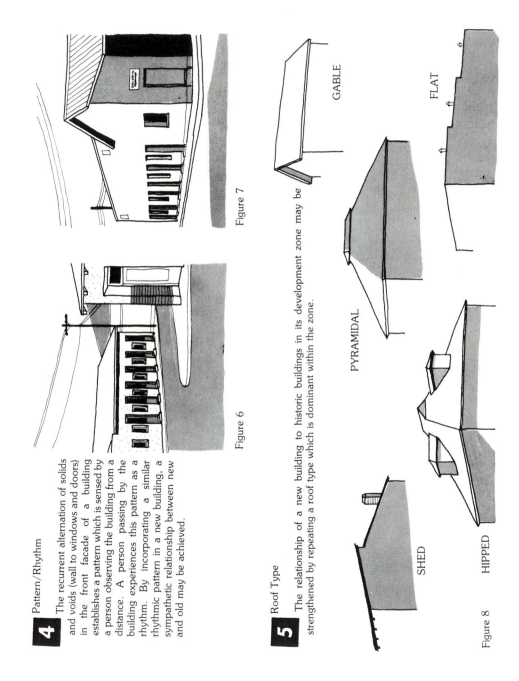

Figure 6

Figure 7

4 Pattern/Rhythm

The recurrent alternation of solids and voids (wall to windows and doors) in the front facade of a building establishes a pattern which is sensed by a person observing the building from a distance. A person passing by the building experiences this pattern as a rhythm. By incorporating a similar rhythmic pattern in a new building, a sympathetic relationship between new and old may be achieved.

5 Roof Type

The relationship of a new building to historic buildings in its development zone may be strengthened by repeating a roof type which is dominant within the zone.

GABLE

PYRAMIDAL

FLAT

SHED

HIPPED

Figure 8

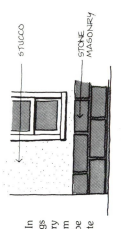

Figure 9

6 Surface Texture

Most of the buildings in Tucson contructed before 1890 were of mud adobe. In almost all cases, the adobe was subsequently covered with stucco. Thus, the buildings shared the common texture of their stucco surfaces. Many of the houses in the Armory Park and university areas are built of brick, the texture of which is quite different from that of stucco. The suitability of new development in any of these areas would be enhanced by the use of building materials which possess a texture which is appropriate in the context of the other buildings within its development zone.

7 Color

Color is both an intrinsic quality of a building material, such as stucco, brick, wood, or metal, and an applied treatment which covers up the natural color of a material. The exterior surfaces of Tucson's early buildings were generally left without the addition of paint or stain. The natural colors of brick, native stone, and unpainted stucco dominate in the historic areas discussed in this report. Any new buildings or renovations should respect this tradition, as it is manifested in each development zone.

8 Site Utilization

The space between buildings is an important factor which contributes to the character of the entire group of buildings. Figure 10 shows a block face in the university area. The generous side yards visually separate each house from its neighbors. Figure 11 depicts a block in an older part of town where the spacing between buildings is either very narrow or non-existent. A new building should observe the appropriate spacing for its development zone.

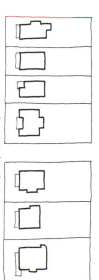

Figure 11

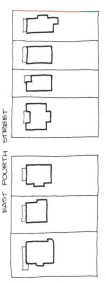

Figure 10

9 Projections

Buildings of the Spanish-Mexican period, for example, the Verdugo House (Figure 12), usually had no projections beyond the facade. As the influence of the Anglo immigrants to Tucson was felt, front porches began to appear on residential structures (Figure 13). The design of remodelings and new buildings in an historic district should take into account the presence or absence of such projections as porches, awnings, and overhangs on other buildings within a development zone.

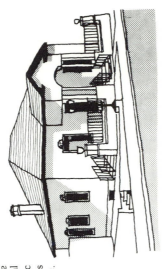

Figure 12

Figure 13

10 Architectural Details

Repetition of architectural details is another way of achieving an harmonious relationship between new and old buildings. But, it is not intended that the details of old buildings be duplicated with exact precision. Rather, they should be regarded as suggestive of the *Extent* and *Scale* of detail that would be appropriate on a new building or remodeling within a development zone.

Figure 14

   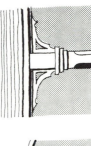  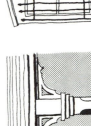 

EAVES   WINDOWS   DOORS   DECORATIVE FEATURES   PORCH COLUMNS   GRILLWORK

Madison, Wisconsin General Ordinances*

Guideline criteria to be considered in the development of historic district plans are as follows:

a. All new structures shall be constructed to a height visually compatible with the buildings and environment with which they are visually related.

b. The gross volume of any new structure shall be visually compatible with the buildings and environment with which it is visually related.

c. In the street elevation(s) of a building, the proportion between the width and height in the facade(s) should be visually compatible with the buildings and environment with which it is visually related.

d. The proportions and relationships between doors and windows in the street facade(s) should be visually compatible with the buildings and environment with which it is visually related.

e. The rhythm of solids to voids, created by openings in the facade, should be visually compatible with the buildings and environment with which it is visually related.

f. The existing rhythm created by existing building masses and spaces between them should be preserved.

g. The materials used in the final facade(s) should be visually compatible with the buildings and environment with which it is visually related.

h. The texture inherent in the facade should be visually compatible with the buildings and environment with which it is visually related.

i. Colors and patterns used on the facade (especially trim) should be visually compatible with the buildings and environment with which it is visually related.

j. The design of the roof should be visually compatible with the buildings and environment with which it is visually related.

k. The landscape plan should be sensitive to the individual building, its occupants and their need. Further, the landscape treatment should be visually compatible with the buildings and environment with which it is visually related.

l. All street facade(s) should blend with other buildings via directional expression. When adjacent buildings have a dominant horizontal or vertical expression, this expression should be carried over and reflected.

m. Architectural details should be incorporated as necessary to relate the new with the old and to preserve and enhance the inherent characteristics of the area.

---

*Sec. 33.01 (6)(d)(2).

Plan for the Creation of a Historic Environment*

Billy G. Garrett and James W. Garrison

1885 Building Characteristics

If the Tombstone restoration program is to be successful, it must be guided by a clear understanding of the city's appearance in 1885. The basic reference for understanding is the photo collection. From this source two types of visual aids have been produced. One is the 1885 Street Elevations, the other is the 1885 Building Characteristics. . . .

Fifteen categories were selected for character explanation. Each category represents an area of physical or perceptual difference between structures built in Tombstone during the years 1882 to 1885 and those built after 1900. Conventional descriptive categories were not used because they were either too technical or failed to adequately explain the *differences* between the periods of consistent character development. . . .

---

*Prepared for the Tombstone Restoration Commission, Inc., Tombstone, Ariz., 1972, pp. B-17-B-27.

Criteria for Building Evaluation

Since restoration work must respect temporal, physical, and financial limitations, the Restoration Commission needed a method by which it could objectively determine the relative importance of buildings within a historic district, and then set rational program priorities. To be fair and objective, the method ought to allow consideration of all critical building factors within the restoration framework. Once determined, the factors should each be given a point count which represents its worth in the whole scheme.

For the purposes of this study, four categories of consideration were selected. The categories are 1885 characteristics, visual impact, historical significance, and structural condition. A short description follows of each category and its component factors.

1885 Characteristics

Factors to be Evaluated	Points
1. Building height	+ 3 or − 3
2. Facade rhythm	+ 3 or − 3
3. Facade proportions	+ 3 or − 3
4. Building materials	+ 3 or − 3
5. Directional expression	+ 3 or − 3
6. Doors	+ 2 or − 2
7. Porches	+ 2 or − 2
8. Windows	+ 2 or − 2
9. Details	+ 2 or − 2
10. Signs	+ 2 or − 2
11. Setbacks	+ 1 or − 1
12. Public accessibility	+ 1 or − 1
13. Building rhythm	+ 1 or − 1
14. Building color	+ 1 or − 1
15. Ground Cover	+ 1 or − 1

. . . to show the importance of building appearance, points are given with a positive value if a building conforms to an 1885 characteristic but the same number of points are given with a negative value if a building does not conform to the 1885 characteristics. Consequently the range of total possible points for this category is from + 30 to − 30. A building with + 30 points would exhibit all 1885 building characteristics. A building with − 30 points would not exhibit any of the 1885 building characteristics. Most buildings will have point counts somewhere in between.

Visual Impact

Factors to be Evaluated	Points
1. Height (choose one)	
One story building	+ 3
Two story building	+ 6
Three story building	+ 9
2. Location in district (choose one)	
On Allen or within one half block	+ 3
On Fremont or within one half block	+ 2
On Toughnut or within one half block	+ 1
3. Location in block (choose one)	
On a corner or an isolated structure	+ 6
Semi–isolated (flanked by one building)	+ 4
Mid–block (between two buildings)	+ 2
4. Degree of individual character (choose one)	
Unique	+ 5
Uncommon	+ 3
Exception	+ 1
Ordinary	0

The visual impact category is based upon the perceptual process by which people create mental images of a new place. These mental images constitute the retained impressions which are carried as memory and to which attitudes are referenced.

The perceptual process begins with determination of two-dimensional shapes, then adds depth, detail, and context. Once a typical pattern is established, the person uses a system of spot checks to identify the particular nature of a new situation.

In a city, identifying features are commonly related to the skyline, major streets, intersections, and local peculiarities. These four elements form the basis of the Visual Impact category.

Of the four evaluative factors only the "degree of individual character" may require elaboration. As it is being used here "individual character" has neither good nor bad connotations. The perceptual process seeks out the *differences* between items before it compares for similarities. Age, historic significance, and presence of historic characteristics are irrelevant in this evaluation. Only the frequency of physical features is important. If one building stands out in the district because it is the only one painted red, then that building has a unique character and would receive + 5 points. Color, texture, shape, and scale are major features which determine individuality.

The points given are all of positive value, since even the commonest building is a part of the perceived subject. The four factors to be evaluated each have three possible answers, only one of which is to be selected. For example, a building is *either* one, *or* two, *or* three stories high. If it is three stories the building receives + 9 points. If it is one story it receives + 3 points. The range of total possible points for the Visual Impact Category is from + 6 to + 23.

Historical Significance

Factors to be Evaluated	Points
(choose one)	
National significance	+ 15
State significance	+ 10
Local significance	+ 5

Historic significance evaluation is based upon the following conditions:

That the structure was significantly associated with the lives of outstanding historic personages
That the structure was associated with significant historic events or occurrences
That the structure contributes information of archaeological, historical, cultural, or social importance to the heritage of the area.

The O.K. Livery, site of the "Gunfight at the O.K. Corral", is of national significance. A building of statewide importance is the old Cochise County courthouse. A building of major local significance is Firehouse No. 1. It represents development of dependable fire protection services.

The total points which a building can receive for this category range from 0 to + 15. Note that if a building is not historically significant it does not receive any points.

Structural Condition

Factors to be Evaluated	Points
(choose one)	
Has structural soundness	+ 5
Needs minor nonstructural repairs (paint, broken windows, etc.)	+ 4
Needs major nonstructural repairs (details missing, roof rusting, etc.)	+ 3
Needs structural repairs (beams, columns, shear stability)	+ 2
Is structurally unsound	+ 1

The range of total points for this category is from + 1 to + 5. Selection of a point count should follow a thorough field survey of each building. The notes from the survey may be useful in estimating project costs when that phase of restoration work begins. . . .

Example No. 2: Block 19 Lot 15
    Post Office Use - Public Built - Post 1910

	Scale:	Points
1.	1885 Characteristics	
	a. Height	+ 3
	b. Facade rhythm	− 3
	c. Facade proportions	− 3
	d. Building materials	− 3
	e. Direction expression	− 3

	Scale:	Points	(continued)

		Scale:	Points
f.	Doors		− 2
g.	Porches		− 2
h.	Windows		− 2
i.	Details		− 2
j.	Signs		+ 2
k.	Setback		+ 1
l.	Public accessibility		+ 1
m.	Building rhythm		+ 1
n.	Building color		+ 1
o.	Ground cover		− 1
	Total 1885 Characteristics		− 12

2.   Visual Impact

a.	Height–1 story	3
b.	District Location Allen	3
c.	Block Location Midblock	2
d.	Individual Character	0
		8

3.   Historical Significance
         None   0

4.   Structural Condition
         Sound   5

5.   Total Contribution to the District

1885 Characteristics	− 12
Visual Impact	8
Subtotal	− 20
Historical Significance	+ 0
Structural Condition	+ 5
Total Contribution to the District	− 15

Proposed Ordinance for the Village of Woodstock, Vermont, 1978*

Design Characteristics of Areas of Woodstock

Woodstock can be divided into areas that have common design characteristics. The following is a description of those areas and the predominant design elements.

I. *The Green*

The Green was left open to provide a communal space for residents, a place that was central to everyone. The importance of village life can be seen in several formal elements: the houses are close to the street and the Green, and the roofline generally takes the direction of the street. The houses are turned toward the Green with their backs to the hills; in fact, the houses along the western side of the Green are like a wall, providing a built edge to the open space. Presently, there is a wide range of architectural styles, but almost all of them have maintained the edge of the Green.

The predominant design elements include:

- Massing of houses and vegetation along the edge of the Green
- Houses 10 to 15 feet from the road, approximately 50 feet of facade
- Buildings 2 stories to roofline
- 8-10 percent of front elevation windows
- Fences providing wall of continuity around the Green
- Sidewalks and curbs
- Brick, stone and wood; horizontal striation; white, red, gray, yellow
- Gabled roofs, symmetrical facades
- Residential and professional use

IV. *High Street*

The houses on High Street are physically separated from the town, not by distance but by height. This separation and the change in style from the center of town gives the street a more rural aspect.

The direction of the facades of the houses is horizontal, but there are strong vertical elements: (1) in the steep roof pitches; (2) the proportions of the buildings (greater height in proportion to length than in the older houses); (3) stairs going up and down from the street; and (4) the presence of the hill behind the houses, rising on one side of the street and falling away on the other. The street itself changes in level and curves along the contour of the hillside.

The predominant design elements include:

- All residential use
- Rich surface articulation; dormers, porches, bay windows

---

*A design control commission responsible for preserving the character of a district needs clear standards on the basis of which it can make its decisions. The ordinance must set these standards. Even in a small town, the various streets may be entirely different, and the standards must make this clear.

- Setbacks of parts of the house (barns, sheds)
- Houses very near road (because of slope)
- Steep gable roofs
- Brick, red and white color

V. Central Business District — Central Street

The central business district is the most urban part of the village. The spaces along the street are defined by buildings. The large windows, level or almost level with the street and sidewalk, provide an indoor-outdoor space. The buildings and the street are completely integrated; not only do the facades assume the direction of the street; they form an edge for it. The first floor provides pedestrian-oriented retail stores; above the first floor display windows, the facades are masonry-stone or brick, and the second and third floors serve as office space, apartments, and storage. The facades extend to three floors on Central Street, making the vertical street frontage and sense of enclosure by buildings greater here than in any other part of the village.

The predominant design elements include:

- Buildings are seen frontally; party walls are typical.
- All roofs are flat with cornices below.
- Glass in display windows does not exceed 8'x 8½'.
- Strong rhythm in 2nd-and 3rd-story windows.
- Light colors on first story.
- Commercial signs are primarily between the space directly above the door and the 2nd story.
- Two or three stories are the rule.
- Buildings are not set back from street more than the sidewalk width.

Common Roof Types

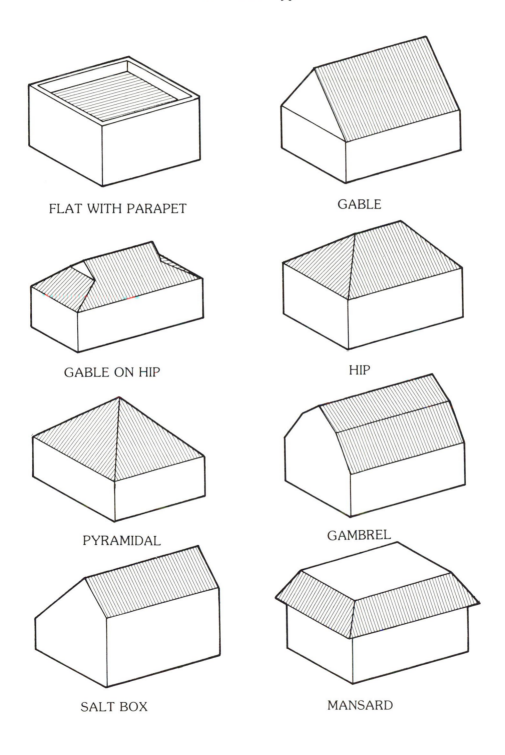

FLAT WITH PARAPET

GABLE

GABLE ON HIP

HIP

PYRAMIDAL

GAMBREL

SALT BOX

MANSARD

Public Commitment and Private Investment*

Weiming Lu

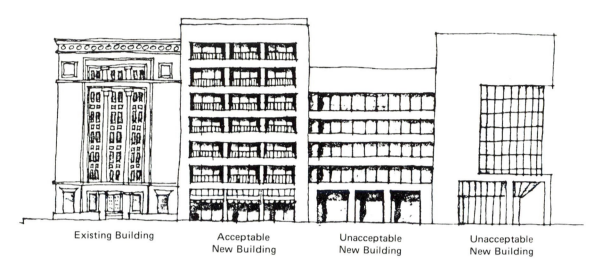

Existing Building   Acceptable New Building   Unacceptable New Building   Unacceptable New Building

Distribution of Window Openings

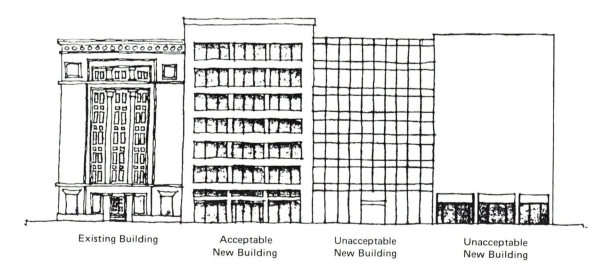

Existing Building   Acceptable New Building   Unacceptable New Building   Unacceptable New Building

Facade Opening/Wall Ratio

*Sketch in National Trust for Historic Preservation, *Economic Benefits of Preserving Old Buildings*. Washington, D. C.: Preservation Press, 1976, p. 36.

6.

Rehabilitation, Restoration, Reconstruction or Stabilization?

Preamble

Historic preservation may be involved with every possible degree of intervention into the physical structure of a building, from mere repainting or repointing on one extreme, to full scale restoration or reproduction of a destroyed building on the other. What degree of intervention would be appropriate naturally depends on the facts of each case, but as the field of historic preservation has matured over the past two centuries, prevailing opinions have increasingly favored a minimum of intervention or "faking" or "earlying-up."

This attitude is reflected in the Venice Charter, the most recent internationally agreed statement of preservation principles. This Charter rules out all reconstruction work (unless unavoidable), and even replacement of missing parts must be made "distinguishable." The same attitude is reflected, to a somewhat less stringent degree, in the regulations of the United States Department of the Interior for the administration of the United States official historic preservation program.

In this chapter the readings show how these attitudes developed, describe the various situations where problems arise, and explain the different attitudes expressed on the matter.

More specifically, this chapter attempts to deal with such questions as:

1. Should the fallen columns of a Greek temple be reerected? If so, should missing "drums" be replaced in similar marble or in some different material to show that they are not original?

2. Should a destroyed building interior in a famous building complex, such as the University of Virginia, be replaced by an approximation of the original or by a similar building designed by a famous architect?

3. How much reconstruction should be permitted at a famous ruin, e.g., Angkor Wat, Knossos, Coventry Cathedral.

4. Is it proper to use modern techniques in rehabilitating old buildings?

5. How should old stones or brickwork be cleaned or repaired? Should Paris have been cleaned as it was in the 1960s by De Gaulle?

6. Is it permissible to fill in a vacant lot in a historic district with a modern but compatible building?

197

7. Is it ever permissible to copy an old style? In what style should a new wing on a historic building be constructed?

8. Is it ever permissible to rehabilitate an old building so that it is all in the same style of architecture? Is it ever permissible so to "renovate" an entire district that the final product is entirely built in the style of one period?

9. When is the readaptation of a historic building not permissible?

10. How far should the original interior of an adapted building be retained?

The Venice Charter

(Statement of Principles drafted by an International Congress of Architects and Technicians involved in preservation and restoration—International Agreement, 1964)

Imbued with a message from the past, the historic monuments of generations of people remain to the present day as living witnesses of their age-old traditions. People are becoming more and more conscious of the unity of human values and regard ancient monuments as a common heritage. The common responsibility to safeguard them for future generations is recognized. It is our duty to hand them on in the full richness of their authenticity.

It is essential that the principles guiding the preservation and restoration of ancient buildings should be agreed and be laid down on an international basis, with each country being responsible for applying the plan within the framework of its own culture and traditions.

By defining these basic principles for the first time, the Athens Charter of 1931 contributed toward the development of an extensive international movement which has assumed concrete form in national documents, in the work of ICOM [International Council of Museums] and UNESCO [United Nations Educational, Scientific, and Cultural Organization] and in the establishment by the latter of the International Centre for the Study of the Preservation and the Restoration of Cultural Property. Increasing awareness and critical study have been brought to bear on problems which have continually become more complex and varied; now the time has come to examine the Charter afresh in order to make a thorough study of the principles involved and to enlarge its scope in a new document.

Accordingly, the Second International Congress of Architects and Technicians of Historic Monuments, which met in Venice from May 25 to 31, 1964, approved the following text:
DEFINITIONS

Article 1. The concept of an historic monument embraces not only the single architectural work but also the urban or rural setting in which is found the evidence of a particular civilization, a significant development or an historic event. This applies not only to great works of art but also to more modest works of the past which have acquired cultural significance with the passing of time.

Article 2. The conservation and restoration of monuments must have recourse to all the sciences and techniques which can contribute to the study and safeguarding of the architectural heritage.

The west facade of Chartres Cathedral is a famous case where an important building has been constructed over a long period and in several styles. All the parts are important and no attempt should be made to "restore" the building to a single style. As stated in Art. 11 of the Venice Charter the "valid contributions of all periods . . .must be respected . . ." *Courtesy of French Government Tourist Office.*

AIM

Article 3. The intention in conserving and restoring monuments is to safeguard them no less as works of art than as historical evidence.

CONSERVATION

Article 4. It is essential to the conservation of monuments that they be maintained on a permanent basis.

Article 5. The conservation of monuments is always facilitated by making use of them for some socially useful purpose. Such use is therefore desirable but it must not change the layout or decoration of the building. It is within these limits only that modifications demanded by a change of function should be envisaged and may be permitted.

Article 6. The conservation of a monument implies preserving a setting which is not out of scale. Wherever the traditional setting exists, it must be kept. No new construction, demolition or modification which would alter the relations of mass and color must be allowed.

Article 7. A monument is inseparable from the history to which it bears witness and from the setting in which it occurs. The moving of all or part of a monument cannot be allowed except where the safeguarding of that monument demands it or where it is justified by national or international interests of paramount importance.

Article 8. Items of sculpture, painting or decoration which form an integral part of a monument may only be removed from it if this is the sole means of ensuring their preservation.

RESTORATION

Article 9. The process of restoration is a highly specialized operation. Its aim is to preserve and reveal the aesthetic and historic value of the monument and is based on respect for original material and authentic documents. It must stop at the point where conjecture begins, and in this case, moreover, any extra work which is indispensable must be distinct from the architectural composition and must bear a contemporary stamp. The restoration in any case must be preceded and followed by an archaeological and historical study of the monument.

Article 10. Where traditional techniques prove inadequate, the consolidation of a monument can be achieved by the use of any modern technique for conservation and construction, the efficacy of which has been shown by scientific data and proved by experience.

Article 11. The valid contributions of all periods to the building of a monument must be respected, since unity of style is not the aim of a restoration. When a building includes the superimposed work of different periods, the revealing of the underlying state can only be justified in exceptional circumstances and when what is removed is of little interest and the material which is brought to light is of great historical, archaeological or aesthetic value, and its state of preservation good enough to justify the action. Evaluation of the importance of the elements involved and the decision as to what may be destroyed cannot rest solely on the individual in charge of the work.

Article 12. Replacements of missing parts must integrate harmoniously with the whole, but at the same time must be distinguishable from the original so that restoration does not falsify the artistic or historic evidence.

Article 13. Additions cannot be allowed except in so far as they do not detract from the interesting parts of the building, its traditional setting, the balance of its composition and its relation with its surroundings.

The Church went out of active use in the 1820s, and the photograph above shows how it had deteriorated by 1920. The photograph on the next page shows its present condition, partly restored and stabilized. *Restoration of the Mission Church, Tumacacori, Arizona.*

HISTORIC SITES

Article 14. The sites of monuments must be the object of special care in order to safeguard their integrity and ensure that they are cleared and presented in a seemly manner. The work of conservation and restoration carried out in such places should be inspired by the principles set forth in the foregoing articles.

EXCAVATIONS

Article 15. Excavations should be carried out in accordance with scientific standards and the recommendation defining international principles to be applied in the case of archaeological excavation adopted by UNESCO in 1956.

Ruins must be maintained and measures necessary for the permanent conservation and protection of architectural features and of objects discovered must be taken. Furthermore, every means must be taken to facilitate the understanding of the monument and to reveal it without ever distorting its meaning.

All reconstruction work should, however, be ruled out a priori. Only anastylosis, that is to say, the reassembling of existing but dismembered parts, can be permitted. The material used for integration should always be recognizable and its use should be the least that will ensure the conservation of a monument and the reinstatement of its form.

PUBLICATION

Article 16. In all works of preservation, restoration or excavation, there should always be precise documentation in the form of analytical and critical reports, illustrated with drawings and photographs.

Every stage of the work of clearing, consolidation, rearrangement and integration, as well as technical and formal features identified during the course of the work, should be included. This record should be placed in the archives of a public institution and made available to research workers. It is recommended that the report be published.

On Formulating New Parameters
For Preservation Policy*

James Marston Fitch

The accelerating interest all over the world in the preservation of the artistic and historic patrimony; the understanding that this patrimony must now be defined as including all sorts of sites, monuments, artifacts and landscapes—urban and rural, high-style and vernacular, historic, primitive and prehistoric; the enormous complexity of the technical problems thus raised; all of these developments require a much broader and more precise definition of both the scope and the levels of intervention that will be required.

---

*From North American International Regional Conference. *Preservation and Conservation: Principles and Practices*. Washington, D.C.: Preservation Press, National Trust for Historic Preservation, 1976, pp. 311-25.

One of the first national monuments, so proclaimed in 1918. The picture, showing the ruin with the Casa Grande-Florence stage coach, dates from the period shortly after the proclamation. *Casa Grande National Monument, Arizona.*

The Scale and Profundity of Intervention

The Venice Charter of 1964, which attempted to identify the parameters of historic preservation, needs to be greatly amplified and much more precisely developed, since it is apparent that a whole spectrum of possibilities, and not merely a few simplistic alternatives, must constitute the core of a viable policy of protection of the artistic and historic patrimony of any country. Table 1 is a suggested classification of such possibilities.

It is apparent that in the modern world any of the levels of intervention listed in Table 1 (or any combination of them) may be mandatory in a given situation. Of course, from a philosophical point of view, the upper parts of both scales are probably the most desirable. That is, since most historic architecture is in an urban setting, optimal protection is necessarily environmental or ambiental in nature. Moreover, a century's experience in both archaeology and architectural preservation indicates that the most conservative intervention is usually the wisest policy, if for no other reason than that it can be most easily rectified subsequently, if that proves necessary.

The question of the *scale* of intervention requires no extended theoretical discussion here, since what is possible in any given case will be largely determined by local exigencies. For example, it was possible to preserve the whole historic core of Williamsburg, Va., intact, whereas none of the approximately 30 buildings now at Old Bethpage Village on Long Island, N.Y., could have been saved except by moving them from their original sites to the architectural museum in Nassau County.

But the problem of the *profundity* of intervention required to save any artifact raises a host of intricate questions, ranging from the philosophical (ethical and aesthetic) to the practical (scientific and technological). All of these questions demand a great deal more theoretical attention than they have hitherto been given.

The recent policy change of the Society for the Preservation of New England Antiquities is highly significant in this respect. The curator of some 60 properties of varying dates, types and conditions, the society has until recently followed a conventional policy, varying between preservation and restoration. But under the new policy, the society will maintain all new accessions in exactly the condition in which they are received. No later and putatively less important elements will be removed; no earlier and putatively more significant elements will be restored or reconstructed. The only form of intervention will be that maintenance required to guarantee the physical integrity of the property in the exact state in which it was acquired.

Objectives of Protection, Preservation

The protection of the artistic and historic patrimony may be said to have two broad objectives: (1) to preserve the cosmetic and structural integrity of the artifact against the attrition caused by environmental forces and (2) to display the artifact to the public in such a way as to minimize a second form of attrition, simple wear and tear.

Table 1: Possibilities for Protecting the
Artistic and Historic Patrimony

Scale of Intervention
(in descending order of physical magnitude)

1. *Entire historic towns*
   Telc, Czechoslovakia
   Venice, Italy
   Williamsburg, Virginia
2. *Historic districts*
   Vieux Carré, New Orleans
   Mala Strana, Prague
   Stare Miasto, Warsaw

3. *Historic building complexes*
   Regent's Park, London
   Lafayette Square, Washington
   Kremlin Palace, Moscow

4. *Individual historic buildings*

   a. *In situ*
      Versailles
      Hampton Court, London
      Mount Vernon, Virginia

   b. *Relocated on new sites*
      Boscobel Garrison, New York
      Abu Simbel, Egypt

   c. *Relocated in groups*
      Skansen, Stockholm
      Cooperstown Farm Museum, New York
      Freiland-museet, Copenhagen

5. *Building fragments — decorative art museums*
   Victoria and Albert Museum, London
   Metropolitan Museum of Art, New York
   National Museum of Anthropology and
   Ethnography, Mexico City

Profundity of Intervention
(in ascending order of severity or radicalness)

1. *Conservation*

   a. *Natural features*
      California redwoods, rare birds and animals

   b. *Works of art*
      Sculpture, painting, frescoes, mosaics

2. *Preservation*
   Hyde Park, New York
   Brighton Royal Pavilion, England
   Wavel Palace, Warsaw

3. *Restoration*
   Independence Hall, Philadelphia
   Hradcany Castle, Prague
   Monticello, Virginia

4. *Adaptive modification*
   Castello Sforszeca, Milano
   Casa Rosa, Genoa
   Opera House, Warsaw
   Ford's Theater, Washington

5. *Structural consolidation*
   The White House, Washington
   York Minister, England
   Norwich Cathedral, England

6. *Reconstitution*

   a. *In situ*
      Santa Trinita Bridge, Florence
      Iwo Treasure Houses, Japan
      Illinois State Capitol, Springfield

   b. *On new sites*
      Skansen, Stockholm
      Abu Simbel, Egypt
      London Bridge, Arizona

7. *Reconstruction*
   Governor's Palace, Williamsburg
   Church of Jan Hus, Prague
   Fort Louisbourg, Canada
   Stoa of Attalus, Athens

8. *Replication*
   Full-scale replica of the Parthenon,
     Nashville, Tenn.
   Use of sculptural replicas outdoors
     Pisa, Florence

The ultimate cultural objective of all preservation activities may be said to be didactic: to teach the citizen to better understand "where he came from" as a means of helping him to decide "where he ought to go." Preservation is thus fundamentally an orientational device—conceptually, intellectually and even psychologically (as in the case of the consolidated ruins of Coventry Cathedral in England or the reconstructed Stare Miasto in Warsaw).

The Importance of Cosmetic Condition

Under these circumstances, the cosmetic condition of the building to be preserved and exhibited is of critical importance. For though it is true that one experiences buildings with all one's senses, the sense of sight is of primordial significance in visiting a historic building. For preservationists, there are two aspects to this question of the cosmetic condition of a building: (1) diagnostic (i.e., as an index of its structural integrity) and (2) aesthetic and associative, as represented by "moss-covered walls," "weathered beams" or "mellowed colors." Although every element of the building will have cosmetic (external appearance) and structural (internal integrity) aspects, the two should not be confused, especially when diagnosis is concerned. For example, many baroque buildings exhibit stained and cracked stucco suggesting walls weakened by years of neglect and decay, even though they may have been carefully restored within the past year or two. This is typically the case in such cities as Prague or Cracow, where the burning of brown coal for heating produces smoke that quickly discolors stuccoed surfaces. For all their unfortunate visual consequences, such practices may continue for decades without serious damage to the stucco. On the other hand, in the case of marble and limestone, the combination of gases resulting from the burning of brown coal sets into motion a complex chemico-physical process, producing serious decay that is concealed by a surface coat of grime. This is typically the case in many Gothic structures in northern Europe. Surface cleaning may be the first stage of therapy in both cases, for aesthetic reasons in the first case and for diagnostic purposes in the latter. But the removal of the discolored surface crust on the fine-scale sculpture can result in the permanent loss of irreplaceable detail, since the crust often conceals an underlayer of desiccated stone.

On the other hand, serious structural defects may display few cosmetic consequences. Wooden beams may be riddled with termites or dry rot without any external evidence. The White House, whose outdoor and indoor surfaces had always been carefully maintained, turned out to be on the verge of collapse when its structure was carefully examined in 1948. Similarly, cracks in the walls of Norwich Cathedral and York Minster were alarming only to specialists, who could tell from the location and direction of the cracks that they indicated grave structural weaknesses requiring immediate attention. Subsequent work revealed that the rubble interiors of these masonry elements (walls, buttresses, vaults) were riddled with voids caused by the desiccation and migration of the Norman cement: Thousands of gallons of cement grout had to be injected into the voids to consolidate them.

Philosophical Aspects of Cosmetic Intervention

Aside from the physical condition of the exposed surface (or of the structural member behind it), there are thorny and complex philosophical aspects of preservation-related cosmetic intervention. They deserve far more attention than they have received to date. One pivotal question is this: When the intervention (whether preservation, restoration, consolidation or reconstitution) is complete, should the building "look old" or "look new"? Should replaced elements be left to weather naturally or should they be antiqued to meld into the older tissue around them? There are competent experts on both sides of this argument. For example, in the restoration of the Collegium Maius in Cracow by the eminent Polish art historian, Carol Estreicher, all the new material was antiqued to match the original. On the other hand, when the curators of the Folkmuseet in Copenhagen must repair one of their old wooden farmhouses, they use new unpainted wood, allowing it to weather just as a peasant who lived in the house would have done.

The same problem is raised to even more critical levels by such activities as the cleaning of entire historic districts, such as the Marais district and the boulevards of Paris, or the restoration of the polychromy in many English churches. The results of such interventions are often startling, compelling many people to readjust radically their ideas of how Paris "ought" to look (i.e., blue gray, the way the Impressionists saw it) or of Westminster "the way it always was" (i.e., before it was cleansed of centuries of soot, smoke and dust).

Criteria for Intervention

While the individual, layman or expert, is entitled to his preferences regarding cosmetic matters, the preservation community must develop broader, more objective and more comprehensive criteria for evaluating decisions about such matters. Certain parameters can be established for different types of preservation project. For example, the preservationist should consider the aesthetic ambitions of the original designers or owners of the structure or site. Most monumental architecture is urbane and upper class, the expression of a life-style that employed precise standards of display, etiquette and propriety, implemented by definite regimes of maintenance, housekeeping and repair. In the Western world, a cosmetic effect of wealth, affluence and good repair, if not shiny newness, was the criterion of owners. And, however fond one may have been of the Louvre when it was still sooty blue gray, one can rest assured that neither the French kings nor their architects conceived of the palace in such colors. Not only was the Louvre, like much of Paris, built largely of tawny pink stone, but much of its architectural ornamentation was conceived in that value and chroma, as is apparent now that the stone has been cleaned. Thus, when the surfaces of monumental upper-class architecture must for one reason or another be disturbed, the cosmetic criteria of restoration should be those of the creators, i.e., newness, brightness (of polychromy and gilt) and good housekeeping.

The reverse probably applies to most vernacular, peasant or primitive architecture. Although all buildings were at one time new and bright, and the builders were probably proud of them in that state, it is doubtful that there were any conscious standards for keeping them that way. Until recent decades, painted woodwork, for example, would have been an unheard-of luxury even for prosperous farmers. Weathered shingles, mossy stones, patched fences and sagging gates would have been standard cosmetic conditions; only the village church may have been painted or whitewashed periodically and its cross or weathervane gilded. The landscape included none of the barbered lawns, clipped hedges or pleached allées associated with urbane upper-class architecture and townscapes. The aesthetic criteria of the restorationist of folk and vernacular buildings should reflect this condition. (Contrast, for example, the laissez-faire maintenance standards adopted by the young archaeologist-anthropologist James Deetz at Plimoth Plantation with the immaculate housekeeping in force at Colonial Williamsburg.)

For ruins (abandoned forts, castles, prehistoric sites, etc.), entirely different aesthetic criteria should apply. The stabilization of above-grade remnants and their maintenance should determine basic policy. In cold, wet climates, protective measures against moisture and freeze-thaw cycles are mandatory (e.g., at Fountains Abbey in England). In hot, humid climates, radical control of vegetation is mandatory, regardless of what the original landscape design may have been (e.g., in Mayan ruins of Yucatan and Guatemala).

For archaeological sites, a certain minimum of restoration is often essential to make the complex more intelligible to the visitor (e.g., at Delphi, Ephesus and Uxmal). Experience with such sites as Knossos suggests that such restorations should be extremely conservative. In certain special circumstances, where the artifacts or structures are both rare and fragile, it may be necessary to build completely new shelters over them (e.g., the glass-and-aluminum canopies over the great mosaics of Piazza Armerina in Sicily or the shelters over some of the rare prehistoric adobe structures in the American Southwest). The design of such devices requires good taste and great discretion on the part of the designer; certainly, all such shelters should be completely contemporary in both design and construction, so that no confusion between the original and the new is possible.

The Question of Cleaning

Since cleaning is a necessary first step in the preservation of most types of structure, the cosmetic state is certain to be affected. Such cleaning, especially of stone and brick masonry and to a somewhat lesser extent of wood and metal, is necessary for two reasons, according to Bernard Fielden, restoration architect for Norwich, York Minster and St. Paul's cathedrals. It is a necessary prerequisite for an inch-by-inch examination of the fabric. It is often an essential step in halting various types of chemical action, such as rust, rot and efflorescence as well as the growth of moss and lichens. In many types of structural consolidation (e.g., injection of liquid grout into masonry structures as was done at York Minster and in many masonry structures in Tuscany), it is also necessary to clean exposed surfaces after the operation.

The palace of Minos at Knossos, Crete, was virtually reconstructed by Evans using old fragments where possible. Reconstruction on this scale is no longer considered acceptable under Art. 15 of the Venice Charter. *Courtesy of the National Tourist Organization of Greece.*

Often there are unanticipated results of complete cleaning: Many forgotten or unknown features of a structure may be revealed, e.g., the vaulted ceiling of the tower at York Minster or the marble polychromy of Garnier's Paris Opera.

There are specialized cases of preservation in the fields of science and technology where immaculate cleanliness and/or perfect maintenance are a sine qua non of the curatorial function. Under such a heading would fall scientific exhibits such as the observatory at Greenwich in England, recently reconstructed and reequipped with great care to re-create 17th-century conditions. To replicate such an atmosphere effectively, equipment is carefully maintained, lenses are polished, metal parts are kept rust free and shining and all moving parts are kept oiled. An example of what happens if such curatorial standards are not observed is the Edison Laboratories in East Orange, N.J. This complex, now under the care of the National Park Service, purports to maintain Thomas A. Edison's personal laboratory exactly as it was on the last day that Edison used it in 1932. Unfortunately, today it falls far short of this goal. Not only is the housekeeping routine, but even more important, the scientific equipment used by Edison is dusty and tarnished. Rectorts and beakers are full of anonymous desiccated materials, which contradict the image of Edison's carefully controlled scientific experiments. (He was actually working on the development of new sources of rubber at the time of his death.) In its present state, the laboratory fails in its central purpose—that of giving a vivid picture of this careful and methodical researcher at work. In preserving a record of this sort of activity for posterity, it is obvious that a new level of curatorial expertise is required.

Of course, the cleaning of any artifact or structure is a hazardous activity, as has been learned at great cost. Here again, a conservative policy is wise, and the rarer the artifact or structure, the more conservative the cleaning methods should be.

There is available now a whole spectrum of cleaning methods that can be arranged in increasing order of radicalness. For the cleaning of masonry buildings, for example, the following choices are available:

1. Continuous film of clean running water (1) without brushing, (2) with brushing and/or (3) with detergent or other chemical cleanser added to the water.
2. Jet of water, with or without brushing or detergent.
3. Steam cleaning.
4. Blasting with abrasives under pressure, using (1) wet or dry sand or (2) softer abrasives (crushed nut shells, buckwheat hulls, etc.).

Sandblasting is too severe for brick constructions and for almost all stone masonry. (It has been employed recently in Paris on the granite revetments of some of the quais without apparent damage, but many experts would argue against even this use.) For buildings of prime importance, pure running water (perhaps even distilled) is recommended, as in the recent cleaning of Notre Dame in Paris. Bernard Fielden used a continuous film of water with brushing at Norwich Cathedral and York Minster.

The cleaning of wood and metal structures requires other methods. Most types of paint are not water soluble; hence, chemical or mechanical means are usually employed to remove them. Sometimes burning off the paint with a small torch is necessary, but this method requires extremely careful workmanship because of the danger of scorching the surface or setting fire to the structure. The cleaning of plaster surfaces, especially if they are decorated, papered or frescoed, lies wholly in the field of the conservator of art and should be entrusted to him.

Correction of Structural Flaws

The correction of purely structural flaws in old buildings poses many complex technical and aesthetic problems, including the following:

1. *Substitution of new materials and techniques.* Because of the scarcity of traditional craftsmen and the expensiveness of their work, there is growing interest in the use of new materials and fabrication methods. Fiber-glass facsimiles are increasingly used as a substitute for hand-carved ornament in wood and stone (e.g., exterior balustrades, cornices or columns). These facsimiles are described as being cheaper, lighter, more durable and more maintenance free. (Thus, the reconstructed cupola of the Merchant's Exchange in Philadelphia is surfaced in a molded fiber-glass facsimile of the wooden original.) Other, more familiar substitutions are asbestos shingles, molded and colored to resemble weathered wood (used at Colonial Williamsburg), and cast-aluminum lampposts substituted for lampposts of cast iron (used at Historic Sacramento).

2. *Correction of previous repairs.* In historic complexes that have been continuously maintained (e.g., Oxford and Cambridge), ashlar stone walls have been cautiously patched for centuries. Since the size, scale and jointing of this masonry was an integral part of the original design and since the stone patches never match exactly in grain or color, the cumulative result of this patchwork is aesthetically disastrous. The new policy is to replace completely any single stone that is deteriorating.

3. *Aesthetic hazards of inserting new tissue into old complexes.* As long as structural intervention is completely concealed, the use of modern materials (e.g., steel or concrete members, modern fireproofing and flashing) is not only justified, it may even be preferable to the use of traditional materials, in that it simplifies future curatorial problems of dating, identification, etc.

When, for adaptive purposes, it becomes necessary to make alterations of any size or of visual importance to a structure, no attempt should be made to replicate the old elements. The only exception to this rule would be a situation in which some kind of serial or repetitive pattern, such as a row of columns or a series of uniform brackets in a cornice, has been disrupted and must be reconstructed to make clear the relationship of the whole composition to its original form. The hazards of not following this rule are painfully evident at Ephesus, where archaeologists have reerected some colonnades to compensate for the missing elements. To dramatize the insertion of new tissue, drums of a different size and cross section from the original columns were used. The result is extremely unsatisfactory, making it actually more difficult to visualize the original building.

Adaptive Use of Old Buildings

There is a growing recognition that the preservation of old buildings as more or less inert museum houses or historic house museums has limits of both practicality and social utility. This is especially true if the buildings in question are a part of living urban tissue. Naturally, there are some buildings of such historical significance (Mount Vernon or Monticello) or of unique artistic merit (the Arena Chapel in Padua with Giotto's frescoes) that they should be restored only as museums. But increasingly, the only way to guarantee the existence of old buildings is to find new, and often unanticipated, uses for them. Architect Giorgio Cavaglieri's conversion of New York City's old Astor Library into a complex of five theaters and his conversion of the old Jefferson Market Court House, also in New York City, into a library are two notable examples of the hundreds of such projects around the world.

Such adaptive uses often result in substantial structural and/or volumetric changes in the building itself and, hence, changes to its visual appearance (e.g., old City Hall, Boston, and New York Bar Association, Albany). Often, adaptive use involves new and unprecedented juxtapositions of small old buildings and large new ones (e.g., the 25-story addition to the original single story banking room of the Bank of California, San Francisco, and South Street Seaport, New York City). Such problems require new aesthetic perspectives on the part of the architect and urban designer and rejection of the misconception that there is something "unnatural" or "artificial" in these new relationships. The very process of urbanization makes such relationships inevitable, and urban planners and architects will have to develop the theoretical capacity to cope with them. Certainly, such new tissue cannot be disguised by draping it in a two-dimensional facsimile of older buildings, as is even now being proposed for new state office buildings in Annapolis. The aesthetic problem is one of real congruency, not mere superficial historicity.

Reconstruction

The reconstruction of vanished buildings, erected on the basis of archaeological and documentary evidence alone, has had a long and distressing history in the past century and a quarter. Examples of reconstruction from the work of Viollet-le-Duc at Pierrefonds to that at Williamsburg and the Stoa of Attalus in Athens makes it difficult not to conclude that reconstruction is a radical and dangerous form of intervention. The many reasons for this opinion need no repetiton here, but it should be observed that the reconstruction of a vanished building alongside the restoration of an extant one is tantamount to a museum curator's hanging known replicas alongside authenticated originals, a situation more apt to confuse the spectator than to raise his aesthetic standards or illuminate his understanding of history.

Nevertheless, there are probably cases in which the reconstruction of vanished buildings or complexes of buildings is ideologically justified and psychologically necessary. One such instance is the restoration-cum-reconstruction of medieval Warsaw. Two famous telegrams from Hitler and his general staff (now displayed in the city's Municipal Museum) ordered the absolute destruction of Warsaw. After the defeat of the Nazi regime, the Poles felt that they had no choice but to reconstruct their capital in its entirety, as symbolic evidence of victory. The policy concerning reconstruction might be generalized thus: The reconstruction of a vanished structure is justified if it is of absolutely prime importance to the society involved and if it is reconstructed during the lifetimes of the people who knew and valued it.

Reconstitution *in Situ* and on New Sites

Modern technology makes possible the complete reconstitution of old buildings, and modern conditions often make it mandatory. The reasons may be purely structural (e.g., the reconstitution of historically important but structurally unsound log cabins in Bethlehem, Pa.) or related to adaptive use of the building in situ (e.g., the dismantling and reerection of the old Illinois State House in Springfield to make possible the installation of an underground garage and the restoration of the mutilated interiors to their condition when the body of President Abraham Lincoln lay in state there in April 1865).

Much more common is the moving of old buildings to new sites. In this process, smaller buildings may be moved intact on trailers or disassembled and trucked to a new site for reassembly. An interesting instance of this latter technique was the disassembly in 1971 of the Edgar Laing Stores building in Manhattan. The disassembly of this 1845 cast-iron facade by James Bogardus was completely documented—all the elements were catalogued and marked, and complete drawings were prepared for its reconstitution as a part of the new campus for Manhattan Community College.*

Facsimiles and Replicas

Largely because of the alarming increase in physical attrition of old structures as a consequence of environmental pollution, there is a new interest in the substitution of facsimiles in situ to permit the original object to be transferred to the controlled environment of a museum. Obviously, this technique is limited by the size of the artifact. Replicas of Michaelangelo's *David* in Florence or the sculptured figures on the Baptistry of Pisa have long acted as surrogates for the originals, which have been moved into museums. There is serious talk of doing the same thing with the portal of St. Trophime in Arles and the metopes on the Parthenon in Athens. The rate of attrition of the limestone masonry of the Spanish Chapel at the Cloisters of the Metropolitan Museum of Art in New York City has proved to be so rapid, and the use of chemical preservatives apparently so ineffective, that there are now plans to encase it completely in an air-conditioned glass-and-metal case. The design of such a protective device will require both taste and discretion on the part of the architect selected for the project, if the role of the Cloisters in the New York skyline is not to be seriously affected.

A new and surprising rationale for the use of facsimiles and reproductions has recently been advanced by James Deetz, the curator of Plimoth Plantation. This entire project has always been a reproduction of the original settlement, not even occupying the original site. Deetz feels that, in the past, this fact was not made sufficiently clear to visitors, who too often left with the impression that

---

*In 1974 the stored pieces of the Bogardus building were stolen from an empty lot where they had been placed after disassembly.

they had "seen the real thing." He has reorganized the entire interpretation program to shift the emphasis from the artifacts and structures to the processes that they supported. The visitor is now made to understand that nothing in the entire project is original or antique. This makes the policing problems much simpler and, incidentally, has reduced thefts to almost zero at a time when they are an increasingly serious problem at most historic restorations. On the other hand, Deetz does everything possible to guarantee that all the activities carried on, tools used and life-styles acted out are as accurate as modern research can make them.

Restoration: An On-Going Process

The restoration of a building does not end when the desired physical state has been attained; on the contrary, although it is seldom anticipated, restoration has only begun. The maintenance of this physical state has been dubbed by Fielden as "four-dimensional preservation." Since no material can be expected to last forever, rational parameters for such maintenance need to be established.

Extrapolating from his experience in restoring three of England's great cathedrals, Fielden has attempted to establish optimal cycles for a continuing preservation program. At York Minster, he has set this cycle at 35 years. In other words, a continuing program of housekeeping and checkups will be phased so that every square foot of the structure's fabric will be examined, cleaned and, if necessary, repaired in not more than 35 years. Emergencies will, of course, be handled as such. However, with continuous inspection, emergency repairs should be held to a minimum. Only basic structural repairs to foundations and towers are exempt from this inspection cycle, because during the restoration, when new reinforced concrete members were introduced at the cathedral, all metal reinforcing rods were executed in stainless steel to assure as long a life as is currently attainable.

The Secretary of the Interior's Standards for Historic Preservation Projects*

Section 68.1 *Intent.*

The intent of this part is to set forth standards for historic preservation projects, containing general standards and specific standards for acquisition, protection, stabilization, preservation, rehabilitation, restoration, and reconstruction. These standards apply to all proposed grant-in-aid projects assisted through the National Historic Preservation Fund.

Section 68.2 *Definitions.*

The standards for historic preservation projects will be used by the National Park Service and State historic preservation officers and their staff members in planning, undertaking, and supervising grant-assisted projects for acquisition, protection, stabilization, preservation, rehabilitation, restoration, and reconstruction. For the purposes of this part: . . .

(b) *Preservation.* Means the act or process of applying measures to sustain the existing form, integrity, and material of a building or structure, and the existing form and vegetative cover of site. It may include initial stabilization work where necessary, as well as ongoing maintenance of the historic building materials.

(c) *Protection.* Means the act or process of applying measures designed to affect the physical condition of a property by defending or guarding it from deterioration, loss, or attack, or to cover or shield the property from danger or injury. In the case of buildings and structures, such treatment is generally of a temporary nature and anticipates future historic preservation treatment; in the case of archaeological sites, the protective measure may be temporary or permanent.

(d) *Reconstruction.* Means the act or process of reproducing by new construction the exact form and detail of a vanished building, structure, or object, or a part thereof, as it appeared at a specific period of time.

(e) *Rehabilitation.* Means the act or process of returning a property to a state of utility through repair or alteration that makes possible an efficient contemporary use while preserving those portions or features of the property that are significant to its historical, architectural, and cultural values.

---

*36 CFR 68.1–68.4, April 1981.

(f) *Restoration*. Means the act or process of accurately recovering the form and details of a property and its setting as it appeared at a particular period of time by means of the removal of later work or by the replacement of missing earlier work.

(g) *Stabilization*. Means the act or process of applying measures designed to reestablish a weather-resistant enclosure and the structural stability of an unsafe or deteriorated property while maintaining the essential form as it exists at present.

Section 68.3 *General standards for historic preservation projects.*

The general standards listed below shall apply to all historic preservation grant-in-aid projects; additional standards in section 68.4 for acquisition, protection, stabilization, preservation, rehabilitation, restoration, and reconstruction apply to specific grant-in-aid projects as appropriate.

Rider A: The standards shall be applied taking into consideration the energy conservation needs and the economic and technical possibility of each project: in the final analysis, however, the treatment must be consistent with the historic character of the structure and, where appropriate, with the district in which it is located.

(a) Every reasonable effort shall be made to provide a compatible use for a property that requires minimal alteration of the building structure, or site and its environment, or to use a property for its originally intended purpose.

(b) The distinguishing original qualities or character of a building, structure, or site and its environment shall not be destroyed. The removal or alteration of any historic material or distinctive architectural features should be avoided when possible.

(c) All buildings, structures, and sites shall be recognized as products of their own time. Alterations which have no historical basis and which seek to create an earlier appearance shall be discouraged.

(d) Changes which may have taken place in the course of time are evidence of the history and development of a building, structure, or site and its environment. These changes may have acquired significance in their own right, and this significance shall be recognized and respected.

(e) Distinctive stylistic features or examples of skilled craftsmanship which characterize a building, structure, or site shall be treated with sensitivity.

(f) Deteriorated architectural features shall be repaired rather than replaced, wherever possible. In the event replacement is necessary, the new material should match the material being replaced in composition, design, color, texture, and other visual qualities. Repair or replacement of missing architectural features should be based on accurate duplications of features substantiated by historical, physical, or pictorial evidence rather than on conjectural designs or the availability of different architectural elements from other buildings or structures.

(g) The surface cleaning of structures shall be undertaken with the gentlest means possible. Sandblasting and other cleaning methods that will damage the historic building materials shall not be undertaken.

(h) Every reasonable effort shall be made to protect and preserve archaeological resources affected by, or adjacent to, any acquisition, protection, stabilization, preservation, rehabilitation, restoration, or reconstruction projects.

Section 68.4 *Specific standards for acquisition, protection, stabilization, preservation, rehabilitation, restoration, and reconstruction projects.*

In addition to the general standards set forth in section 68.3 the following specific standards shall be applied as appropriate: . . .

(b) *Protection.* (1) Before applying protective measures, which are generally of a temporary nature and imply future historic preservation work, an analysis of the actual or anticipated threats to the property shall be made.

(2) Protection shall safeguard the physical condition or environment of a property or archaeological site from further deterioration or damage caused by weather or other natural, animal, or human intrusions.

(3) If any historic material or architectural features are removed, they shall be properly recorded and, if possible, stored for future study or reuse.

(c) *Stabilization.* (1) Stabilization shall reestablish the structural stability of a property through the reinforcement of loadbearing members or by arresting material deterioration leading to structural failure. Stabilization shall also reestablish weather resistant conditions for a property.

(2) Stabilization shall be accomplished in such a manner that it detracts as little as possible from the property's appearance. When reinforcement is required to reestablish structural stability, such work shall be concealed wherever possible so as not to intrude upon or detract from the aesthetic and historical quality of the property, except where concealment would result in the alteration or destruction of historically significant material or spaces.

(d) *Preservation.* (1) Preservation shall maintain the existing form, integrity, and materials of a building, structure, or site. Substantial reconstruction or restoration of lost features generally are not included in a preservation undertaking.

(2) Preservation shall include techniques of arresting or retarding the deterioration of a property through a program of ongoing maintenance.

(e) *Rehabilitation.* (1) Contemporary design for alterations and additions to existing properties shall not be discouraged when such alterations and additions do not destroy significant historic, architectural, or cultural material, and such design is compatible with the size, scale, color, material, and character of the property, neighborhood, or environment.

(2) Wherever possible, new additions or alterations to structures shall be done in such a manner that if such additions or alterations were to be removed in the future, the essential form and integrity of the structure would be unimpaired.

(f) *Restoration.* (1) Every reasonable effort shall be made to use a property for its originally intended purpose or to provide a compatible use that will require minimum alteration to the property and its environment.

(2) Reinforcement required for structural stability or the installation of protective or code-required mechanical systems shall be concealed whenever possible so as not to intrude on or detract from the property's esthetic and historic qualities, except where concealment would result in the alteration or destruction of historically significant materials or spaces.

(3) When archaeological resources must be disturbed by restoration work, recovery of archaeological material shall be undertaken in conformance with current professional practices.

(g) *Reconstruction.* (1) Reconstruction of a part or all of a property shall be undertaken only when such work is essential to reproduce a significant missing feature in a historic district or scene, and when a contemporary design solution is not acceptable.

(2) Reconstruction of all or a part of a historic property shall be appropriate when the reconstruction is essential for understanding and interpreting the value of a historic district, or when no other building, structure, object, or landscape feature with the same associative value has survived and sufficient historical documentation exists to insure an accurate reproduction of the original.

(3) The reproduction of missing elements accomplished with new materials shall duplicate the composition, design, color, texture, and other visual qualities of the missing element. Reconstruction of missing architectural features shall be based upon accurate duplication of original features, substantiated by historical, physical, or pictorial evidence rather than upon conjectural designs or the availability of different architectural features from other buildings.

(4) Reconstruction of a building or structure on an original site shall be preceded by a thorough archaeological investigation to locate and identify all subsurface features and artifacts.

(5) Reconstruction shall include measures to preserve any remaining original fabric, including foundations, subsurface, and ancillary elements. The reconstruction of missing elements and features shall be done in such a manner that the essential form and integrity of the original surviving features are unimpaired.

What Time is This Place?*

Kevin Lynch

There are several ways of dealing with a valued piece of an old environment. What remains can simply be saved from destruction, perhaps by moving it away from danger. It can be restored by minor repairs and refurbishings. Or it can be rebuilt in as careful a copy of its "original" state as is currently known. This may be done with original material, judiciously pieced out and refinished, or with covert new material, or even with obviously new material. Put another way, the patina of time may be retained, imitated, or removed. When there is a frank and complete reconstruction, using new material, on a new site, the aim may be an appearance of having just been built, an aim that may be carried out even to the details of equipment and perhaps the use of costumed actors. Such a reconstruction will often shock contemporary taste (Greek temples were gaudily painted in their day), and sometimes it will be made ridiculous by subsequent scholarship. But it can be a strong evocation of the past for a general audience.

The official priority rankings of historical societies usually range from the least to the most disturbance, that is, from preservation through restoration, reconstitution, and relocation to complete reconstruction. But this simple formula cloaks many subtleties and invites controversies. What, for

*Cambridge, Mass: MIT Press, 1972, pp. 31-35.

example, happens to later historical additions to the original structure? Since historic structures are thought of as having been built all at one time and then potentially eternal, but have actually undergone a continuous process of physical change and human occupation, and since our view of history itself changes constantly, the controversies may be heated and scholastic. Robert Scott's Antarctic hut, unused since his fatal expedition sixty years ago, survives intact in the polar cold: papers, food, and equipment are just as they were. The effect is powerful—it corresponds to our wish to arrest the past—but we cannot easily reproduce the circumstances that created it.

Sometimes the historical object is reconstructed at regular intervals, preserving not the old materials but rather the ancient form. The 2000-year outline of the White Horse of Uffington is still visible on the downs because it is renewed by its annual "scouring." The temple at Ise, completely rebuilt with new material on a new site every twenty years, conserves the most primitive form of any building in Japan. Such periodic reconstructions, because they do not depend on a single effort, evade some of the issues posed here. . . .

According to another doctrine, only the external historical shell need be preserved or reconstructed. It can then shelter current, active uses, and internal physical modifications suitable to those new uses are allowable. "Outsides" are public, historic, and regulated, while "insides" are private, fluid, and free. An aversion to an unused or "museum" environment is connected with this doctrine. Even then, there are difficult decisions to be made: the interior-exterior dichotomy is a convenient distinction to make, but what kinds of specific modifications are, in fact, allowable? In restoring the Nash terraces around Regent's Park in London for modern offices, the facades were rebuilt according to the original designs, but enough of the former internal arrangement was also imposed so that the view from the street would have the right sense of depth. How far can we go in subsidizing activities that are likely to survive in preserved surroundings? To what degree does contemporary utility, however discreetly provided, rupture the sense of historical integrity? The ceramic bathrooms of colonial Williamsburg come as a shock. And what is to be done where inside and outside are hard to separate, as in a large public building or in a landscape?

Strict preservation is the more pessimistic view. It considers any reconstruction as fraudulent and thinks of time as a process of regrettable but inevitable dissolution. We can protect only what still remains by a variety of means, principally passive but including removal to a protected place (then the loss of the museum itself can erase the concentrated harvest of generations!). The object to be preserved can be presented for better public view, but the process of decay is only slowed down—not stopped.

One may also take a purely intellectual view, aiming to learn as much and as accurately about the past as possible and only secondarily to preserve, use, or exhibit it. One is then justified in destroying remains by dissection or excavation or in reburying them after inspection so that they are kept intact for later generations of scientists, even though they may not then be seen or used by the general public.

Coventry Cathedral was a major casualty of the German air raids early in World War II (November 1940). After the war, the shell of the old cathedral (or what remained of it) was left intact, and a new cathedral built adjacent at right angles to the old. Several features of the new cathedral have been dedicated to promoting international understanding and reconciliation. *Courtesy of the British Tourist Authority*.

Conservation of Historic and Cultural Resources*

Ralph W. Miner

Purity or continuity? Another basic issue is how far restoration should go. We have a tendency in this country to develop preconceived notions about the "best" architectural period of a particular area and then to restore buildings in it to that particular style. This has often been called "*to early-up a building.*" The restoration attempts to be exacting in terms of known (or assumed) details in order to represent the purity of the particular style. This effort to recreate authenticity (even though new materials, and often new methods, are frequently used) tends to inflate restoration costs. While this approach might be acceptable for the occasional building appropriate for museum use, another alternative may be much more relevant for those structures for which adaptive uses are sought. This is the European approach reflected in "The Venice Charter" of 1964. . . . This approach of retaining additions and alterations reflects the continuity of a building over a period of time. It is a more flexible approach in terms of fitting old structures to new uses.

While the purity approach to restoration may be relevant in certain circumstances, caution should be exercised so that this objective does not emerge as false purity—restoring a building to something it never was because of a preference for a particular style or series of details. This danger exists on an area basis also, as for example in a proposal to demolish a nineteenth century shopping street in order to rebuild in an eighteenth century idiom.

European Governmental Experience**

Raymonde A. Frin

Preservation of Materials

This first aspect lies within the competence of chemists through the analysis of materials and their reactions to external factors; and of biochemists in their study of the effects of parasites and microorganisms upon these materials. So it is easily understandable that large laboratories equipped

---

*A.S.P.O. *Planning Advisory Service,* Report no. 244, 1969, p.13.

**From National Trust for Historic Preservation, *Historic Preservation Today.* Charlottesville, Va.: University Press of Virginia, 1966, pp. 88-92.

with the latest technical instruments have been established throughout Europe, the most important being l'Institut Royal du Patrimoine Artistique in Brussels, l'Istituto Centrale delle Restauro, and l'Istituto di Patologia del Libro, both in Rome. The latter is particularly concerned with the danger of parasites, such as termites. Similar work is being carried out in England, France, Poland, Sweden, the USSR, etc. UNESCO has established, also in Rome, the International Centre for the Study of the Preservation and the Restoration of Cultural Property. The function of the UNESCO center is to insure international exchange of information, to stimulate further research on a cooperative basis, and to assist countries who apply for help.

Stone

To retain what one might call the "skin of the stone," i.e., the exterior surface that throughout the centuries has acquired a beautiful and irreplaceable patina, is today of great concern to all those interested in historic and artistic monuments. The patina is sometimes produced by the alteration of the stone. Who would wish, however, to remove the honey-colored patina of the Parthenon, caused by the oxidation of the iron salts contained in the Pentilic marble; or the ivory quality of the sandstone blocks of the casemates at Mycenae where, long after the citadel was abandoned, shepherds brought their sheep to shelter, the greasy wool having rubbed the raw stone smooth; or the warm tone of the Orvieto Cathedral's low reliefs?

Unfortunately, patina alone does not cover the surfaces. Layers of dirt, soot, and gas fumes lie on the original facades and gnaw into the stone. In such cases, cleaning becomes imperative (on condition, of course, that the methods employed do not attack the surface or the delicately sculptured elements). Thus have the monuments of Paris, completely blackened in a little less than a century and a half, been "washed" with a powerful jet of water. Some have revealed beauty never even dreamed of by the most enlightened connoisseurs, who have beheld in wonder the Cour Carrée of the Louvre, for example.

Pigeons are also a perpetual threat to monuments, and a campaign is being organized against the tourist-beloved pigeons in Venice, which left to their own devices would soon reduce the aspect of the monument to that of the off-coast islands of Peru! In other cases, silicate compounds have been used for protective coating over the surfaces, thus preventing the deterioration of soluble materials; calcareous incrustations have been removed with the aid of a chisel; atmospheric humidity has been fought by the installation of air conditioning plants; and the disintegration of mortar is parried by high pressure injections of concrete.

Wood

Xylophagous insects, parasites, and molds are the most deadly enemies of wood, and when the wood fulfills a structural function, not very much can be done. Attacked by parasites, wood becomes pulverized and loses all resistance. It will be seen later that the solution resides in relieving the wooden elements from their structural function. Research is being carried out on a large scale to try to stop the havoc caused by the insects. Various methods are being investigated: injections of curative or prophylactic insecticides, spraying, coating, etc.

Metals

Oxidation, rust, and patina have often caused complete destruction of parts exposed to climatic variations and humidity. Likewise, the corrosion of elements incorporated within the stone structure has caused it to split and crack. Examples of columns, the bases and capitals of which have cracked because of the swelling of the rusted iron tenons, are innumerable. Only the delicate operation of substituting bronze or stainless steel tenons for iron tenons can remedy this state of affairs. Various experiments are being carried out which show that methods to render metals inactive can be developed.

Efforts of the scientists are also being directed toward obtaining stabilization of the ancient elements without, unless unavoidable, replacing them by new elements. The methods adopted vary according to the case. Each one presents very different problems, and the old saying "there are no diseases, only diseased," may be applied to monuments.

Preservation of Stability

The aforementioned proverb applies especially to structural problems, and because of variations in their static stability, one seeks in vain for analogous situations among the monuments. Thus no system valid for all cases can be advocated. Each problem of stability requires its own methods. This is particularly true in Europe because of the extraordinary variety of monuments from all periods and places. It will suffice to consider for a moment the different conceptions of static stability.

Greek architecture is based upon the principle of the trilith—a pediment on supporting elements exercising a vertical weight; on the other hand, in Roman architecture the thrust of the vaults is oblique and shored up by enormous engaged piers. In Byzantine architecture the skillful balance of the component parts achieves stability, avoiding thick walls and jambs. This principle was applied in medieval architecture, gradually leading to the miracle of Gothic architecture, which reduced supporting structures to a minimum of piers shored up by flying buttresses.

It is the task of civil engineering to find remedies for the weaknesses of ancient buildings. In bygone times, additions were made to strengthen the monuments (the supplementary piers to St. Sophia in Constantinople, extra flying buttresses to San Vitale in Ravenna), windows and porticos were scaled, and other means were employed that either disfigured the monument or altered its original character. An example of this is the Royal Palace in Naples. At the beginning of the eighteenth century the portico threatened to collapse. In order to reinforce the walls the arcade was sealed, but the masonry was handled in a way to organize a series of niches that conferred on the monument a different and richer architectural rhythm. Today such a method is no longer acceptable, for however ingenious or brilliant it may be, it nevertheless appears as an alteration to the original architecture. So the efforts of the architect-restorers are concentrated on a kind of reinforcement of the structures that does not affect their original appearance.

For classical monuments built of large blocks in which mortar plays but a secondary role, an ingenious system has been devised to ensure the cohesion of the monument. It has been used to preserve the Ala of the Verona arena and the Arch of Constantine in Rome. The whole height of the building has been bored through and steel stakes or cables driven through the perforations and sealed at each end. Highly resistant liquid concrete has been injected to restore the cohesion of the monument without either the help of props or the dismantling of elements.

The use of concrete and steel gives excellent results, for these materials can be modelled according to the various shapes and forms, particularly when whole structures must be internally renewed, and they are far more resistant than the ancient materials used as stays. Needless to say, owing to the discovery of these new methods, it is no longer necessary to take down sloping walls and rebuild them; the thrust of vaults can be completely absorbed and excessive weights removed from feeble structures. In the case of sloping walls another bold device has been employed: it consists of digging a trench at the base of the walls and (after having encased them provisionally) pulling them plumb with the aid of ropes and cables. (It is regrettable that such a method cannot be used for the tower of Pisa!)

The role of steel and concrete in the case of reinforcement of the substructure of buildings is also important, for these materials insure an equitable distribution of weight and thrust on the ground. As a matter of fact, modern techniques applied to the restoration of monuments have become a common practice, particularly with regard to the replacement of ancient elements—ceilings, framework, roofs, and rafters—by more durable and more resistant materials.

Plan for the Creation of a Historic Environment[*]

Billy G. Garrett and James W. Garrison

The 1885 Reference Data

At the beginning of work on Tombstone's restoration plan, no reference date had been firmly fixed. In part, this lack of definition was because of an information void. Few people had an accurate mental picture of what the city really looked like during the 1880s. So the entire period was treated as if it were a single, characteristically consistent entity. The photographs quickly revealed this fallacy.

After some discussion it was decided to establish a date to which design decisions could be related. The year 1885 was selected for this purpose. The choice was based upon the following facts:

1. Many of the important buildings which stood during Tombstone's best publicized years (1880-1882) were destroyed by fires in 1881 and 1882. Very little reliable information exists about them today. Furthermore, quite a few of the city's most notable structures were not built until after those dates.

2. A good number of buildings from the 1880s time frame are still standing in Tombstone. Since the town peaked out before 1885 and declined rapidly after 1885, it may be assumed that no major structures were raised after 1885. Existing 1880s buildings were therefore probably a part of the 1885 setting.

3. Well-designed, permanent structures were usually not built in Tombstone until after the fire prevention problem was solved in 1882. From that point on, until the mines closed, community

---

[*]Prepared for the Tombstone Restoration Commission, Inc., Tombstone, Ariz., 1972, pp. 45-47.

character steadily matured. The peak physical development most likely occurred sometime in 1885.

4. Restoration work has to go from the present backward, if existing historic resources are to be properly conserved. It was felt that the reference date selected should allow for inclusion of all 1880s buildings remaining. Only 1885 could satisfy this requirement.

5. The reference data had to correlate with available photographic material. A comprehensive but detailed set of images from one point in the city's first decade was needed. Pictures of and from the buildings which stood in 1885 comprised the largest category of this kind.

Once 1885 was chosen, work moved ahead on the street elevation references and the zoning ordinance. Neither could have been done without the time definition. But both needed to be qualified after they were completed.

In Evicting a Stanford White Design, Virginians Gain Apparent Jefferson *

Paul Goldberger

Charlottesville, Va.—Stanford White, whose buildings epitomized the free use of historical styles in the late 19th century, is usually the hero of preservation efforts. But here at the University of Virginia, he is the villain. The reason is that White redesigned the Rotunda, the central building of the Thomas Jefferson-designed campus here, after an 1895 fire destroyed Jefferson's interior. For years the Rotunda was, thus, more a White building than a Jefferson one.

Then, in the mid-1950s, Prof. Frederick D. Nichols, the architectural historian and Jefferson scholar, started a campaign to restore the building to its Jeffersonian form. Persuading the university's board and finding money, including a Department of Housing and Urban Development grant, took years but the restoration finally went ahead in 1972.

It was completed last spring, and the university now has what might be described as an unreal Jefferson building, instead of a real Stanford White one. For the White design had to be demolished to permit the re-creation of the Jefferson one, and there were some grumblings to the effect that, whatever the merits as an architect of "Mr. Jefferson," the university's founder, they did not justify the demolition of a Stanford White building in favor of what is, everyone admits, a somewhat conjectural re-creation of the Jefferson design.

Now that the rebuilding is complete, most of White's defenders, including Joseph Bosserman, dean of the School of Architecture here, have made their peace with it, but the question the project

---

New York Times, Nov. 9, 1976, p. 30.

The Rotunda at the University of Virginia, designed by Thomas Jefferson. *Courtesy of the National Trust.*

poses still remains—when a building has one layer of history covering up another, which should take priority?

The University of Virginia as built to Jefferson's designs in 1817-27 is, quite possibly, the finest group of public buildings in the United States. It is a vision of classical order. The Rotunda, a brick model at half-diameter of the Pantheon in Rome, is the visual center and, since it originally housed the library, was a symbolic center as well.

The Rotunda faces a 750-foot-wide expanse of grass, lined on both sides by a gracious Doric colonnade containing student dormitories. Five larger buildings are set at uneven intervals along each side of the colonnade; these are faculty residences, and each is designed to illustrate a different classical order.

The buildings are sited on a ridge, and Jefferson intended the fourth side of the rectangle that his buildings form to be left open to the view of the valley and the mountains beyond. It was closed with another building by the university's nemesis, Stanford White ("I told my students in the 1960s that if they felt like protesting they should blow up that building," Professor Nichols said). But in spite of the closed vista, the open space between the colonnades remains a remarkably restful outdoor room, perfectly proportioned and skillfully balanced between a sense of openness and enclosure.

Inside the Rotunda, Jefferson designed what Professor Nichols has called "the first free-form space in America." He divided the round building's main floor into three eliptical rooms, leaving an hourglass-shaped hall in the center. One floor up, Jefferson placed his dome room, reproducing the proportions of the Pantheon in a delicate and majestic space that was the original home of the university library.

It is these interiors that White destroyed. He removed the main floor to permit a two-story-high room under the dome, altering the Pantheon proportions and creating a space that is more Renaissance in quality than classical. But in the White building, "you entered into the great hall, whereas in the Jefferson design, the dome room is upstairs, unrelated to the rest of the building," according to Dean Bosserman.

Some Intrusions of Modernism

The re-creation of the Jefferson design was done by the firm of Ballou & Justice, with Professor Nichols as advisor. Much of it is conjectural—there are no records as to the precise design of cornices or chandeliers, for example, and while those chosen are elegant and surely Jeffersonian in feeling, no one can be certain that they are like the originals. And the re-creation also includes some intrusions of modernism that seem utterly unnecessary—visible air-conditioning vents, for example, and recessed downlights.

But the university seems confident that it has opted for the better layer of history. Looking at the re-creation, with the "free-form" hourglass hall back and the splendid dome room once again low-ceilinged, one is tempted to agree; it is difficult to imagine that White's hall could have been any better.

But still, the nagging question remains. Undoubtedly, in an ideal situation, Jefferson's design is the finer of the two versions. White, the flamboyant New York stylist, "never really understood what Jefferson was trying to do," as Professor Nichols said.

But the university never had the chance to truly turn the clock back to the days before Stanford White arrived in Charlottesville. Its choice was not between White and Jefferson, but between real White and not entirely real Jefferson. By going back in time to celebrate one part of its history, the University of Virginia has necessarily obscured another part of it.

Historic Preservation in Inner City Areas
A Manual of Practice*

Arthur P. Ziegler

Here are a few examples of corner-cutting to achieve minimal restorations.

Stud old interior walls and sheet with drywall rather than replastering.
Paint over old wallpaper if possible.
Scrape and paint old floors.
If a floor covering is required, use linoleum.
Use rubber stair treads, not carpet, on hall stairs.
If new bathroom plumbing is needed, do not tear up the old floor; lay the pipes over it and build a raised new floor on top.
Keep the existing sinks, bathtub, lights and other fixtures insofar as possible.
Paint woodwork; don't try to refinish it.
Have tenants help with the work, like painting.
Enlist federally funded Neighborhood Youth Corps youngsters to help.

This list is meant only to indicate the direction in which you should be thinking. Other economies will manifest themselves as you work. Obviously minimal restoration work should be done only where full funding cannot be obtained and only as a temporary (1-5 years) measure. It is not a final solution but it will enable you to save more buildings and improve the living conditions of the residents without unduly disturbing the rental levels, and you spread you money further.

For a more useful and permanent solution, you must utilize a federal subsidy program (or that of a state or local government, if available). These are few in number and niggling in appropriations, but they do exist and you should make every effort to tap them.

*Pittsburgh: Allegheny Press, 1971, p. 44-45. The process described below was adopted in order to make it easier for original inhabitants to remain in the buildings. (See chapter 9.)

Special Aspects of Urbanism*

James Marston Fitch

I would prohibit building on one square foot of unspoiled American soil until every square foot of urban tissue had been made habitable again.

---

*From *Back to the City: A Guide to Urban Preservation*. Proceedings of the "Back to the City" Conference, New York City, Sept. 13-16, 1974, p. 8.

7.

Adaptive Reuse

Preamble

The adaptive reuse of old and historic buildings is becoming increasingly accepted as a normal, attractive, and less expensive way both to provide space and to save historic buildings and areas. This is true for a number of reasons. Among them are:

1. Museums and museum towns like Williamsburg, Virginia, are not, except in unusual cases, a desirable way to carry out preservation. Such arrangements are expensive, and create an artificial atmosphere. At best, they can only preserve a small part of the building stock which needs preservation.

2. Old buildings are usually energy-saving in operation, while the materials in them already represent the use of much energy in their preparation.

3. Inflation has now made the use of old buildings economically advantageous.

4. The reuse of old buildings helps revitalize decayed downtown areas.

5. Adaptation of old buildings is labor-intensive, and creates jobs rather than wastes resources.

6. Adapted buildings tend to offer special amenities, and have good-quality, handmade features, while the average new construction tends to avoid handmade details and uses the cheapest materials. It all tends to look the same.

7. Old buildings adaptable to modern conditions are frequently in areas already supplied with utilities and will not require new utility installation.

The arranging and financing of this type of project has recently become more familiar to American banks, developers, and architects, so that it will become increasingly easy to finance the work and to obtain the necesary skills.

The disadvantages have not proved as great as anticipated, and, in fact, people using adapted buildings like them and prefer them to new buildings.

This chapter discusses comparative costs of new and adaptation construction; how local governments can and do help in rehabilitating older areas; and how and why certain specific projects were carried out.

Conservation of Historic and Cultural Resources*

Ralph W. Miner

Issues in Maintaining Historic Areas

Unfortunately, establishment of historic areas will not solve all the problems. Numerous issues will arise in the administration and maintenance of a historic conservation program. Three of the major policy decisions to be made locally will involve the use of historic structures, the extent of restoration, and the impact of new construction on historic areas.

Active or passive? An early question will probably concern the use to be made of historic buildings. A quick response from some groups might be to use them as period museums. This may be appropriate if there are one or two buildings of exceptional architectural merit and/or historic associations. No community, however, can afford to turn too many of its old buildings into museums. This would take considerable property off the tax rolls and create a superfluous number of competing facilities, none of which could hold its own. A period museum is essentially a passive use; the building is viewed as a monument, a landmark, or an abstract art object. Its appearance is frozen at a certain stage of development, and its potential for more productive use is withdrawn.

Many old structures can continue in their original uses. If the original use is no longer economical, adaptive uses must be found which will allow continued functional and productive use of the structure in its environment. The public interest in preservation relates, except in the case of the occasional noteworthy museum, to the public views of the building and its setting. Adapting structures to economically viable new uses will almost certainly require interior alterations. Either approach, museum or adaptive use, will stimulate aditional problems to be solved in the preservation plan, such as the provision of adequate parking space to serve the new uses.

National Benefits of Rehabilitating Existing Buildings**

Baird Smith

The rehabilitation of urban buildings, largely composed of residential, office, and commercial space, is increasing. Rehabilitation, known also as repair and alteration or renovation, for nonresidential buildings has grown from 13.5% in 1970 to 21.5% in 1975 and is projected to reach

---

*A.S.P.O. *Planning Advisory Service* report no. 244, 1969, p.12.
**11593, U.S. Department of the Interior, 1977.

24.8% this year. That will represent nearly $19.9 billion of construction this year. The rehabilitation of residential property may reach 38% of the market, which accounts for an expenditure of $32 billion. Thus, we will spend about $52 billion, about 32% of all construction dollars, on the rehabilitation of existing buildings. Of course, buildings that are recognized as historic would represent a small increment of this overall effort; nonetheless, this extensive effort results in recycling, that is, extending the life of existing building stock. . . .

There are several positive attributes of the rehabilitation of buildings in our urban centers:

- General revitalization of the city
- Increased property tax base and revenues
- Support for the commercial business segment
- Re-creation of community/neighborhood feelings in urban centers
- Reduction of energy outlay resulting from fewer commuting workers
- Increased use of neglected utility systems
- Feelings of identity and pride of ownership

Some disadvantages include

- Displacement of low-income persons
- Increased demand for city services (police, fire, etc.)

In addition to the attributes that have a localized effect, there are two other contributions that have a national impact. First, rehabilitation projects are heavily labor intensive; often 75% of the dollars expended are for labor costs. New construction is usually about 50% labor and 50% materials. That means for money invested in rehabilitation, the greatest part of it goes directly into the local economy to support commerce and increase employment. This is a recognized spin-off value of rehabilitation, which certainly has a positive national impact.

The second major national contribution to the rehabilitation movement may be in energy conservation. As with many aspects of energy research and energy consumption, we are just beginning to discover information about energy use patterns. There is little doubt that a large amount of energy is consumed to build, rehabilitate, and operate all the buildings in the country. An important recent study prepared for the Energy Research and Development Administration (ERDA) has investigated the amount of energy needed to build new buildings and the amount necessary to rehabilitate existing ones. The report is *Energy Use for Building Construction* by Richard G. Stein and Associates, Architects, and the Energy Research Group, Center for Advanced Computation, University of Illinois at Champaign-Urbana. The study surveyed all publicly advertised new construction and rehabilitation work for a base year (1967) in the United States to measure how many BTUs of energy is taken, on a square-foot basis, to extract, manufacture, deliver, and install all building materials, such as lumber, brick, and concrete. The researchers determined that it took 23% less energy to rehabilitate existing buildings. Specifically, it took an average of 49,900 BTUs/sq. ft. to rehabilitate as opposed to 65,200 BTUs/sq. ft. to build anew. This included all building types—residential, office, commercial, and industrial. (Farm buildings, highways, sewer lines, and other similar non-building construction is excluded from both categories.) This lower energy consumption can be attributed to the fact that most of the structural systems and building materials were in place and reuseable in the rehabilitation project. . . .

How do historic buildings fit into this picture, and can we make any generalizations about energy usage in these older buildings? It may be a recognized fact that old buildings are deficient with regard to meeting modern health, safety and general welfare standards; however, important new evidence would suggest that certain old buildings may be excellent energy conservers requiring only changes in building operation and minor physical alterations.

This evidence is reported in an important research report prepared for ERDA, *Energy Conservation in Existing Office Buildings*, written by Syska and Hennessy and the Tishman Research Corporation, both of New York City. The research involved contacting the owners of over 1,000 office buildings in New York, from which 436 were selected for further investigation based on such criteria as (1) willingness to cooperate with the study, and (2) existence of complete financial records covering fuel and energy expenditures for the five-year period 1970-1975. From this building subpopulation, 44 sample buildings were chosen for an in-depth analysis of the energy consumption. The consumption was measured by evaluating money expended for utilities (electricity, fuel oil, coal, etc.) through the five-year period.

After analyzing the data, the researchers found that energy usage had dropped about 12% after the oil embargo of 1973. Interviews with the owners determined that simple operational controls such as fewer hours of operation, lowering the thermostats in winter, and turning off lights accounted for the reduction. There was little evidence of analytical approaches or any quantitative knowledge of energy usage in the buildings. Nevertheless, there was a substantial drop in energy consumption.

The report studied several aspects of the energy usage in these buildings. The most important, relative to historic buildings, were the results of analyzing the age of buildings to determine energy use. When building age and energy use per square foot of space were compared, the report found that the *oldest* buildings used the *least* energy. The following table indicates this comparison.

Dates	No. of Bldgs.	% of Bldgs.	% of Area	Energy Consumption Range (1000s of BTUs/sq. ft.)	Average Consumption (1000s of BTUs/sq. ft.)
Before 1900	3	6.8	1.1	83–115	95
1901–1919	8	18.2	12.8	76–135	105
1920–1940	18	40.9	28.3	68–223	109
1941–1962	12	27.3	36.2	66–198	126
1962–1970	3	6.8	21.6	78–163	115

Syska, Hennessy, Tishman Research Corporation, *Energy Conservation in Existing Buildings*, ERDA contract no. EY-76-C-02-2799,000, June 1977, unpublished, p. 111-20.

The results clearly show that the oldest buildings, those built before 1900, used only 95,000 BTUs/sq. ft. per year, whereas those built after 1941 consume the most energy. It is not surprising that the newer buildings, often characterized as glass boxes, were found to consume the most energy.

Some of the physical characteristics of the buildings and the various mechanical systems used are quite interesting. For instance, the average building area was over 300,000 square feet and the buildings averaged over 1,000 occupants. Nearly three fourths of the buildings had cavity wall construction and only 2% used doubled-paned glass. Additionally, over 60% of the buildings were heated with radiators, with only 13% having fan coil units.

The results of this study are impressive. They point out that old buildings use less energy than newer ones. But what does this really mean, and why did these old buildings use less energy? Apparently, the answer can be attributed to two principal characteristics of these buildings. First, the buildings were heated and cooled by an accumulation of outdated mechanical equipment which probably provides a level of comfort below that which is provided in most new construction. The buildings may have been cooler in the winter, hotter in the summer, and had a lower level of light. Fortunately, this is the goal of most energy conservation programs since it has been established that many of the comfort levels established for new construction are too high and waste energy. Thus, it would seem that the type of mechanical equipment existing in these buildings, and the lower comfort level provided, partially contributed to the lower energy usage.

The second important physical characteristic that resulted in these buildings using less energy relates to the older types of building construction. The following characteristics, typical of old buildings, apparently contribute to the lower use of energy in both heating and cooling cycles.

Wall Mass It has been determined that existing walls of large mass (thick brick or stone) have the advantage of "high thermal inertia." This inertia modifies the thermal resistance (R factor) of the wall by lengthening the time scale of heat transmission. For instance, a wall of high thermal inertia, subjected to solar radiation for an hour, will absorb the heat at its outside surface, but transfer it to the interior over a period as long as 6 hours. Conversely, a wall having the same R factor, but low thermal inertia, will transfer the heat in perhaps 2 hours.

Ratio of Glass to Wall Old buildings which have low ratio of glass to wall, less than 20%, will be better energy conservers than buildings with high glass-to-wall ratios because windows are a principal source of heat loss and gain.

Operable Windows The fact that most old buildings have operable windows will result in measurable energy savings because the fresh outside air is readily available during mild months so that energy consuming heating and cooling systems will not have to be operated.

Cavity Wall Construction The presence of cavities in most masonry and wooden construction in old buildings provides a definite increase in the thermal resistance of the wall and increases the positive benefits of thermal inertia.

Business and Preservation: A Survey of Business Conservation of Buildings and Neighborhoods*

Raynor M. Warner, Sybil McCormac Groff, and Ranne P. Warner

Preface

This book could not have been written ten years ago, and it would not have been written five years ago. It expresses a truth become tolerable. By the time it goes into its second printing, what is now tolerable may have become self-evident. We are so quick to adapt to changed circumstances that we may not recognize how much has changed and how rapidly. The peril is that, having adapted, we may fail to see that the tide of events still swells, and that what has become easy is already insufficient.

Therefore, it may be well to note why urban and industrial preservation is beginning to seem a

*New York: McGraw Hill, 1978, pp.vii-x, 5-18.

necessary response to economic reality, and also why it has not been so in past decades. Recycling buildings may be as much an expression of the 1980s as disposable clothing and planned obsolescence were of the 1950s and 1960s. We are no more pious than our predecessors; we are responding to a different normalcy. Let us review the record and then ask whether mere adaptation to the obtrusive present is enough to prepare us for the future.

I was born while the nation was keeping cool with Coolidge. Construction costs had been constant for fifty years. A building could be put up for the same dollars in 1926 as in 1876. There was no need to explain in 1926 what kind of dollars you were spending. For half a century, "nominal" dollars had equaled "real dollars" for houses or factories. Indeed, inflation for all goods and services averaged less than one-half percent per year for forty years until World War I. That was my father's experience.

My grandfather had learned economics during a long deflationary boom during which most of the downtown area in my hometown was built. St. Paul, Minnesota, like Chicago and most other places built around railroad depots, tripled its size in the 1880s, while construction costs declined steadily. Logs jammed the rivers on the way to the mills, wheat glutted the elevators, labor was cheap, and there were plenty of eager replacements coming ashore. Land? Some land was still $2 an acre along James J. Hill's shiny new rails. (Most was more, but still very cheap by present standards.)

Although Frederick Jackson Turner told us that the frontier was closing in 1893, more land was homesteaded after that date than before it, and the frontier could be defined as the edge of the unused, plentiful and cheap. The common experience of my parents and grandparents was profusion and steady prices. On the microeconomic level, there were privation and hard work, bleached bones on the prairie, and squalor in the immigrant slums, but speaking in macroeconomic terms (as we are wont to do in short introductions like this) there was plenty for Cal to be cool about.

The Depression came as an abrupt deflationary shock. Bond holders in corporations which stayed solvent made fortunes, but as the NRA told us, the rest of the nation suffered from glut: too much unemployed labor, and too many goods. The War of 1941 produced a recovery from that Depression. Its shortages were perceived as sufficiently abnormal to permit those at home a little easy heroism in self-denial. Profusion was still our natural setting, and we feared a postwar depression because we did not know what to do with profusion. Wartime self-restraint was an economic necessity because government expenditure, financed by debt and taxes, accompanied a program of government employment on a scale which made the WPA seem trifling. The money, of course, went for what might be called single-purpose goods, more quickly depreciable than usual, and the work was perilous but (again speaking from the perspective of macroeconomics) we had always been an unusually wasteful people, and we were just wasting more than usual.

After the war, there was no depression, but there was, after a while, a second amazingly profusive aberration in our economic history: the capital glut which seemed to condition the normalcy of the middle classes of my generation. Our parents and grandparents grew up with cheap labor and steady prices. We grew up with the cheapest capital in the history of American capitalism. The postwar boom had such enormous momentum that a businessman selling stock could sell a dollar of current earnings (and, of course, the hope of capital gains) to a new shareholder for twice as much in 1958 as he could in 1948, and five years later, buyers of common stock on the New York Stock Exchange were willing to pay twice as much—again—for a dollar of current earnings.

During the 1950s, the large corporations were still paying rates of interest for borrowed money less than a third of those prevailing today.* That meant, of course, that even though construction costs

---

*Computing the effect of money cost, of interest, upon construction is a dicey business. But if one could imagine zero interest cost—a Swiss instance, perhaps—that would differ from the 12 percent construction loans of 1974 atop what we *now* think to be an underlying inflation rate of 6 percent and differ again from 5 percent construction loans atop a 3 percent inflation rate of earlier years.

had begun to escalate in the late 1920s it was easy to take in partners (new equity owners) for the purpose of building new plants. It is possible, although the figures are slippery, that the decline of the cost of capital just about offset the increase of the cost of construction between 1926 and 1966.

What has all this to do with this book? The discovery of preservation is natural to my generation because we live in a time of steadily rising costs and expensive capital. We owe our predecessors some graceful acknowledgment that their normalcy is no longer accessible to us. We are, therefore, free to adapt to circumstances which have now prevailed long enough for them to become normalcy to us.

There are examples in this book of action which anticipates necessity by so wide a space as to be remarkable. Why remarkable? A businessman operating to protect his shareholders cannot go too far ahead of what appears likely to be required of him lest he be caught by changes of economic climate or of governmental requirements which turn a good plan into an embarrassing anachronism.

Yet, the only greater danger than planning too far in advance is refusing to plan far enough. As the corporate managers described in this book looked about at the inventory of buildings which they could include in their plans, they had to make computations about alternative ways of housing their plants. They knew what an existing building would cost, and they could get respectable estimates of what conversion would cost. All they could know about new facilities was that they would go up in cost the longer their construction was delayed.

Computations produced more preservation, I'll bet, than sentiment did. And having written more books and articles about architectural history than I like to count, and having given more lectures about historic buildings than I can remember, I am fully prepared to put my faith in computation as the better hope for the future than moral suasion or aesthetic admonition.

When it makes economic sense to reuse an existing plant, there is presented an opportunity to do the job well. When among one's choices for reuse there are ugly buildings and handsome buildings, at nearly the same price, one will be likely to use a handsome one, as several case studies in this book demonstrate. Solving an aesthetic and economic puzzle simultaneously is fun, like Chinese checkers. And there are good reasons for doing so.

There are very few corporate managers who are indifferent to the multiple constituencies who surround them: stockholders, workers, customers, bankers, suppliers, and journalists. When the economics are close to right, it is pleasant to have something good to report.

Businessmen occupy places of power quite briefly, and they know it. The long progression up the corporate Jungle Gym consumes decades, for most people, and when the summit is reached, the person who becomes boss looks about to make a mark while he may; and for interesting ways to make that mark. This is as true in a corporation as it was in the feudality or the Renaissance church, in Pharaoh's Egypt, or in any People's Republic. And throughout human society, a sound economic decision may be to create something beautiful, or save something beautiful, which may be associated with the boss for many years. It may be his best way of proclaiming his survival as well as his taste.

I do not mean to discredit this impulse. It is hardly derogatory to classify anyone with Lorenzo de'Medici, Urban II, Cheops, the Earl of Carlisle, Louis XIV, or Pericles. What this book adds to the earnest work of architectural historians, and to the education which has refined the taste of those who hold economic power, is a series of examples of sound business arguments for the cause of old buildings.

There are, of course, less numerical arguments to be made. We could speak of used buildings as constructed natural resources, to be regarded with as much, or even more, reverence as natural resources. We would emphasize the fact that the environment for most people is an urban environment, not a bucolic or sylvan one. Bombed-out and brutalized neighborhoods are inhabited by more people than bosky dells, and we should use public policy to make it easier, not harder, for the individual local choices of businessmen to serve these people.

Finally, I must express a personal apprehension which I cannot support with any elaborate statistical base. The largest unknown cost of future construction is energy or, to be more precise, oil. We have adjusted to a large single price increase in oil and are adjusting to the syphoning off of consumer disposal income from industrial countries toward producing countries. But there are good economists who say that we are growing more slowly, as an economy, than in the past.

Slower growth coupled with intractable unemployment (possibly occasioned by the gap between the requirements of high technology and the attainments of popular education, possibly by deeper causes related to the nature of human services actually required by modern, mechanized society) constitute heavy weights on a society already burdened by a need to buy much of its energy from others. An economy which has an oil leak, out of which flows consumer purchasing power, *and* which grows slowly, cannot afford waste.

This book suggests that we are beginning to learn how to diminish our waste of old buildings: to return our empty bottles. We are going to have to learn these lessons and a lot more. The corporate managers who created these test cases can take satisfaction in having led the way through what was desirable in the present toward what will be necessary in the future.

Roger G. Kennedy
Vice President
The Ford Foundation

Historical Inflation Data for the U.S.A.

Period of time	Annual Inflation Rate	Total Change in the Cost of Living
1865 to 1940	approx. 0	fell 9% in 75 years
1940 to 1952	5.5%	rose 89% in 12 years
1952 to 1965	1.3%	rose 19% in 13 years
1965 to 1972	4.1%	rose 33% in 7 years

Year	Inflation Rate
1973	8.8%
1974	12.2%
1975	7.0%
1976	4.8%
1977	6.8%
1978	9.0%
1979 so far	13.3%

NOTE: Chart prepared by Prof. Alan S. Blinder, Princeton University, for Alumni Panel, June 1979.

Benefits*

The projects profiled in this study suggest that many economic, aesthetic, and public-relations benefits have accrued to the companies involved.

Economics. The recycling and continued use of existing buildings can usually be justified on economic grounds alone. The shell of an office or factory building, including the foundation, supporting structure, and outer enclosure, represents a substantial cost in construction dollars and time. The cost of demolition and new construction, both from a dollars-and-cents and an energy standpoint, is often high. While there are no universal rules, INFORM found that at most of the seventeen reuse projects profiled, the costs ran from 30 percent to 40 percent less than replacement new construction. Lawyers Co-operative, a Rochester publishing company, spent about $15 per square foot to convert a nineteenth-century mill complex to office space. This represented a considerable saving over the approximately $45-per-square-foot cost of similar new construction. Adaptive reuse exceeded the cost of new construction in only three of seventeen cases. . . .

Aesthetics. Aesthetic benefits, while more difficult to categorize, also accrue to company employees and society at large. A look at any American city or town today affirms that new construction, often standardized to reduce cost, tends to produce a bland similarity of spaces and appearance. Several companies, on the other hand, have noted that recycling buildings is good for employee morale and has brought a favorable response from the community. Employees of Digital Equipment Corporation like the option of designing their own office space in a former textile-mill complex. SEDCO's conversion of an old school in Dallas to corporate offices has brought the company acclaim from local historical and architectural groups.

New additions can harmonize with older buildings through the use of modern materials, techniques, and details. In the six such cases profiled, an effort was made to develop stylistically compatible new designs. Old residential areas often contain architectural diamonds in the rough, like Brooklyn Union's brownstones in Brooklyn or Lakewood Bank's Dallas project which contained prairie-style homes inspired and in one case designed by Frank Lloyd Wright. . . .

Company Public Relations. Probably the most consistently cited benefit among all of the projects surveyed is that of enhanced image. Preservation activities can provide a sophisticated advertising vehicle whereby awareness of both the company and its products is increased. Older buildings usually reflect quality, stability, and continuity in the community. This may, in fact, be one major reason why 11 of the 29 recycled-building cases surveyed involved the conversion of older buildings by banks. The First New Haven National Bank's renovation of an eighteenth-century house as its Westbrook branch brought the bank extensive local publicity. In addition, new accounts and deposits in the branch exceeded projections. The experience was similar for the Connecticut Savings Bank, which turned another eighteenth-century house into one of its branches.

On the other hand, recycled buildings need not project a conservative image or rely on nostalgia for acceptance. With much of modern architecture resulting in look-alike anonymity, the unique identity an old building provides is often a positive business benefit in itself. McGraw-Hill is pleased

---

*The book from which these excerpts are taken profiles a number of specific adaptive reuse projects. The Lawyers' Cooperative Case (presented later in this chapter) is one of them.

with both the location and individuality of its publications company's Western Regions Office located in a converted ice cream factory. Although the company is only a tenant, the building was renamed the McGraw-Hill Building.

Support of community revitalization also brings public-relations benefits. Most such projects have resulted in extensive local publicity. Some have brought industry recognition, and state and national attention as well. Frederic Rider, the Brooklyn Union official in charge of the company's residential-redevelopment activities, has been interviewed by newspapers across the country. Trend Publications received the 1976 Annual Governor's Award in the Arts for its conversion of an old cigar factory in Tampa, Florida, into a commercial center. . . .

Problems

In the 71 cases in this survey INFORM found three general problem areas to be associated with business-sponsored preservation activities: problems in obtaining adequate capital, uncertainties and delays resulting from the unconventional nature of the projects, and employee apprehensiveness about recycling and revitalizing. These problems relate largely to recycling buildings and revitalizing neighborhoods, and do not apply to charitable contributions to preservation. While preservation groups are frequently hard pressed to raise money, the giving of donations does not involve many problems for companies. The problems found were real enough, but in most cases not insoluble. As preservation projects proliferate, construction problems will lessen and financial backing should become easier to obtain. If commercial and residential revitalization projects are successful, apprehension should decrease.

Availability of Capital. The novel and—for now—somewhat uncommon nature of many preservation projects leads to greater technical and financial uncertainty than is generally encountered in new construction. Difficulties in obtaining mortgages and loans because of banks' perceptions of greater risk were found to cause delays and/or to require changes in the plans of 9 of 22 community-revitalization projects. The more ambitious the project, the more prevalent the problem seemed to be. The Jefferson Company's $20 million project to redevelop the neglected Minneapolis river front was delayed nearly three years while the company searched for bank financing. The company finally obtained partial financing, and was able to proceed with the first phase of the project.

Uncertainties in Construction. Contractors and architects are often hesitant to provide firm bids and guaranteed completion dates on recycling projects. Structural problems, initially hidden from view, are at times exposed as work progresses, resulting in extensive delays and/or cost overruns. Replacing the existing plumbing in Cleveland's Cuyahoga Building, an unexpected part of the renovation of the structure, resulted in a $300,000 overrun in the Sohio case. Obtaining variances for zoning or code violations can also cause delays and cost money.

Such uncertainties could, of course, be reduced by employing architects and contractors with previous experience in recycling, and by thoroughly inspecting a building before making a reuse decision. Nevertheless, there is no way to eliminate all risks involved.

Community, Employee, and Management Apprehension. Employees and management alike often have not been exposed to the good qualities of recycled buildings. Managers of public companies are also reluctant to invest in properties that might not appear profitable to stockholders. In addition, communities and sometimes, ironically, preservation groups are hesitant to allow a business to reuse a historic building for fear that the use might destroy the landmark's original character. Many Philadelphians resisted Design Research's efforts to convert an old mansion to its Philadelphia branch, until local efforts to find an alternate use failed. . . .

Companies and financial institutions that have decided to adaptively reuse old buildings give a variety of reasons for their decision. In thirteen of the seventeen cases profiled by INFORM, the firms wanted and believed they received enhanced public images. This was particularly important to the First New Haven National Bank, which was moving into a new market in Westbrook, Connecticut. However, it seemed to be equally important to a firm like Lawyers Co-operative, a law publisher long established in Rochester.

Economic considerations were another strong reason given for recycling. Space in an adapted older structure is often less expensive than that acquired through new construction. This was true for Digital in Maynard, Massachusetts, which obtained office and manuacturing space for $15 per square foot as opposed to the $25 to $30 per square foot it would have had to pay for new construction; and for Wachovia Bank, where recycling proved to be 20 percent cheaper than new construction. Costs varied according to the degree of renovation, the nature of the business, the availability of materials, and regional pay scales. Among the cases studied by INFORM, the per-square-foot cost of renovation ranged from a low of $15 in the Lawyers Co-operative and Digital cases to a high of $110 in the San Diego Federal Savings and Loan case. Adaptive reuse was reported to be as much as two-thirds less expensive than new construction. In only three cases—San Diego Federal, Design Research, and Commonwealth Bank and Trust—did the cost of rehabilitation exceed the estimated cost of new construction designed for similiar use.

Location was also often a key factor in the decision to reuse existing buildings. The study includes nine cases of companies who were looking for a new location for a branch or other facility in an established area. They found that construction of a new building would generally necessitate demolition of an existing structure. Demolition is often expensive, and the approvals required are not easily obtained. Thus, the adaptive reuse of structures already existing in good locations became a logical alternative. Connecticut Savings Bank found a location for its Cheshire branch in a badly neglected old house on a main commercial street. Instead of demolishing the building, the bank restored the exterior and renovated the interior, turning the old home into a productive branch and helping maintain the character of the area.

INFORM also profiled six cases of companies which were established in an area and needed to expand their facilities. Building on adjacent sites often proved to be the most feasible plan. Harbridge House, a Boston-based consulting firm, purchased a house adjacent to its Back Bay offices (also located in old houses), and is using it for additional office space. The reused houses provide the cheapest office space of any of the company's locations.

In almost every building-recycling project studied by INFORM, aesthetic considerations played a significant role. Often the force behind the project was a concerned executive to whom aesthetics were important. This top-level individual often had participated in local preservation and community activities. While companies tend to stress economic or "image enhancement" grounds as justification for their projects, aesthetics and that special interest of a high-level official seemed to have triggered the initial consideration and study of reuse as an option in almost every case. One example is Morris Newspaper's president, Charles Morris. A trustee of Historic Savannah, Morris wanted a historic building to house his offices in that city.

Although not a major motivating factor, five of the companies INFORM studied felt that reusing older buildings resulted in improved employee morale. The employees of Digital Equipment Corporation like the option they have of personalizing their office space in the company's converted textile mill.

Adaptive Use: A Survey of Construction Costs*

U.S. Advisory Council on Historic Preservation

The concept of historic preservation has gained broad popular support over the last decade, but, in a society oriented toward profit-making, the conservation of historic buildings cannot have the far reaching acceptance envisioned by its supporters unless it can be made economically feasible. To have the greatest impact, the reuse of historic buildings must be accepted and adopted by those responsible for shaping human settlements—the architects, planners, city officials, real estate developers, and investment bankers. Various proposals designed to make preservation profitable have been suggested in the form of tax incentives, easements, the transfer of development rights, and funding assistance programs for historic properties, to name just a few. Generally, such efforts have been directed at providing public support or subsidy for preservation actions. However, one of the most successful solutions to date has been to work within the existing framework of the commercial real estate market and adapt vacant or underused buildings of historical or architectural value to fit the needs of contemporary tenants. Made marketable, these recycled buildings stay on the tax rolls and return a profit to their owners, frequently at a better rate than new construction. . . .

About the same time, planners and city officials began to acknowledge the failure of many of the grandiose schemes of urban renewal and slum clearance programs of the 1950s and 60s and started studying alternative ways to deal with the problem. It was recognized that rehabilitation instead of demolition of sound but decayed structures offered a more economically and socially less disruptive means of renewing cities. Planners and city officials were coming full circle and joining with the environmentalists and the inhabitants of the neighborhoods that were originally slated for destruction to come up with new ideas such as neighborhood conservation and urban homesteading. By the mid-seventies, it became evident that conservation of the built environment had become a basic tenet of many community development programs. . . .

There are obvious benefits to reusing existing buildings, beyond pure costs and broader social values. Older buildings are frequently better built, with craftsmanship and materials that cannot be duplicated in today's market. Late nineteenth and early twentieth century buildings were constructed with care and lavish decoration seldom possible in contemporary buildings. These structures have thicker walls, windows that open, higher ceilings, and other amenities not found in new buildings.

---

*Washington, D. C., June 1976, pp. 21-27. The figures in this article are all pre-1976. Projects since 1976 have been far more advantageous for adaptive use owing to the tax incentives adopted by Congress in that year.

Also, these buildings were designed to use natural light and ventilation, often being natural energy savers. In sum, old buildings provide more interesting and varied environments for people to live, work, shop and eat.

Adaptive use of historic buildings is finally being accepted by the broader world of government agencies, national professional organizations, city officials and lending institutions. An example of this occurred in the late 1960s by the movement of artists and sculptors into unused warehouses in Soho, New York City's Cast Iron District in lower Manhattan. These large spaces above ground floor loading platforms provided excellent and inexpensive studio spaces for artists. Unfortunately, certain zoning restrictions technically barred this activity. The city authorities, after applying rather ineffective punitive measures, finally accepted the situation and changed the laws. Others began to move to this area and it became a lively neighborhood, complete with shops, restaurants, and art galleries. Eventually, through the interest generated by the residents and architectural historians, the area was designated a historic district. What had been a neglected and dismal part of the city is now a revitalized neighborhood and an asset to the broader community. . . .

In 1974, the Housing and Community Development Act administered by the Department of Housing and Urban Development authorized funds that, at the discretion of the individual community, may be used for a variety of urban programs including neighborhood conservation, historic preservation and rehabilitation. Many communities have taken their grants to fund wholesale neighborhood rehabilitation programs, often including significant adaptive use programs. Also in 1974, the Amtrak Improvement Act authorized demonstration and planning funds for the adaptive use of significant railroad stations. . . .

While not unusual in Europe, it is refreshing to see American businesses working with communities to help conserve neighborhoods and significant urban landmarks. In 1976, a firm requiring additional office space is as likely to think about moving into a recycled warehouse or railroad station as to invest in a steel and glass structure that has just been erected. Increasingly, developers and lenders are willing to invest money into an adaptive reuse project such as recycling an abandoned hotel or former piano factory into contemporary apartments. Experience has shown there will be no difficulty in renting such apartments to tenants eager to live in the center of the city in a soundly constructed older building, with high ceilings, and unique architectural features, where each living unit is distinct from its neighbor. . . .

On each cost data summary sheet are cost figures from the Robert Snow Means Company, Inc. which publishes annually *Building Construction Cost Data*, including data from over 7,500 building projects nationwide. Included in this survey are three cost figures from the Means book: the lowest per-square-foot cost for a building in a particular category; the median cost for all buildings in the category; and the cost for the most expensive building in the category. There are, therefore, five cost data summary sheets immediately following for each of the five building categories. Attached to each are brief descriptive sketches containing supplementary information on each project. These sketches are listed alphabetically within each building type.

All costs are based on January 1976 indexes and are shown in dollars. The degree of work required in each category is defined as: (M)—Minimal; (N)—Normal; and (S)—Substantial. These letters will accompany each cost figure. Where data was not supplied by the architect the space has been left blank.

Building Type: Office
(Cost Per Square Foot)

Building	Demolition	Architectural	Structural	Mechanical	Total
Webster House 31,800 sf	M	M	M	M	3.74
Bank of Newburgh Building 3,900 sf	.53 N	6.57 N	1.06 M	3.50 S	11.66
Means—Lowest					12.10
China Basin Building 500,000 sf	.62 M	7.80 N	.62 M	7.94 S	16.98
Butler Square 500,000 sf	.26 N	9.48 N	2.90 N	6.12 S	18.76
Grand Central Arcade 80,000 sf	.73 N	14.16 N	.44 N	4.77 N	20.10
Pioneer Building 88,550 sf	M	N	N	N	23.89
Dodge—Average		13.47	6.67	9.48	29.62
Teknor Apex Company 25,000 sf	M	N	M	N	30.06
Baltimore City Hall 203,000 sf	3.75 S	15.75 S	S*	13.50 S	33.00
Old Boston City Hall 40,000 sf	I.99 S	15.18 S	2.64 S	13.20 S	33.00
Actors Theatre 42,125 sf	.54 N	18.76 N	2.14 N	12.06 N	33.50
Means—Median					35.48
Saturday Review Building 27,657 sf		18.83	6.12	11.88	36.83
21 Merchants Row 25,000 sf	3.96	19.80	6.60	6.60	36.96
One Winthrop Square 105,000 sf	3.39 S	24.86 S	2.26 N	10.17 S	40.68
Blackwell House 6,348 sf	.57 M	21.13 S	2.26 N	19.55 S	43.51
Means—Highest					101.52

*Structural costs included in architectural.

Webster House, Boston

This masonry residence was built in 1872 and was designed by John Sturgis. This home, which was in excellent condition, was adapted to office space for the sum of $90,000. The architectural firm of Childs Bertman Tseckares Associates completed the project in late 1972. The building is 100 percent occupied, with a citywide average of 85 percent. (Bainbridge Bunting, *Houses of Boston's Backbay*, Cambridge: Harvard University Press, 1967)

Bank of Newburgh Building, Ithaca, New York

This 1821 combination bank building and residence is thought to have been designed by Luther Gere and features graceful Greek temple front with pediment and four pilasters. The wooden building, an important component of the DeWitt National Register Historic District, was adapted to office space by November of 1974 by the firm of O'Brien and Taube, Architects of Ithaca, for the sum of $45,000. (*Ithaca Journal*, December 2, 1974, p. 3)

China Basin Building, San Francisco

This 1920s concrete building was originally a food storage facility with 500,000 square feet. The building was adapted to include 520,000 square feet of office space. The project, costing $1.7 million, was completed in late 1973 by the architectural firm of Robinson and Mills of San Francisco. It is currently 65 percent occupied, compared to a citywide average of 85 percent. (*Architectural Record*, December 1975, p. 90)

Butler Square, Minneapolis

Originally a warehouse, this 1906 building appears austere and simple, an effect produced by the skillful handling of scale and proportion by designer Harry Wild Jones. The nine-story red brick facade originally enclosed 500,000 square feet of space. Half of the masonry building was adapted to include 83 percent office, 16 percent retail, and 1 percent restaurant space. The project was completed in December of 1974 for the sum of $3.84 million by the architectural firm of Miller, Hanson, Westerbeck, Bell, Architects, Inc. of Minneapolis. The building, listed in the National Register of Historic Places, is currently 60 percent occupied. (*AIA Journal*, April 1976, p. 42)

Grand Central Arcade, Seattle

In 1889 this masonry building was built to include 80,000 square feet. The building, listed in the National Register as part of the Pioneer Square Historic District, was adapted to include 58 percent office, 29 percent retail and 13 percent restaurant space. The $1.28 million project was completed by December of 1973 by the architectural firm of Ralph D. Anderson of Seattle. The building is currently 95 percent occupied, which compares favorably to the city average of 85 percent. (*Progressive Architecture*, August 1974, pp. 46-48)

Pioneer Building, Seattle

Elmer Fisher designed this beautifully scaled masonry building in 1892 after fire badly destroyed most of Seattle's docks and business district in 1889. The Pioneer became the prestige address for the new Seattle, and is the centerpiece of the Pioneer Square Historic District listed in the National Register. The building, which originally was a combination of office and retail space, was renovated to include 71 percent office, 12 percent retail and 17 percent restaurant space. The $1.872 million project was completed in January of 1975 by the architectural firm of Ralph D. Anderson of Seattle. The building is currently 95 percent occupied, compared with a citywide average of 85 percent. (*Fortune*, May 1975, p. 196)

Teknor Apex Company Offices, Pawtucket, Rhode Island

This steel frame factory building was built about 1900 and included 20,000 square feet. The building was adapted to office space totaling 25,000 square feet by the architectural firm of Warren Platner Associates of New Haven, Connecticut. The project was completed in late 1974. (*Architectural Record*, January 1975, pp. 111-115)

Baltimore City Hall, Baltimore

This 1875 masonry building, designed by George Fredericks, is an early example of French Renaissance Revival in this country. Of bluestone, faced with cut marble, it features an imposing dome flanked by three-story wings detailed with elaborate pilasters, window keystones and semicircular archivaults, all capped by a mansard roof with marble dormers. The renovation of this National Register property cost $6.7 million and includes 203,000 square feet of office space. The project, to be completed by October of 1976, is being undertaken by the architectural firm of Architectural Heritage-Baltimore Inc. and Meyers and D'Aleo of Boston. (*Architectural Record*, March 1975, p. 37)

Old Boston City Hall, Boston

This 1865 masonry city hall was designed by the firm of Bridley and Bryant in monumental Second Empire style, resembling the Louvre in Paris. The building's 10,000 square feet of space was adapted to include 80 percent office, 10 percent retail and 20 percent* restaurant space with a total floor area of 40,000 square feet. The $2.25 million restoration of this National Historic Landmark was undertaken by the architectural firm of Anderson-Notter of Boston and was completed in late 1972. The building is 97 percent occupied when the citywide average is only 85 percent. (*AIA Journal*, April 1976, pp. 38-39)

Actors Theatre, Louisville Warehouse, Louisville, Kentucky

Gideon Shryock designed this brick and limestone bank building in 1836 in the Greek Revival style, which features an interior skylighted elliptical dome. Together with an adjacent masonry warehouse of Italianate design, the buildings have become the new home of the Actors Theatre of Louisville, offering 36,000 square feet of versatile space. The adaptive use project, totaling 42,125 square feet, includes 65 percent office, 5 percent retail, 5 percent restaurant and 25 percent assembly space. The architectural firm of Harry Weese and Associates of Chicago completed the

---

*In Boston, all things are possible.

The old Boston City Hall has been readapted as offices and a restaurant with outstanding success. *Courtesy of the National Trust.*

The buildings of the Actors' Theatre in Louisville, Kentucky. *Courtesy of the National Trust*.

project, listed as a National Historic Landmark, in late 1972 for the sum of $1.035 million. (*AIA Journal*, August 1974, p. 52)

Saturday Review Building, San Francisco

This simple masonry building was built about 1910 for use as a Chinese cigar factory. The building was adapted to 27,657 square feet of office space by the architectural firm of Bull, Field, Volkman, and Stockwell of San Francisco. The project was completed in February of 1973 for the sum of $736,200. (*Architectural Record*, August 1973, pp. 99-100)

21 Merchants Row, Boston

This historically significant masonry mercantile building included 25,000 square feet and is in the heart of Boston's historic waterfront. The architectural firm of Childs Bertman Tseckares Associates of Boston adapted the building to include 80 percent office space and 20 percent restaurant. The project was completed in July of 1972 for the sum of $725,000. The building is 100 percent occupied compared with a city average of 85 percent.

One Winthrop Square, Boston

This stone mercantile building was built in 1873 and was designed by the firm of Fehmer and Emerson in the elegant French Second Empire style. Originally a quality apparel store, until 1972 it was the home of the Boston Record American newspaper. It originally had 100,000 square feet, but with its adaptation to 80 percent office and 20 percent retail space, the floor area totaled 105,000 square feet. The $3.6 million project was undertaken by the architectural firm of Childs Bertman Tseckares Associates of Boston and was completed in August of 1974. The building is 100 percent occupied, compared with a citywide average of 85 percent. (*Economic Benefits of Preserving Old Buildings*, Washington: Preservation Press, The National Trust for Historic Preservation, 1976, pp. 75-80)

Blackwell House Restoration, Roosevelt Island, New York

This 1810 wood frame farm house includes 6,348 square feet. The adaptive use project transformed the building into office space for the sum of $244,000 and was completed in late 1973. The architectural firm of Giorgio Cavaglieri of New York undertook the restoration of this National Register property. (*Preservation and Building Codes*, Washington: Preservation Press, The National Trust for Historic Preservation, 1975, p. 16)

Results of the Survey

A number of general observations may be made on the survey data. The data confirm that, although adaptive use is not always cheaper than new construction, the cost of adaptive use falls within the range of new construction costs. It would seem, then, that adaptive use stands as an equally feasible alternative to new construction to meet the space needs of a tenant. Actual cost differences for any given project are, of course, going to vary with the amount of work needed to adapt a particular building to the desired use. The survey results provide some insight as to the relative cost of various components of that adaptation work.

The survey indicates that demolition costs inside the buildings being recycled are minimal, normally only one to four percent of the total project cost. Structural costs are also low, normally varying from about five to twelve percent of the total project cost, which is less than half the average expenditure for new construction. This reflects the fact that little structural work is normally required when reusing an old building. Architectural costs vary above and below the average for new construction. Generally, in projects where the maximum effort was made to reuse the existing interior and exterior materials, the costs are substantially below those for new construction. Conversely, where decisions were made to substantially alter the existing fabric, the costs rose.

Mechanical costs, like those for architectural, were both above and below those for new construction. Again, where the costs were low, normally complex climate control equipment and fire protection systems were not installed. Where the costs were high, extensive fire protection equipment was necessary due to the nonfireproof nature of certain old buildings. In addition, because many old buildings do not easily lend themselves to the installation of the tremendous quantity of ductwork and chases normally required with sophisticated mechanical equipment, mechanical equipment will likely remain an expensive item in adaptive-use construction.

Since the survey shows that demolition and structural costs are minimal and represent areas where considerable savings can be made, it appears that the real determining factors of the overall cost of adaptive-use construction will be in the architectural and mechanical work. Through ingenuity and inventiveness by the architect, the costs may be kept down.

These survey results support the opinion of Hugh Hardy, senior partner of Hardy Holzman Pfeiffer Associates, that the key to successful adaptive use is an inventive matching up of the new plan to the existing building. This view is shared by the architect of the Cast Iron Building in New York City, who noted the challenge and opportunity of adaptive use: "Ultimately, the main difference between rehabilitation and new construction lies in the fact that the developer working with an existing structure must be alert for both unexpected and unique opportunities."

While the survey, as expected, did not show a uniform cost advantage for every adaptive use project over new construction, it does reflect the ability to provide varied and interesting space for reasonably comparable cost. In this regard, the reader is strongly urged to examine some of the published accounts of the various projects surveyed here. Appreciation of the quality of the finished product is essential to place the comparative cost figures in perspective. Amenities provided by these recycled buildings frequently produce sound economic benefits through higher occupancy rates and rents. George Notter, a Boston architect with an extensive adaptive use practice, summarizes the real economic aspects of adaptive use: "More often than not, the total dollar expenditure for preservation, including the acquisition of the property involved, is about the same as new construction. Thus the plus factor is achieved by developing the potential assets into a final project of greater amenity—one having the right location, more space in either height or volume, more area or more character, materials of special quality or a potential for time savings in construction."

So far the focus has been on the benefits of adaptive use for the developer and the occupant. It is important to consider adaptive use projects in broader policy terms, in their contribution to the urban framework. Two of the surveyed projects, a retail shopping center and an apartment complex, are particularly representative of the positive effects adaptive use projects can have on a community.

The Trolley Square project in Salt Lake City was completed for less than nineteen dollars per square foot and has rewarded the occupants with a rich array of interior visual and textural delights. The character and ambiance achieved there is the current goal of many new shopping center developments. Trolley Square is successful because it combines stores, shops and restaurants which not only appeal to the casual visitor, but also provide a market for regular visits by the residents of the neighborhood. The mix of retail stores and shops is an important ingredient to this popularity.

In addition to the services it offers to those who visit it, Trolley Square has stimulated the rejuvenation of the surrounding neighborhood. Typified by deteriorating housing stock, the area is now experiencing revitalization with new people moving in and renovating houses throughout the area. The benefits of this project to the neighborhood and city as a whole extend well beyond those measurable in dollars and cents.

The second project is the Chickering Piano Factory in Boston, now an apartment complex with 116 studio and one-bedroom units, 52 two-bedroom units and six three-bedroom units. This formerly rundown factory building is now providing highly desirable housing for nearly 300 renters and was adapted for less than twelve dollars per square foot.

Thus, an urban commercial/industrial site, which was thought to be nonfunctional in today's city, has found new meaning through conversion to a new use as a housing project. One is only too painfully aware of the numerous obsolete commercial and industrial structures that, in disuse and decay, currently exert a blighting influence on our cities. Such creative reuse can have an obvious impact on the whole urban fabric.

The broader benefits to society from various adaptive use projects are just beginning to be felt. Fortunately, as public awareness of the inherent qualities of old buildings heightens, the costs for such projects seem to be becoming increasingly competitive with new construction. The entire construction market, which formerly encouraged the destruction of these buildings, is now responding to both public and economic conditions demanding the retention, development and resulting conservation of these valuable urban resources. Bruce Chapman, Secretary of State for the State of Washington, says,

Urban conservation, then, is one of government's legitimately expanding fields of endeavor. The value of beautiful wilderness parks and scenic rivers is vitiated if our daily environment is one of cancerous schlock. The economic benefits of spectacular corporate monuments likewise are diluted when the American economy simply discards old buildings and neighborhoods and then finds itself paying the enormous costs of resulting social problems. Urban conservation is not just romantic indulgence in nostalgia. It is a physical restatement of long hallowed American values of frugality, good craftsmanship and community responsibility.

Therefore, although adaptive use projects can be undertaken and cost less than new construction, the real bonus comes at the conclusion of the project. There is no comparison to a project which creatively reuses and adapts an old building, rich in decades of character and life, to a new building of only average construction. Adaptive use projects not only reward the investors and the occupants, but also the community by being the primary ingredients of an urban conservation scheme. This fresh new look at the urban fabric has the potential of redefining and reestablishing the promise of America's cities.

Making Historic Preservation Profitable — If You're Willing to Wait*

Alan F. Black

In January 1962, a young architect named Ralph Anderson took the plunge that, in retrospect, triggered the gradual renaissance of Skid Road, which today carries the more polite name Pioneer Square. He purchased the three-story, 36-by-110-foot Jackson Building for $30,000. He sand-blasted and cleaned the exterior, cleaned and refurbished the inside and moved his office to the second floor. The third floor was remodeled into a spacious, skylit, walkup apartment. He rented the main street level, originally the Old Tum Water Tavern, with a beautiful mosaic tile floor, to an able and established decorator. In addition to a spacious and unique office for his own architectural practice on the second floor, he had a tenant on the main floor who attracted important, so-called establishment people to that section of town.

In 1965 Ralph Anderson's close friend Richard White negotiated a long-term lease on the 60-by-110-foot Liberty Building around the corner. The following year, Ralph Anderson bought the four-story, 60-by-110-foot Union Trust Building for $75,000; it adjoined the Liberty Building. Both these

---

*From *Economic Benefits of Preserving Old Buildings*. Washington, D.C.: National Trust for Historic Preservation, 1976, p.21.

buildings were gradually cleaned and refurbished as tenants were found for the space. White started an art gallery in the Liberty Building and rented space to a miscellany of other tenants for prices in the range of 80 cents to $1 a square foot per year, unserviced, and with tenants responsible for finishing their own space. These three buildings began not only to carry themselves but to produce enough cash flow to allow the owners to make additional improvements to them.

In December 1968, Richard White purchased the four-story, 60-by-110-foot Globe Building for $55,000 in the same block as the other three buildings controlled by himself and Ralph Anderson. With this purchase, the available buildings in the square block bounded by South Jackson, South Main, First Avenue and Occidental were fairly well consolidated in the hands of two men who had a strong feeling for the area and were putting substantial money into improvement of their buildings. Being the first to make financial commitments to the area, they had "bought right" at figures of around $10 or less a square foot for the ground area. Except for White's leased building, they had bought on favorable low-down-payment real estate contracts. Modest additional cash outlays by the owners brought the buildings into rentable condition without the need for major improvements or financing.

During this period another architect, David Gray, bought and remodeled the 30-by-110-foot Maud Building. He converted the space to small offices and successfully leased them at $2 to $3 per square foot per year, with janitorial services included.

More and more people were coming into the area to the several newly established galleries and shops. The purchase and rehabilitation of the buildings in this block established a new identity for Skid Road. It was becoming a more vital area known by the new arrivals as Pioneer Square.

The period from January 1962 through approximately 1970 should be thought of as a somewhat separate and distinct phase in the revival of Pioneer Square. It was a period of speculative pioneering by a few visionary and venturesome souls who moved into this run-down and economically depressed area. They "bought right," buying relatively small buildings that were in fairly good shape at bargain prices before most people realized what was going on. Improvements were made to these buildings without major structural changes and with a minimum of attention to code requirements. The buildings were rehabilitated with a minimum of cost on a "seat-of-the-pants" basis and with a minimum of fuss. Existing plumbing and much of the existing electrical systems were used, a practice that made costs substantially less than later owners would incur under strict code enforcement.

As a result, these buildings could be rented for $1 to $2 a square foot per year. These were bargain prices in anyone's book and allowed a wide range of tenants to rent large square footage at minimal cost. In addition, the space was in a convenient central area that showed signs of really coming alive. All this occurred in what is termed here the phase 1 period in the redevelopment of Pioneer Square, the 1960s.

Poineer Square: Phase 2 Begins

Phase 2 began in May 1970 with passage by the Seattle City Council of the ordinance establishing the Pioneer Square Historic District. This was the first legislation of its type in the state of Washington. The ordinance gave the area an identity in a legal sense. Finally there was a set of standards with the force of law to keep the area from being turned into a massive parking lot. A building of significance could no longer be torn down by a slumlord faced with a roof repair. The razing of buildings for parking lots was stopped and the concept of areawide restoration began.

Phase 2 is the period in which there was a commitment of substantial risk capital by private individuals to the restoration of major buildings in the district. It is also the time when the city actively began supporting restoration work and spending municipal funds—matched in some cases with federal money—on parks, malls, tree planting and other major improvements in the Pioneer Square area.

Until this time, most of the upgrading and restoration of buildings had taken place south of Main Street in one square-block area. No significant rehabilitation had been done in the two blocks north of Main Street. It seemed in 1970 that some major restoration would have to take place in the latter section. Otherwise the work done to date would be only an isolated pocket, cut off from the rest of the downtown mainstream.

The Grand Central Project

In July 1971, Ralph Anderson, Richard White and I purchased the derelict and long vacant Grand Central Hotel Building on the corner of First Avenue South and South Main Street, in the block north of the area where all the work had been done to date. It was a big, homely, four-story box of a building covering an area of 111 by 150 feet on First Avenue, with an alley and parking lot on one side. The building was bought for the same illogical and unintelligible reason the mountain climber gives for climbing: because it's there. We did not know what we would do with it; we had absolutely no financing for it, and certainly no prospective tenants. I suppose we felt someone had to do something, and that we might as well give it a try. Essentially, there was never a more totally emotional and unprofessional purchase of a major building.

The 66,000-square-foot building was purchased on a real estate contract for $230,000. The building had long been vacant, the roof was ruined, the windows broken and anything of value in the way of hardware or woodwork had been stolen. We signed the purchase documents, looked at the building, and wondered why! The only thing going for us was a first-class pigeon rookery. We had more pigeons per square foot roosting in the building than anywhere west of the Mississippi.

With no financing and no master plan, we hired three laborers at $2 an hour to start clearing out the years of accumulated refuse and rubble. We next turned them loose beating off plaster and pulling down 85-year-old lath.

The Plan for Grand Central

During the summer of 1971 there was earnest thinking about what to do with the building. About the time of purchase there had been rumors of the possibility of the city's purchasing the half-block east of the Grand Central for a park. In the fall of 1971 the city did indeed buy the parking lot property to the east, which put a new light on plans for the building. What had been the back alley side of the structure could now be considered an important visual and access point. It would also be possible to have two fronts to the building: First Avenue on the west and the proposed park on the east.

Out of this the arcade concept developed, with passage from First Avenue through the building to the park with shops opening onto an arcade. In addition to this pedestrian-oriented main floor, we planned three floors of office space above. Work was to be done in stages or phases, with the first stage being the main floor arcade area and retail shops. The three upper floors would be the second, third, and fourth stages, completed as space there was rented.

With the plan established, Ralph Anderson's office began the design and working drawings, while the three partner-owners began worrying in earnest about where the money would come from.

Financing

The building had been bought on contract for $230,000, about $15 a square foot for land area. This was about $5 a square foot more than was paid for the buildings purchased during the middle and late 1960s. Unlike those smaller buildings, this project was going to need major financing. The purchase contract did not allow subordination to future financing, so a major lender who would take out the underlying contract and supply adequate funds for the proposed project was required.

The presentation for financing was made to a nearby bank that had shown considerable interest in the area. It seemed natural that this bank would help with the financing for this first major restoration there. The local manager was enthusiastic and developed a carefully prepared presentation. A phased loan in the total amount of $650,000 was requested. Of this, $200,000 would be for the main floor and exterior, and $150,000 for each of the other three floors. This was to be an interim construction loan with permanent financing to be sought on completion when the project had proved itself. Each of the three owners would have to put in enough money to pay off the underlying contract of about $200,000 and be willing to personally guarantee the $650,000 loan.

The application for the loan was turned down January 19, 1972. This was a dark day for the three of us. We each had contributed considerable cash to keep the demolition and cleanup going through the summer and fall of 1971, and major restoration would not proceed on the building until someone was willing to commit substantial funds to the area. We felt that if anyone could get financing for a major building we should be able to, because of the buildings already owned and improved by Anderson and White and because of our overall record and reputation in respective areas of work in the community. The project was well into the working drawings and the gutting of the building was nearly completed, so the need for financing was immediate.

Each of the partners had had some contact with the Seattle Trust and Savings Bank and knew some of the officers and principals. They were presented with the program for the building and the financing needs. Seattle Trust made a study of the area, reviewed the proposal and plans carefully and decided to help. With a projection of rents and income for the building when completed, Seattle Trust appraised the completed, fully restored building at $1 million and gave a 75 percent loan of $900,000 at 8.5 percent interest with a 15-year term. Besides the $30,000 already personally invested in the building, each partner was required to put up an additional $75,000, a total of

$225,000 new equity. In addition, the loan required personal guarantees. The Seattle Trust agreement was a phased loan with disbursements tied to completion of the exterior and main floor as one stage, and each of the three upper floors as an additional stage. In mid-February 1972 we mortgaged other property and signed the papers to close the loan.

Structural Reinforcement

Meanwhile, during this period of planning for the Grand Central and searching for financing, something rather significant was happening in another area. In September 1971, some officials from the Seattle Building Department visited Los Angeles for a firsthand view of the damage caused by the severe quake of the previous spring. The Building Department people returned obviously impressed by the damage they had seen and alarmed about the risk of unreinforced brick buildings, the primary type of construction used for the buildings in Pioneer Square during the post-Seattle Fire period of 1889 to about 1910. In any major seismographic disturbance there was the chance that the brick walls might pull away from the floors and the totally unreinforced buildings would collapse.

The building code required that whenever more than 50 percent of the assessed value of a building was spent on improvements in any one year the building would have to meet current building code seismographic requirements. Because no major building had been restored to this time and because any work that had been done in the area had been spread over several years, this provision of the code had not been applied. However, the Grand Central was not going to escape some major reinforcing work.

The architects and structural engineers for the building, together with the Building Department staff, developed a compromise solution for this type of unreinforced masonry building. The walls on each floor of the building had to be tied to the floors by the installation of a properly sized steel angle around the inside perimeter of the floor, with 4-foot-on-center steel strips welded to the channel and running back along the surface of the floor. These strips were then nailed and bolted to a new plywood overlaid floor, which tied the floor together so it would act as a single diaphragm. The perimeter steel angle member was then tied to the outside of the walls by bolts drilled through the walls and fastened on the outside with escutcheon-like plates that could be decorative in design.

The Grand Central was faced with this major structural requirement, the first of many unforeseen cost overruns. It was a reasonable and proper requirement in the interest of public safety, although costly to the developers.

As soon as the building had been cleaned out, which included the removal of all plaster and wood lath, a contract was let for the structural reinforcing work, which needed to be done while the ceilings and walls were exposed and before any reconstruction work proceeded. Concurrently with this, a contract was let for the repair of all exterior masonry, including the rebuilding of the parapet. To meet the building permit requirements, the parapet was lowered and the upper section rebuilt incorporating a bond beam that would tie the parapet together.

Substantial portions of the building elevation required the removal of rotten brick and mortar and replacement while tuck pointing was being done. Finally, neglected roof drains and downspouts had allowed water to run down the face of portions of the building and during a period of many years this process had made a soft mush of much of the brick for a depth of several courses. While the staging was in place for the tuck pointing, this rather substantial exterior brickwork repair, another unbudgeted item, was done.

The cleaning, tuck pointing and repairing of the exterior were completed in early 1972. We waited until dry weather in the late spring to do the silicone sealing of the exterior.

Interior Work

In February 1972, eight months after purchase of the building, the interior reconstruction was begun. Electrical and mechanical contracts were let for stage 1, the main floor, with runs to be installed to the top three floors for the later stages. Concurrently, workers began cutting through the 18-inch brick bearing walls for the interior archways, which formed the new entryways to the shops and opened up the arcade to other sections of the main floor.

This process of cutting large archways through the brick walls of the building was one of the large-expense items in the reconstruction of the Grand Central. The work could not properly be bid, and many of the archways were located as the work proceeded—a procedure that illustrates an important phenomenon in restoration work.

The fact is that the Grand Central restoration was an evolutionary design process. We felt our way along. As the building was opened up, many things that would add significantly to its usability and improve the aesthetics became apparent.

The Grand Central was a big, ugly box of a building. Out of this box were carved entirely new spaces, putting the building, which was originally a hotel, to an entirely new use.

The Basement

One illustration of the evolutionary nature of restoration was the basement of the Grand Central. When the building was bought the basement appeared to be unusable. However, as work on the main floor arcade proceeded, it became apparent that a major stairway from the arcade to the basement might open up some usable space. A cleanup crew cleared out the mass of rotting timbers, old heating plant boilers and hydraulic water-powered elevator equipment, most of which had to be cut up with acetylene torches to be removed. The ceilings were high enough to make attractive space and the area could be dried out with drain tile to allow the pouring of concrete slab floors. Because this basement level was too low to be served by the existing sewers, sump pumps were installed to pump back up to the street sewer level.

If the basement were ever to be used, it had to be tied in with the work on the main floor. Most of the costs for the basement were unbudgeted, but we believed that eventually rental revenue from this area would justify the cost. In retrospect, this was a correct decision, but at the time it was a bit unnerving in light of the funds.

One amusing sidelight concerning the basement involved a wrought-iron pipe, 4 inches in diameter, that was uncovered. Sticking several inches up through the dirt floor of the basement, it was capped off and seemed to be there to stay. We did not want to bury an unidentified pipe under the new basement floor, so it was investigated. The job foreman drilled a small ¼-inch hole in the cap, and water spouted to the ceiling. We thought a branch of an old water main had been hit, but city records showed no line there. Water samples were taken; it was 100 percent pure, with no chlorine, which would have indicated city water. We had a high-pressure artesian well in our basement! We drove a wooden plug in the little hole we had tapped and poured the new concrete floor over it.

The Project Completed

By May 1972, the main-floor arcade was ready for tenants. Since the autumn of 1971, people had been making inquiries about possible space for shops in the building. Informally people were signed up, maintaining a reasonable mix of tenants. Shop space on the main arcade was rented for approximately $2 a square foot on three- to five-year leases with no percentage of escalation clauses. We were grateful just to have some tenants!

By the summer of 1972, one year after purchase of the building, the main floor was fully rented and the basement arcade shops would be ready for occupancy by fall. Attention then turned to the three upper floors. By later summer, this space was ready for partitioning and finishing off to tenant specifications.

In September a major tenant signed a five-year lease for the entire fourth floor at $4.50 a square foot. This price covered fully improved space to the tenant's specifications, except for janitorial services, for which the tenant wanted to contract separately. These services were worth about 60 cents a square foot per year. By renting the entire floor we were able to gain additional net rentable area, which put the return close to $5 a square foot, excluding janitorial.

The fourth-floor tenants moved into their space on December 31, 1972, a year and a half after our purchase of the building.

With the fourth floor occupied and looking attractive, inquiries concerning office space on the second and third floors began. Tenants for these floors signed up at $5.50 to $6.00 a square foot per year. However, we were virtually out of money from the $900,000 loan and still had two floors to complete. Some of the funds projected for the upper floors had been used on the basement instead, and the budget had been exceeded in a multitude of other areas. Faced with this dilemma, we took the actual and projected rent roll to Seattle Trust and reviewed the overall financial situation.

We now had the basement area rented (a situation never contemplated in the original appraisal), the fourth floor fully rented at a figure of approximately $5 a square foot and additional tenants signed for space at $5.50 to $6.00 a square foot on the remaining two floors. Thus the building was given a new look by the lenders. Based on the existing rent roll and signed future tenants, a reappraisal of the building produced a value of $1.6 million.

Seattle Trust was willing to loan 75 percent of this new appraised figure, which increased the take-out loan from $900,000 to $1.2 million. This revised loan commitment was based on a new schedule of proven rents for the building. These were rents that to date had not been charged in the area, but the Grand Central was the first air-conditioned, totally restored and fully serviced building in Pioneer Square. By "uptown" standards for comparable space, these rents were still a bargain. Seattle Trust could see the rental income to justify the new appraisal and gave us the means to finish the building. By the summer of 1973 the last two floors of office space were completed and rented at $6.00 to $6.50 per square foot.

A little more than two years after the Grand Central was purchased, it was finished and rented. We had paid $230,000 for the ugly box in July 1971. Over a period of two years an additional $1,375,000 had been spent on renovation and reconstruction. Of this, $1,260,000 was for permanent capitalized reconstruction costs to the building and $115,000 for loan fees and interest.

The funds came from the $125,000 put in by each partner (totaling $375,000 equity or "front-end" money) and $1.2 million of borrowed funds, for a total investment of $1,575,000. In addition, there was some rental income during the latter part of this period when the building was partially occupied.

The 1974 annual gross revenue, based on existing leases, was approximately $275,000 a year. This gives the owners a cash flow of about $2,000 a month or $24,000 a year after debt service and operating costs. To date, this cash flow has gone back into the building in the form of nonrecurring operating costs and additional improvements. There will be no appreciable return on the $375,000 equity investment until the original leases expire and new leases are negotiated to reflect current rental market conditions.

The three upper office floors presently rent at between $5 and $6.50 a square foot, substantially below the $7.50 to $8 a square foot that this type of air-conditioned, fully serviced space brings today in Pioneer Square. Similarly, the retail shops on the main floor and basement are on leases with no percentages and below-market rates for the area.

The Grand Central would not have been bought and restored as it is today if cold logic and feasibility studies had been the deciding factors. We did it because the building was there, because we believed in the area and its future and because, with our experience and previous record, we could act as a development team that could obtain the necessary financing to get the job done. We believe that as the area develops there will be a reasonable return on the investment, though perhaps never a return on all the personal time, work and headaches (except through some strange satisfaction in seeing it done). However, I do not regret for one moment the two years spent on this project.

The Maynard Building

When the Grand Central was finished I swore I would not do it again for a long while, but here I am, a partner with Richard White, a year into the restoration of the Maynard Building, a block north of the Grand Central. Unlike the Grand Central, the Maynard is an intrinsically beautiful building.

We bought it because it was simply too handsome to ignore and offered too much potential not to be restored properly. The Maynard Building is 90 percent complete and 75 percent occupied. It is such a beautiful building I am confident it will fill up with rents in the $7 to $8 range. These rents are now established in Pioneer Square for fully serviced, air-conditioned space in the three major building completed to date.

Phase 3 in Pioneer Square

With completion of these three major buildings, phase 2 is ending and the phase 3 development period lies ahead for Pioneer Square. In phase 1, from 1962 to 1970, modest but important renovation work was done on an informal and somewhat amateur basis with limited outside financing. Phase 2, beginning with passage of the Pioneer Square Historic District Ordinance in 1970, saw the complete restoration of three major buildings and important municipal recognition and support for the area. Phase 2 also established the financial feasibility of restoring major buildings. Proven rent structures were established for these buildings and financing became available. Phase 3 is beginning now, in the summer of 1975. The Pioneer Square area is an established and recognized vital part of the city, where many buildings remain to be restored. There is a market for attractive, first-class space and financing is available for the right development team.

The major stumbling blocks remaining are the few slumlords who sit on these old buildings and will not spend one penny to fix them up, let alone to restore them. Neither will they sell their buildings at prices that will allow someone else to put together the risk capital and financing necessary to restore them. As in so many cities, the slumlords still have a negative power. I have hopes, however, that the Minimum Maintenance Ordinance passed recently by the city council will give the slumlords pause for thought. They will have to fix up or sell out. Thus many of the remaining buildings in this neglected category should gradually find their way to restoration. If the properties are realistically priced, which means a modest value put on the buildings, investor-developers will find it profitable to restore them.

The investment and restoration that took place in Pioneer Square from 1962 to 1970 during the phase 1 period certainly was the most profitable. Indeed, it should have been, because it demanded the imagination and courage that started the area going.

Phase 2 was a period of high risk and long wait for a return on investment—in short, a testing period for Pioneer Square. Expensive restoration work was done before rental rates had adjusted to reflect the true cost of the work or the fine quality of the product.

Phase 3 can be approached less emotionally and with more logic. Rents are established for top quality space in well-restored buildings. Financing is easier to obtain for projects that show economic feasibility based on the record of work recently done in the area. The period of highest risk is over, and others will now come into the area and profitably restore some of the many remaining buildings that cry out for a little love and attention.

The Lawyers Co-operative Publishing Company*

Raynor M. Warner, Sybil McCormac Groff, and Ranne P. Warner

Summary

In 1971, Lawyers Co-operative, located in a vintage mill complex in downtown Rochester, needed additional space for its expanded operations. The company, one of the nation's leading law publishers, asked its architects, Handler/Grosso, to determine whether it would be practical to recycle the existing structures. The architect's feasibility study showed that renovating the 125,000 square feet of the existing buildings would cost approximately $15 per square foot as compared to $45 per square foot for demolition and new construction. Completed in one year, the Lawyers Co-operative recycling, the first major rehabilitation project in downtown Rochester, has served as an instructive example. The success of the first project inspired Lawyers Co-operative to recycle another building in the complex, as well as to create a new park adjacent to its headquarters.

Background

Lawyers Co-operative is located in six brick buildings along the Genesee River. In 1901, the company occupied the Aqueduct Building, the oldest structure in the complex, a former shoe factory dating from about 1880. As business increased, Lawyers Co-operative gradually expanded to the adjacent buildings: a warehouse dating from 1890; a smaller pre-1900 industrial building; and a 1950 addition to the 1880s mill. Two other buildings, yet to be renovated, complete the complex. Floor space for the four renovated buildings measures approximately 125,000 square feet.

Through the years, the company continued to grow. In 1965, it also leased additional space outside the complex to house administrative offices, and two years later it expanded into suburban Rochester, adding a new manufacturing plant for printing and binding. In 1971, management asked Handler/Grosso, architects, to study the feasibility of recycling their historic building complex to meet their space requirements.

---

*New York: McGraw-Hill, 1978, pp. 49-51.

Execution

Handler/Grosso found the buildings to be structurally sound and in excellent condition, and concluded that renovation would be economically feasible. The company decided to proceed.

The recycling of the buildings took one year, and was done in stages so that production would not be disrupted. The exterior masonry was cleaned, using dry grit, and waterproofed—except where ivy-covered—with a silicone coating. Some of the finer architectural details, the brick-arched floors, cast-iron columns, and wrought-iron beams, typical of nineteenth-century mill construction, were left exposed. Many interior walls were cleaned, highlighting the brick. Windows were replaced, and air conditioning was installed throughout the complex. All new heating, wiring, and plumbing systems were added. The newly retrofitted buildings now serve as administrative and editorial offices. All manufacturing previously done in the complex has been transferred to the suburban Rochester facility.

The crowning feat of the renovation was the construction of an Italianate tower, topped by a statue of Mercury 163 feet above street level, on an existing elevator shaft. A familiar landmark, the 21-foot, 700-pound copperplated statue, dating from 1881, had been atop the nearby Peerless Tobacco Works. It had been kept in storage by the City of Rochester since Peerless's demolition in 1950.

Relying on this experience, the company has recently retrofitted another smaller building in its complex and is now leasing the space. Handler/Grosso revitalized the 1890 structure, exposing the brickwork, installing new plumbing, heating, air-conditioning and electric systems, as well as new windows, a new elevator, and an acoustical ceiling. This renovation took ten months.

Adjacent to its buildings, along the Genesee River, Lawyers Co-operative created a pleasant public park. Designed by Carol R. Johnson and Associates, the park effectively links the complex with the rest of downtown, and provides increased green space for Rochester's citizens.

Costs

The cost of recycling the vintage buildings was much lower than the cost of new construction: about $15 per square foot as compared to about $45 per square foot. Handler/Grosso provided a breakdown on the comparative costs (see below).

The renovation cost an estimated $1.8 million. Development of the park cost about $250,000.

	Retrofitting		New
Land value	$ 300,000		$ 300,000
Value of existing shell	1,250,000		—
Cost to demolish	—		100,000
Total square feet need	125,000		125,000
Renovation costs, including:	1,800,000	New construction costs, including:	$6,250,000
Mechanical systems	700,000		700,000
Floor finish	150,000		150,000
Window replacement	100,000		—
Time for renovation	1 year	Time for new construction	1½ yrs.

Problems

The temperature of the condensate from the steam used to heat the renovated buildings had to be lowered before it was returned to the city's sewers. To solve this problem, condensate-cooling pipes were installed below the sidewalks. In winter, the pipes serve to melt the abundant snow, while at the same time lowering the condensate temperature.

Benefits

Richard Handler, of Handler/Grosso, enthusiastically assessed the results of the rehabilitation: *At a cost of less than one-half of a new building, this office building provides functional area equal to any new building with the elements of charm and historic continuity for the company as well as historic significance for the community.*

In addition to the cost savings, rehabilitation, unlike new construction, made it unnecessary for the company to reshuffle its operations and employees. The newly decorated, bright, and spacious interiors also enhance the working environment. Employees take pride in their offices and in Mercury, a Rochester landmark for years.

The new park is popular with both employees and city residents; it has even led to the establishment of a bocce league among the employees. In addition, some local citizens have telephoned the company to express their appreciation. The company has received a good deal of favorable publicity in local newspapers and magazines.

Following the Lawyers Co-operative example, other businesses have chosen to remain and retrofit rather than flee to the suburbs. Rochester Telephone Company has recently completed a new mini-park, and Handler/Grosso is renovating a vintage former Federal Building (c. 1890) as the City Hall.

In June 1975, Handler/Grosso received a Design Award from the Rochester Chapter of the American Institute of Architects for the Mercury statue and tower. The Award read, "Chosen for its imaginative contribution to the city of a meaningful landmark and its sensitive relationship to existing buildings."

Information: Economic Analyses
of Adaptive Use Projects — Guernsey Hall*

National Trust for Historic Preservation

Old mansions that have outlived their usefulness as single-family dwellings often are demolished to make way for new construction or they are turned into museum pieces. Guernsey Hall in Princeton, N.J., nearly met the former fate, yet today it is certainly not a museum. The mid-19th century house has been converted into five luxury apartments under a condominium form of ownership. Situated on an extensively landscaped 2.5-acre site, the mansion contains parking for residents and guests and a formal garden.

The mansion is located in an area of single-family detached houses on large lots, and there were some complaints that the Guernsey Hall condominium would be the catalyst for turning other large and historic houses in Princeton into apartments—to some a sign of decline. Formerly the residence of Richard Stockton Field, New Jersey state attorney general, a founder of a short-lived Princeton University Law School, and United States Senator, the structure is of stone masonry construction, designed in the Italianate villa style. Originally, the Field estate consisted of 40 acres, planted with trees from around the world. Now half of it is a public park, owned by the borough of Princeton.

---

*1976

Guernsey Hall, or Fieldwood as it was first known, was designed by John Notman, a Scottish-born Philadelphia architect, and was erected around 1852. The stone used for construction is a golden yellow, local sandstone. Exterior trim is of brownstone and wood, the latter painted a deep buff color to blend.

An unusual feature of the house is a large, square, three-story tower, off center and pierced with arched windows. The house itself is bulky with low, hipped roofs of tin, accentuated by clusters of hexagonal chimneys. The west front terminates in two large bays.

All major rooms had marble fireplaces and elaborate, molded, plaster cornices. By far the most spectacular space in the house, however, is the octagonal center stairhall, rising 40 feet to a glazed dome. The stairhall walls were painted to simulate stone. Around the walls a winding staircase appears to be supported by fluted, plaster corbels.

Field died in 1870, and one year later his heirs sold the property to Mrs. David Brown. In 1887, Mrs. Brown sold the property to Allan Marquand, who changed the name of the house to Guernsey Hall, for the island of Guernsey from which his ancestors had come. Marquand modernized the house in 1912 since at that time it was still lit by gas, heated in large part by fireplaces and had only one bath. The house was enlarged by one-third through a three-story addition.

The cast-iron porch on the south and west fronts was removed and, on the south front, replaced with heavy piers and arches holding a flat roof. Many of the original marble mantels were replaced, but the elaborate plaster cornice work was left intact. The Minton tile flooring in the stairhall was removed and replaced with hardwood. In addition, clear glass was substituted in the skylight for etched glass. Formal gardens were constructed on the west and northwest parts of the property, but only the former remains.

In 1951 the property was sold by the estate of Eleanor Marquand. When it was learned that the new owners intended to subdivide the property, approximately 20 acres were repurchased by the Marquand daughters and donated to the borough of Princeton as a public park. Eventually the new owners sold four house lots from the property on the south and west.

Preservation of a Landmark

Guernsey Hall and the remaining three acres came up for sale in 1970 after the death of its last private owner. It was zoned in a category (R-1) permitting only single-family residences, but it was obvious that only someone of great wealth could maintain the house as a private residence.

The building came to public attention when a prospective purchaser wished to demolish the house and replace it with a combined house and studio for organ instruction. This was permissible under the existing zoning, but the zoning restricts home occupations to 40 percent of the total area. The organ loft required more space, so the prospective buyer sought a variance from the zoning regulations. At public hearings, the opponents of the variance pointed out the historical significance of the building and the loss to Princeton if the mansion, which was in good condition, were razed. Moreover, opponents objected to the studio use and especially the noise that would be generated. The request for the variance was denied, but it was still unlikely that this 42-room mansion could be maintained as a single, private residence. William Short, who had testified at the earlier variance hearing, believed that a multiple dwelling would be the most feasible way to save the landmark. Others believed that conversion to office use for nonprofit institutions would be possible too, but that was not actively pursued.

From the outset, the intent of the Guernsey Hall venture was preservation of a Princeton landmark and not necessarily realization of a profit. Along with Short, eight other persons formed a Subchapter S. corporation (in which there can be more than 10 stockholders) called Guernsey Hall, Inc., with the intent of purchasing the property for conversion to a multifamily dwelling under a condominium form of ownership. Short believed that the project had to be a condominium because the interest of the corporation's investors was to save the building, not to become rental apartment owners. Moreover, rents would have had to be more than $1,000 per month to justify conversion in this manner.

Guernsey Hall, Inc., entered into a nonconditional purchase agreement and took possession in February 1972. The property was still zoned R-1 so it was necessary to petition the local zoning board for a use variance. At a public hearing it was pointed out that the neighborhood would be worse off if the house were torn down and the acreage subdivided into five lots requiring more roads, more utilities, etc. Subsequently, the use variance was granted.

Guernsey Hall, Inc., is a nonprofit Subchapter S. corporation consisting of nine stockholders, three of whom are Marquand daughters. Under this organization, the corporation can elect to have its income taxed directly to the shareholders, an arrangement similar to a partnership but with limited liability to the participants. However, losses in a Subchapter S. corporation cannot exceed the total of the capital stock and the loans by the shareholders to the corporation.

Rehabilitation Process

The nine shareholders made a capital investment of $95,000. In addition, the corporation borrowed $180,000 for construction from the Princeton Savings and Loan Association at 8 percent interest. The loan had a life-span of 18 months. The corporation was allowed to borrow money as needed and was only charged for money actually used. The mansion and grounds were purchased for $125,000, using $50,000 of the initial capital investment and $75,000 from the Princeton Savings and Loan. The remainder of the money was treated as working capital. Furthermore, four of five condominiums were presold and the down payments used as working capital. The last condominium was sold in an even trade for the new owner's single-family house. In all, the project incurred some $400,000 in construction costs.

In addition, a half-acre parcel was sold from the mansion grounds for $45,000. This brought the Guernsey Hall site down to 2.5 acres and resulted in the irregular shape of the property.

Out of an initial capital investment of $95,000, shareholders will realize a return of $85,000. However, most of the corporation shareholders are in a position to realize some annual tax shelter benefits with a limited liability. In a regular corporation, these losses could not be transmitted to the participants.

The two overriding design objectives of Guernsey Hall, Inc., were to save a fine, old, single-family residence by adaptation and to keep as much of the good original details as possible. Working from old drawings, Short, as project architect, tried to match the stone color in the trim to make the house look as it did when built. In addition, honeycomb concrete block was laid outside the north front and grass planted in the holes, providing additional, inconspicuous guest parking. There were three garages extant when reconstruction began; two more were added, giving each unit one garage space plus at least one guest space.

Interior reconstruction consisted of dividing the 42 rooms into six apartments, the sixth being a caretaker's apartment on the top level. The existing plaster and woodwork were retained where possible and the main stairhall was repainted to simulate stone.

The mansion contained a poorly located passenger elevator that was incorporated as part of the largest condominium, which spans three levels, and a new hydraulic elevator was added in the vestibule of the main entrance.

The house has five levels, due to the fact that there are 14-foot-high ceilings in some areas and nine-foot ceilings in others, reflecting the difference between servants' quarters and owner's quarters. Also, the former servants' sections lack the elaborate plaster detailing on the ceilings and cornices that is found in the owner's quarters.

The state building code required that there be two fire exits. The large center stairhall serves as one, and a new fire escape was added to the east front and painted a buff color to match the wood trim and the sandstone. The code does not permit winders on stairs used for fire egress, but exemption from this portion of the code was secured to permit retention of the stairs when it was argued that the winders were, in fact, wider than an average stair without them.

The building code for multiple dwellings also required that the main stairhall under the dome in Guernsey Hall be a two-hour fire stair. Fortunately, the code was met by the 12-inch brick wall under that plaster exterior. In addition, doors that were considered to be primary apartment entrances off the main stairhall had to be steel rather than wood. Moldings were applied to the flush steel doors to match the paneling of the original doors.

Improvements to individual apartments were not made until the units were actually sold. In this way, interior amenities could be tailored to fit the individual tenant. The corporation had a base figure for individual unit improvements. If the owner wished improvements that cost more, it was the owner's responsibility to pay for them. In all, the five tenants spent $32,578 in custom refinishing.

In the redesign scheme, four of the five apartments have one of the big formal rooms for a living room. One apartment has the original morning room and library; another the formal dining room; and the last two have the big bedrooms. The fifth apartment, a duplex or two-story apartment on the east side, consists of servant space entirely, but the owner is compensated for the size by a private garden. The basement of the mansion consists of storage space for each unit, a workshop for the caretaker, and laundry facilities.

Completed Project

The last unit was occupied in July 1974. With the exception of improved main entrance security, an elevator, and two new garages, the mansion looks much as it did after the 1912 modernization.

The formal garden still exists and is owned in common by all residents. A caretaker has been hired to keep up the garden. No trees have been removed, and, therefore, the site remains heavily wooded. Some of the specimens—cedars of Lebanon, yews, larches, horse chestnuts, white oaks, and beeches—date from Judge Field's time.

Marketing

There is no comparable project of this type in Princeton. In fact, multiple dwellings are only now being introduced into the borough. Hence, the market for this type of project was unknown. Guernsey Hall, Inc., conducted a trial marketing study before it committed itself to the project. Of 16 prospective purchasers, only two made firm offers, but it was on this basis that the decision to go ahead was made.

Cost was not the major consideration to the tenants, all of whom have above average incomes. The units sold in the $90,000 to $115,000 range. Advertising expenses were minimal ($200 to $300) since the project had remained in the public eye because of the variance proceedings. Four units were taken quickly either on the basis of the project's publicity or through referrals. There was a delay in selling the last apartment, which ultimately cost the corporation $4,025 in maintenance payments while it was held for sale. A willing buyer was found for this unit initially, but he had trouble selling his single-family house and was reluctant to commit himself totally to the condominium. Renting the unit temporarily was decided against because that would have required interior refinishing, and the corporation wanted it finished for an owner rather than a renter. Also, renting would have held up a possible sale for the period of the lease. In the end, the corporation made an even trade with the owner, the house for the condominium, the reasoning being that there would be a better market for renting the house than for the condominium. Subsequently, the house was sold. Nevertheless, the corporation lost money by having to spend $4,025 to carry the last condominium unit for a year. At present, the mansion is fully occupied.

Management

Maintenance expenses amount to over $19,000 yearly, a major cost being the caretaker at about $10,000. In light of the mansion's size, a caretaker seemed mandatory, although 8-10 condominium units would have made the per-unit costs more palatable.

Expenses for grounds maintenance, general fees, the caretaker's salary and liability insurance and workman's compensation are split evenly among the five tenants, regardless of ownership interest. Apartments are not metered separately, a construction decision that saved the developer $2,000. In another project, however, the developer would install separate metering. The initial intention was to charge electricity on pro rata share based on the number of outlets, occupancy not considered. In the end, costs for electricity as well as building maintenance, fire and machinery insurance, and water were divided on a percentage basis according to ownership interest. Heating costs are allocated on a percentage basis according to the cubic footage, or volume, of each unit. There are individual hot water controls in each apartment.

The administration and management of the condominium is vested in the Board of Managers of the Guernsey Hall Condominium. Each of the five unit owners designates one member. Residents own their individual units from face of wall to face of wall and floor to ceiling and are restricted from altering the central stairhall, exterior cornices, windows and doorways. Each unit owner has a joint access easement to use the common elements located in any other unit but serving his unit.

Units are served by a master television antenna. In addition, certain outside areas have been set aside for the exclusive use of individual tenants. The remainder of the outside space, including the formal garden, is common property.

Conclusions

Reuse, as an alternative to demolition and new construction, can be cheaper for a municipality. In the case of Guernsey Hall, which remains on the local tax rolls, the taxes collected are probably equal to or exceed the taxes that would be levied if five single-family houses were built. In addition, the reuse plan creates less of a burden on city services—roads, sewers, schools, etc.—than would five single-family dwellings.

Without Notman's main center stairhall, it would have been more difficult to satisfy the building code requirements for multifamily housing. Overall, Notman's plan with thick masonry bearing walls throughout limited the flexibility in actually changing the spaces, but it made compliance with the fire code easier.

Although it saved the developer $2,000, it would have been better to have installed five separate meters for utilities, given the fact that the occupants own their individual units and that occupants now pay their percentage of heating costs regardless of whether they are there or not.

It probably would have been possible to charge more for the individual condominium units and thereby make up some of the loss to the investors. However, since four out of five units had been presold prior to construction, there was no way to make up for increased costs brought about by unforeseen circumstances. It might have been advantageous to have had some form of escalator clause built into the presale agreements, which would have accounted for the unforeseen circumstances.

8.

Preservation through Area Planning

Preamble

A major factor in the modern approach to historic preservation has been the enlargement of perspective, from the individual structure (or artifact) to a broader context. This has happened in two quite different ways. First, the early consideration of individual structures has gradually been supplemented by a realization that their surroundings have often contributed to their value—and, conversely, that their value depended in part upon the quality of their surroundings. Similarly, the New York City Landmarks Commission began with a focus on individual landmarks, but soon broadened its outlook to the designation of large historic districts—and this has been one of the most successful parts of the entire program, as discussed in chapter 2 above. If the valuable area is larger than an individual building, the removal of a single building (perhaps even a not particularly distinguished building) may change the mood of the entire area.

In the second place, considering the whole matter in a broader and quite different context, problems of historic preservation are often closely related to various other major questions of public policy. In recent times work on historic preservation has therefore often been assimilated into and based on the overall planning operation. The obvious examples include Baltimore and Los Angeles, for in both cities plans for historic preservation have been prepared and adopted as part of the central planning operation. Examples of these interrelationships are legion, and increasingly obvious, for in many instances, planning agencies are already deeply involved in work which is at least closely related. The interrelationships between historic preservation and other major planning problems are increasingly clear. Any substantial historic preservation program is likely to affect the supply of housing at various income levels and various locations. Many of the valuable older buildings are likely to be located in the downtown areas, and their future is an important item in downtown development. Historic districts may be an important part of the local economic base, as most obviously in New Orleans, and so inevitably play an important role in an economic development program.

Large Scale Preservation, Saving Places for People*

Sharon Lee Ryder

It's one thing to save a single building, but it's something else again to preserve a place. To begin with, it's more complicated. Everything that has to be done to save an individual building gets multiplied in saving an area; the spaces as well as buildings that give an area its character must be identified; interdependent uses must be worked out for them; the political strategies are more intricate because there are more parties involved. And while one building may conceivably be out of use while it is being restored, an entire area can't be taken out of service.

It is a knotty problem, partly because a place, as opposed to a single building, is apt to loom large in the public mind. Saving one takes clairvoyance (to read the public mind), political acumen (because the decisions often end up in the political arena), a grasp of guerilla tactics (for the infighting that comes with preservation projects), and a touch of paranoia (because the threats to a place can be far more subtle than the threats to a building)

Some Thoughts on Preservation**

Osbert Lancaster

Of all three of our grounds for defense this is the most difficult upon which to take a stand and by no means the least important. For the number of people who consciously realize the vital part played by one small unit in a landscape, or an architectural ensemble from which they subconsiously derive pleasure, is always very small. Conscious awareness, alas, only comes when the effect has been ruined by the disappearance of the unit in question. It is, largely, a question of scale and contrast and as such is not amenable to generalization. I will therefore confine myself to a concrete example. In the case of Varley House it will, I think, become obvious upon reflection by any person of sensibility standing in Parliament Square and looking upstream toward Millbank, first how much the height and vertical emphasis of the Victoria Tower is increased by the low horizontal lines of the facade of Varley House, and second, how greatly the romantic exuberance of Barry and Pugin's great work gains by contrast with the restrained and unenthusiastic classicism of its tiny neighbor across the road.

---

*From *Progressive Architecture*, Nov., 1972, p. 70.
**Historic Preservation Today*, Charlottesville, Va.: University Press of Virginia, 1966, pp. 191-92.

And finally one becomes aware that Varley House acts as a most valuable nonconductor, as it were, between the sixteenth-century Gothic of Henry VII's Chapel and the Victorian version of Perpendicular opposite, both of which would stand to lose from the close proximity of each other were it to be destroyed. Conversely, the value of a building can be totally destroyed if the surrounding landscape is removed.

For example, Abu Simbel. The staggering effect of that extraordinary site as one rounds the corner of the Nile at dawn is one that no one who has experienced it would be likely to forget. But it is one of landscape rather than of architecture. It has more in common with that created by the Grand Canyon or by the mountains of the Argolis seen through the Lion Gate at Mycenae than that evoked by, say, the facade of the Louvre. Considered aesthetically, the temples are not only defiantly second-rate but faintly ridiculous—the ham-fisted expression of a tedious megalomania. Therefore, while one may bitterly regret their immersion, it would be, in my view, idiotic to spend vast sums in removing them from their present position on the water's edge, which constitutes their sole *raison d'être*, to a site where they would be quite without significance and, owing to the prevailing winds, in 50 years time almost certainly unrecognizable.

Problems of this magnitude are, however, fortunately rare. But the task of maintaining the proper relationship between new buildings and their environment is, in England at any rate, a constant preoccupation.

Here the practicing architect can be of the greatest assistance if he will but bear in mind how much the effect of even the most excellent building can be enhanced by a carefully preserved neighbor. Let me give you a striking and familiar example. Some years ago Dr. Sigfried Giedion, in the course of one of his interesting lectures on modern architecture, threw upon the screen a photograph of Rockefeller Center, the severe beauty and simple structure of which we were, quite rightly, exhorted to admire. But the photographer had cunningly included in his plate the adorned steeple and fretted roof of a neighboring neo-Gothic church on Fifth Avenue, now, alas, no more. Afterward, at question time, I asked the lecturer if he did not think that some of the effect created by this undoubtedly impressive but not outstandingly subtle building was in this photograph due to the happy inclusion of its humbler neighbor? My question was not well received.

That the building to be preserved for these reasons is not itself of any great merit is beside the point; its function in the scheme of things has become quite different from its original one and such considerations are, therefore, pointless.

Adapting the Past to the Present[*]

Jacques Houlet

The concept of conservation has constantly evolved over the years. Limited at first to monuments restored almost as museum pieces, conservation now takes in old groups of more modest buildings and city centers whose modern needs have given rise to the idea of "conservationist town planning."

---

[*]Council of Europe, *Forum*, 3d quarter, 1979, p. iv.

Originally only palaces, castles, and great sanctuaries were thought worthy of conservation, but then less noble buildings were included and today vernacular architecture is being protected on the countryside as well as in towns. This prodigious growth of the architectural heritage, or conservationists' realization of its importance, has had consequences to which the Council of Europe has been particularly attentive. In this area it has been a major trend-setter. The first consequence was the realization that a heritage on such a scale could only be preserved if it was used. The upkeep of buildings is always costly; buildings that are not properly maintained are in constant danger of decay and ruin; and dilapidation is all the more rapid when they are badly built. The absolute necessity that they be used gave rise to the concept of integrated conservation, and it is this emphasis on use that distinguishes that concept from scientific conservation.

The second consequence was recognition of the value of groups of buildings or "ensembles." Be they centers of historic cities or traditional villages, "ensembles" like Salzburg, Heidelberg, Bath, Florence, Conques, and hundreds of others are precious for themselves, and not just for the monuments of major importance they may contain. "Ensembles" may be prestigious even without important monuments: San Gimignano in Italy, for instance, or Pérouges and Sarlat in France. All the countries of Europe contain examples.

If maintaining contemporary life in buildings thought worthy of conservation makes for their survival, all the more does it apply to ensembles. For, although it is possible to fall back on conservation of buildings as museum pieces—the Roman gates at Trier, the Colosseum in Rome, the Maison Carrée at Nimes serve no useful purpose—it is quite out of the question in the case of "ensembles." It is a truism to say that a town or village from which life departs dies. And it loses everything.

Modern Needs

While maintaining activity in a building poses problems, especially when the activity changes, the adaptation of a medieval group of buildings to modern living, particularly if it is to be at all pleasant, presents much more difficult problems. They are all the more complex because we are often concerned with historic centers in more recent urban surroundings, and because these historic districts are often the administrative and commercial nerve-center of the city.

One instance of a challenging problem here is that of motor traffic. It is relatively simple to ordain that private cars are no longer to have access to historic centers, but less so to decide that deliveries are no longer to be made to shops, and that ambulances and fire engines are to be excluded. The problems are so complex that we are witnessing the start of what might be called conservationist town planning. It is not easy to define this kind of town planning in theoretical terms, since it sets out conditions which at first sight appear irreconcilable: retaining ancient structures as far as possible, and recreating a town which is highly agreeable to present-day men and women with all their impedimenta: cars, household appliances, plumbing, television, etc.

In practice, the ingeniousness of our architects seems to be boundless, and the symposia organized by the Council of Europe have indicated a wide range of solutions to the basic problems, despite their highly paradoxical appearance. Have the solutions been universally acceptable? It would be too good to be true if they had, and in fact all the cases presented have provoked criticism and comments, not to say totally negative reactions. But what seems to be of the essence in this nascent discipline is that the only way in which it can successfully adapt ancient patterns to present-day living is through searching analyses of the historic urban fabric and of the needs of present-day people. And these analyses have shown that our theoretical town-planners of the first half of the twentieth century overlooked factors of which our ancestors were probably aware.

Street Life

To take just one example, the use of collective space. Streets and squares are not only the conduits, reservoirs and drains which allow for the circulation of motorcars and pedestrians, like so much fluid. The street has its importance as a place in which people come together, communicate, celebrate or indeed lose their tempers, in the case of political and other kinds of events. This was something realized by the Greeks, whose cities' heartbeats resounded on the *agora*. Public spaces may be taken over for various uses: one group (however hospitable) may take over a place where it feels at home, and something very like rejection occurs when another group attempts the same operation in the same place.

Some areas are "general purpose," lending themselves to both movement and sojourn. This applies to Place des Vosges in Paris, Piazza Navona in Rome, apparently to Trafalgar Square in London. Other places, despite their architectural splendor, do not have the power to retain people, one instance being Place Vendôme in Paris, or they fall prey to the motor car, as with Place de la Concorde. And others, despite the cars, are so magnificent that at all times they attract both inhabitants and visitors. This is the case with Place Stanislas in Nancy.

Pedestrian Precincts

To some extent we are only at the start of our researches. They are essentially practical, and we too have probably made a lot of mistakes. A critical analysis of pedestrian precincts would be welcome, because notwithstanding their success, some present serious deficiencies. But we have broken with a form of urban planning that neglected not only values belonging to the past, but mankind's spiritual needs as well. This painstaking work of analysis, these cautious efforts to save historic centers, which perhaps overpompously we have called conservationist town planning, do not really represent a new discipline. The whole endeavor leads to the practical and critical appraisal, in vivo, of a form of town planning which was drunk with the apparently unbounded scope of modern technology and failed to take into account many factors which are vital to man's life in society. And such appraisals must make it possible to rectify the errors of what might be called perennial town-planning.

Landmarks of Beauty and History*

Christopher Tunnard

Another approach has been taken by . . . Brooklyn Heights, the first residential suburb for ferry commuters to Manhattan, which contains 13,000 residences, many built in the aristocratic era of the mid-nineteenth century and 600 of them dating from before the Civil War. The present residents have requested the Landmarks Commission to designate as a historic district a 50-block area which has been investigated by architectural historian Clay Lancaster, who has published a detailed study of 619 houses in the old Brooklyn Heights area. Parts of Greenwich Village in Manhattan will also be designated as historic districts, and in lower Manhattan a section of Greene Street between Canal and Broome Streets will be preserved as the Cast Iron District.

It should be obvious by now that although the defined historic area has certain legal and administrative clarity, it cannot serve for all preservation purposes. It cannot cover the architecture of region or of types of community, like the ghost towns of Colorado, the early canal towns of Ohio or the watering places of Virginia.

In the future it would be desirable to extend the restoration principle to groups of communities in distressed areas, or those threatened by sudden change or slow deterioration. After the example of a Wallace Nutting, the antiquarian who in 1915 established his "chain of houses" in New England, it should be possible nowadays to substitute a chain of White River Valley towns in Vermont (say Chelsea, Tunbridge, and South Royalton) or some of the steamboat towns on the Ohio, Missouri, and Mississippi Rivers, or gold mining towns in California. Some of these are already preserved as individual communities as in the case of Columbia, California, a gold rush town which is now in the state park.

As President Johnson said in his message, "our concern is not with nature alone but the total relationship between man and the world around him." These regional towns and villages, which are not necessarily remarkable for the quality of their architecture, are nevertheless unique in character and plan. Those which are still inhabited and have no protection are prey to depredation by nationwide retail chain operations or single-function public agencies like the state highway departments. The latter, in fact, can have a great role to play in the preservation of our urban heritage. They should consider the view of a village from the highway as well as the effect produced by a truck-load of trees and shrubs which they apply as cosmetics to the paved ribbon. They, too, should treat these older communities as precious reminders of a past not entirely forgotten.

*From Special Committee on Historic Preservation, U.S. Conference of Mayors, *With Heritage So Rich,* New York: Random House, 1966, pp. 32-33.

Views of the town greens in Chelsea and South Royalton, Vermont. *Courtesy of the Vermont Law School.*

Promoted to Glory . . .*

Walter Muir Whitehill

A Modern Dream of the Past

Although it is unlikely that second, third, fourth, and fifth Williamsburgs will spring up, the practice of lookir.g at a town as a whole, or certain large areas of a city, as appropriate fields for preservation, has become widespread during the past quarter of a century. Country towns, well isolated from industrial areas, present a more manageable problem than larger places. Of these the Connecticut valley frontier town of Deerfield, Mass., is a remarkable example. There, through the joint efforts of the Pocumtuck Valley Memorial Association, a historical society organized in 1870, Deerfield Academy, a boys' school of national reputation, and the Heritage Foundation, established by Henry N. Flynt of Greenwich, Conn. (the president of the association and a trustee of the academy) and his wife, Deerfield has unobtrusively become one of the most attractive towns in New England. It is a small country town, centered on a single long, tree-shaded main street. The object has been, not an antiquarian restoration to any particular period—for everything from the seventeenth to the twentieth century is to be found along this street—but the maintenance of a town in which people live, teach, and learn, where the best of the past is enhanced by thoughtful improvements and additions. Half-a-dozen houses are open to visitors; the rest are occupied by the academy and townspeople. As Deerfield Academy has required new buildings, these have been designed to blend unobtrusively into the scene. The Heritage Foundation has bought a number of houses, and even brought some (threatened with destruction elsewhere) into the town. Some of these are admirably furnished as exhibits, while others are rented to provide living space and to help support the museum houses. The Pocumtuck Valley Memorial Assocaition maintains the seventeenth-century Fray House and a museum in Memorial Hall. The trappings of the tourist trade are completely absent, for the Heritage Foundation recognizes that a venture of this kind can never be made self-supporting. The remarkable thing about Deerfield is that one can never tell at a glance what organization is responsible for a given agreeable feature, for individuals and institutions alike work together for Deerfield with uncommon skill, taste, generosity, and reticence. (*See photographs on p. 37—Ed.*)

---

*From Special Committee on Historic Preservation, U.S. Conference of Mayors, *With Heritage So Rich*, New York: Random House, 1966, pp. 32-33.

Conservation of Historic and Cultural Resources *

Ralph W. Miner

Preservation activities occur at all levels of government as well as within various private organizations, with programs ranging from a national to a local focus. It is a premise of this report, without detracting in any way from the value of other efforts, that developing and coordinating a program for historic and cultural conservation is a proper function of the local comprehensive planning agency. In this manner, preservation activities can be undertaken within the framework of overall developmental objectives and programs of the community. Notable structures and places are rooted in the local community, and relatively few are of state or national significance from either an architectural or an historic viewpoint. Also, most of the tools to accomplish preservation must be either developed or applied locally. Historic and cultural conservation, therefore, can properly be viewed as matter of local public policy within the overall developmental perspective established by comprehensive planning.

Preservation of the City's Character * *

Baltimore Department of Planning

Incorporation of Historic Districts and Sites in the Master Plan

Baltimore's historic districts and sites, and the role they are to play in our future, must be carefully considered in the formulation of the Comprehensive Plan. Since the Comprehensive Plan deals with the interrelationship of all forms of City development, it concerns the connections between preservation and expressways and transit, urban renewal, park development, and the character of the City.

Expressways and other public improvements should be planned to avoid historically important areas and, where this is impossible, should be designed to be compatible with them. Urban renewal projects which encompass historic buildings and sites should take full advantage of them in planning

---

*A.S.P.O. *Planning Advisory Service*, report no. 244, 1969, p.3.
* *Baltimore, Md., 1967, pp. 16-17.`

for reuse; the same applies to development of existing or future parks. The value of elements of character, Lexington Market for example, must be recognized, and general development should take advantage of them. Sensitive design controls should be included in the Comprehensive Plan. As a framework for such design, a relationship between the building and its surroundings can be established by choosing compatible uses and intensities of uses.

French Proposal to Amend the Venice Charter for the Conservation and Restoration of Monuments and Sites *

Historic Towns and Villages

Art. 14 The aim in conserving and rehabilitating historic towns and villages is to ensure the continuing life, unity and continuity of human settlements, in town or country, which are of value for their plan or their architecture, and which bear witness to a political, social, economic or cultural structure. To this end, any functions maintained in or introduced into such towns and villages must be compatible with the structure and with the character of the buildings, and with the open spaces and setting of which they are a part.

Art. 15 In conserving and rehabilitating historic towns and villages, particular attention should be paid to the rights of the existing inhabitants whose economic activity and social relationships often depend upon the physical structure of their surroundings.

Art. 16 The conservation and rehabilitation of historic towns, quarters and villages require their effective integration into the physical framework of social life, to which they can offer a vital sense of the past as a factor in cultural identity.

Art. 17 All works of conservation and restoration carried out in historic towns and villages should be inspired by the principles set forth in the foregoing articles, while taking due account of the economic factors involved in their execution.

Art. 18 If it is going to be successful, the conservation of historic towns and villages must be given full consideration as a part of normal planning process at national, regional and local levels. Conservation is an essential element of such planning, and has particular urgency because of the unique and irreplaceable character of historic towns and villages.

Art. 19 The rehabilitation of historic towns and the adaptation of their fabric to modern living conditions must be both planned and executed in such a way as to respect their historic character and their

---

*Proposed amendment by French delegation to Venice Charter, offered at ICOMO's Fifth Assembly, Moscow, June 1978.

spatial and architectural qualities. Any change in the proportion, structure, materials or other characteristic features of their buildings must be avoided. The integration of new buildings into historic towns and villages is possible so long as they respect the historic character, aesthetic quality and social balance of their old surroundings, and their design represents a harmonious development of local architectural traditions. On the other hand demolition and reconstruction behind identical facades should be avoided.

Part IV

A Major Problem, Often Overlooked

9.

The Effect on the Poor and Minorities

Preamble

Many older areas of our cities are worn down and in need of substantial (and expensive) repairs. Such areas frequently are occupied by minority racial and ethnic groups. These areas are often also historically valuable, and the cost of renovation and preservation is likely to be substantial. In such areas a preservation program is likely to involve relocation, except in those instances where great care is being taken to control the cost of renovation.

Taking care to do so is not inconceivable, or even all that difficult. Indeed, as Ziegler points out below, minimal renovation of older buildings, in order to remove real health and safety hazards without a cost so great as to throw a burden on low-income residents, is one of the long-neglected major opportunities in American housing policy. Whenever architects begin to consider renovating a building, many other things inevitably turn up that would make the finished job nicer and then the cost of the job escalates. The first consideration in historic preservation is simply the appearance of the exterior facade and in this area there may be opportunities for following a policy of minimal interior renovation in order to control costs and minimize the need for relocation.

Considered more broadly, what is involved here is one of the major questions of public urban policy—the possibilities for the rehabilitation of residential (and other) areas in older cities. (Not all of these are neighborhoods with historic values, but clearly many of them are.) Although federal aid has clearly been available for such a program since the Housing Act of 1954, major emphasis on rehabilitation had to wait until the fascination with large-scale clearance ran its course. But by the late 1970s, the rehabilitation process had become so widespread that it had generated a new word—"gentrification", i.e., the process by which low-income occupants of such areas are replaced by higher-income people. Here again, well-meant public policy has resulted in an unfavorable impact on the poor, who had largely been excluded from the new suburban areas. With gentrification, they began to be chased out of some of their strongholds in older central-city neighborhoods. The problem is in part, but by no means entirely, the result of the high cost of rehabilitation. The principal purpose of most urban renewal/rehabilitation operations is to revive a profitable ("normal") real estate market in the area; if this is successful, the usual result will be to increase the demand for houses there, thereby increasing property values and making it tempting for people to sell out—and of course increasing taxes on those who would like to remain. Moreover, the increasing numbers of new higher-income residents may begin to resist measures being taken on behalf of the pre-existing poorer population. The problem should be faced directly. "Gentrification" is the normal sign of a successful rehabilitation program conventionally considered.

The process described above is recurring in many historically valuable areas, all over the world. To note the problem is not to argue against a historic preservation program, but to consider the probable consequences thereof, and to prepare to deal with them. If nothing is done, those concerned with historic preservation should be prepared for the same sort of vigorous resistance that resulted from the minority clearance programs carried out in the name of slum clearance and urban renewal. Dealing with the problem later will not be any easier than facing it directly early in the process.

Blacks and Historic Preservation*

Michael DeHaven Newsom

Why should black people be so concerned about historic preservation? Consider, by way of example, Georgetown, a predominantly white enclave populated by the white aristocracy. Its reputation as a chic, expensive place to live is well known. The trouble is that we used to live there too—until the historical preservationists, in league with the real estate developers, decided that Georgetown's historic value was ripe for takeover.

Georgetown is a very old place, and blacks had been living there since before the Civil War.[1] By 1930 over forty percent of the residents of Georgetown were black.[2] The housing they lived in was not grand, perhaps, but it was housing and it was theirs. Real estate brokers, however, recognized that the historically significant origins of Georgetown could, upon rehabilitation of the area, attract new white residents willing to pay handsomely for an association with history. Black homeowners could not resist the prices offered them, nor could they afford the significantly higher rents that the restored houses could command, and by 1950 most blacks had moved from Georgetown. The Georgetown syndrome has been aptly described by the Taeubers, who point out that other examples exist in other cities, including Charleston and Philadelphia.[3]

A close examination of the Georgetown syndrome reveals its galling effects. It contains most of the elements of an all-too-common pattern that has devastating effects on blacks. The first difficulty with this form of Negro displacement is that it is another example of whites deciding what is best for blacks. When Georgetown was taken over, blacks probably did not offer much resistance. The

*Law and Contemporary Problems, vol. 36, 1971, pp. 423-26.

View of Wisconsin Avenue, a shopping area in Georgetown, District of Columbia, formerly inhabited by a mixed black and white population. Most of the blacks were forced out by economic pressures when the area became fashionable. *Courtesy of the National Trust for Historic Preservation.*

"white liberal" was thought of as a friend of the blacks. He would lead them to the promised land, but only as long as they did what was expected of them. The fact that he wanted to move into Georgetown was not supposed to be a matter of concern to blacks. Today that kind of approach does not command respect in the black community. The need for and the imperative of black power with its tenet of self-determination is here to stay.

The second difficulty with the Georgetown syndrome is that blacks have no place to move once they leave. What happens is that the white middle and upper classes, which already have the greatest number of housing choices, are given one more option, the old black neighborhood, and blacks, who have the smallest number of housing choices, are deprived of an option. The situation might be less obnoxious if preservationists showed some concern for relocation of the blacks, and put as much effort into that endeavor as they put into restoration. But of course this concern and effort have been conspicuously absent.[4]

There is, however, another more philosophical objection to the Georgetown syndrome. It is not clear that it properly qualifies as "historic preservation" at all. The true history of Georgetown—until the preservationists' interest in it—was an integrated history. The black elements in that history have now been destroyed, resulting in a perversion and distortion of history. An equally dramatic example of this distortion is found in the treatment of the role of the black man in the development of the South. It was he who labored to build the houses that preservationists are so eager to restore. There were no white building construction unions in those days. Slaves and free men of color built the houses.[5] Of even more interest, some of those houses were built as homes for black people.[6]

What the preservationists have done to black history is not unique. Black men have been reduced to smiling, shuffling, banjo-playing indolents by many historians who should have known better.[7] Blacks have attempted to correct the distortions in the teaching of history, and they are attempting to do the same thing with history as seen and as acted upon by the preservationists.

Much historic preservation in the Georgetown style more accurately reflects desires to profit and to provide a new area for white residents near the city core than a concern for history. A genuine concern for history would not countenance a course of action designed to distort that very history. A concern for social implications of a restoration project would compel the participation and involvement of blacks presently residing in historic neighborhoods in any preservation activities affecting that neighborhood.

The point of this discussion is that some historic preservation projects have been accompanied by wrongs perpetrated against blacks. It is the contention of the author that elimination of the wrongs may require the elimination or at least the drastic redesign of some historic preservation projects. Alternatives and compromises may exist. Some of them will be suggested here, but the focus is on the methods that might be available to end the Georgetown syndrome. The point is serious. Historic preservation work will confront black people who are tired of the things white people have done to them, and preservation activities will therefore have to change.

The Georgetown type of restoration project is one that reflects the efforts of private enterprise. Preservation work could, however, be publicly financed.[8] The methods that might be helpful in stopping the latter type of project might differ from the first. The focus of this paper, however, is on the private enterprise project.

The central elements of this type of project can be briefly summarized. A real estate developer or speculator decides that there is a profit in restoring a particular old neighborhood. The speculator may have been inspired by the local preservationists who have concluded that the neighborhood in question has fundamentally attractive qualities. The developer, appropriately fortified, proceeds to purchase a large portion of the land. He will probably obtain the aid of the building department or other appropriate governmental agency as means of "stimulating" the present owners to sell.[9] After acquiring title, the developer will proceed to obtain financing for the actual restoration and, upon completion of the restoration, will sell the restored unit at a high price to a white family. The developer would steadfastly maintain, of course, that he would sell to anybody, but there do not happen to be many blacks who can meet his price.

The black response to this scenario will depend in large part on their political power. The specific tactics available fall into two major categories: those that require relatively little political power and those that require a great deal. When blacks will gain a great deal of political power is a matter of some debate. Realistically, it has to be conceded that they may never get as much power as they want. But the potential for acquiring some degree of political power is great.

An obvious answer to this threatened displacement would be for the black owner to say "no" to the developer. There have been instances of this behavior, as on East Capitol Hill. Unfortunately, whites are seldom disposed to accept a negative answer from blacks. The building inspector might decide that the neighborhood in question requires strict enforcement of the building code. The black owner usually cannot meet the standards because he is poor or because, even if he could afford it, financing is not available to bring the property up to code. He may sell rather than go through the rigors of housing court and its threats of fines and possible imprisonment. Furthermore, not all of the property owners will necessarily be black. The slum landlords would probably be more than willing to sell at the price offered by the developer. Indeed, it would appear that he is the first to sell.[10] On balance, then, refusal to cooperate may not work where blacks possess little political power, or where other tactics are not available.

Notes

1. C. Green, *The Secret City: A History of Race Relations in the Nation's Capital*, 1967, 53-54.

2. Id. at 235-36.

3. K. Taeuber & A. Taeuber, *Negroes in Cities: Residential Segregation and Neighborhood Change*, 1965.

4. See Rohrbach, "The Poignant Dilemma of Spontaneous Restoration," *Historic Preservation*, Oct.-Dec. 1970, p. 4.

5. An excellent discussion of the artistic activities of black men in the antebellum South can be found in J. Porter, *Modern Negro Art*, 1942.

6. See W. Overdyke, *Louisiana Plantation Homes* 1965. See also *The Negro Almanac*, ed. Ploski and Brown, 1967.

7. See, for example, S. Morison & H. Commager, *The Growth of the American Republic*, 3rd ed. 1937.

8. 16 U.S.C. §470a (1970), authorizes the Secretary of the Interior to make grants to the states for the preparation of statewide historic surveys and plans for the preservation—for the public benefit—of districts, sites, buildings, and structures of historic significance.

42 U.S.C. §1500d-1 (1970) provides for grants by HUD to state or local public bodies of up to 50 percent of the cost of acquiring, restoring, or improving urban sites, structures, or areas of historic or architectural significance. This program will be merged, effective July 1, 1971, with HUD's Open Space Land Program. Housing Act of 1970, P.L. 91-609, Dec. 401 (1970).

None of these programs is particularly suitable, however, for projects like Georgetown or East Capitol Hill. Others that might be applicable will be considered herein. *See* notes 15-29 and accompanying text *infra*.

9. Rohrbach, *supra*, note 4, at 7.

10. *Id.*

Urban Revival Poses Some Hard Choices*

Robert Lindsey

Middle-Class Interest in Older Housing Presses Poor

An awakened interest in urban living is causing a quandary for many American cities. City officials are being asked to choose between encouraging the middle class to live in the city and rehabilitate old homes or protecting low-income people from being outbid for these homes by the middle class.

This situation is already a political issue in Washington and San Francisco. Housing specialists say that if recent patterns continue, the result could be a series of confrontations between the poor and the affluent.

Tom Gale, housing director of the Urban League of New York, speaking of renovation projects in Brooklyn, the Upper West Side and elsewhere in the city, asserted in an interview:

"Blacks are being uprooted by the middle class from the suburbs and other areas in the city."

The Rev. Vinny Quayle of the St. Ambrose Housing Center in Baltimore said the competition for housing in that city first became apparent last year. "Real estate prices soared and middle income families began to reconsider moving to the suburbs," he said, and many poor tenant families have lost their homes.

"Working-class families can no longer afford working-class neighborhoods," he said.

Racial Tensions

In Philadelphia, a firebombing incident occurred last summer in a dispute between Puerto Ricans and middle-class whites who are buying more and more rental units in the Spring Garden area, one of several neighborhoods near the center of Philadelphia that are being rehabilitated.

In Chicago, a transition has occurred in a 15-block area around DePaul University on the North Side that was largely inhabited by people of Latin descent three years ago. The same buildings are now occupied principally by young middle-class families who have settled in the area because they could not afford homes in Chicago's Gold Coast and Lincoln Park areas.

Robert Moore, director of the Houston Housing Authority, said the renovation of old urban housing "is called 'historic preservation,' but it is displacement" of poor people.

David Crane, former dean of architecture at Rice University, said of the situation in Houston:

*New York Times, April 21, 1978, Sec. D, p. 15.

"The poor are simply being squeezed out of the few old neighborhoods that the white middle class want most, resulting in further concentration of poor and minorities in slum areas."

Interest in the Cities

The collision between the poor and well-off has grown recently as a product of increasing interest by the affluent in moving into old urban neighborhoods and upgrading them—a process called "gentrification" in Europe, where it is also occurring in some cities.

Proponents of the process have said that it is potentially one of the most important trends in the recent history of American cities. While most acknowledge that dislocation of the poor is a problem, they maintain that, on balance, the cities are better off if they can lure and keep middle-income wage earners.

Judy Morris, a real estate agent in a section of Baltimore that is undergoing a rapid change in low-rent, multiunit apartments to renovated single family homes, said: "Houses cannot exist on such low rent; they are deteriorating, and if they are not reclaimed they will be bulldozed in another couple of years."

Other proponents of the movement say that in many cities low-income people own some of the houses being coveted by the middle class. As a result, they assert, some low-income families will be able to sell their homes at large profits and move to the suburbs, where more and more blue-collar jobs are located. This is an effective transition, they said, because cities are shifting from manufacturing centers to service industry centers.

Moreover, they argue, the renovation movement and the potential for displacement of the poor is not a racial issue. Many of the middle-class families who are now attempting to rehabilitate neighborhoods, they say, are members of racial minorities.

Housing experts attribute the new interest in old housing to the soaring cost of new homes in the suburbs; birth patterns that have placed large numbers of young people who are unable to buy today's expensive new homes in the home buying market at the same time; demographic patterns that have reduced family size, sent more wives to work, and made problem-plagued urban schools less important in deciding where to live; and the disenchantment with suburban living among some young people.

Beginnings of Bias

In some cities—San Francisco, Dallas and Washington, for example—the increased popularity of the older homes that have a potential for rehabilitation has caused a surge in real estate speculation.

Speculators are being accused of driving up the price of homes, forcing up taxes, and forcing landlords to evict their low-income renters. Speculators, according to real estate industry sources, are not merely professional real estate investors but middle-income couples who have renovated a home, discovered they could make a profit, and then decided to renovate others.

"The big irony of gentrification is that today, in these traditionally poor black neighborhoods, people won't rent to blacks," said David Prowler, a housing specialist with the San Francisco Human Rights Commission. "I'm actually beginning to get discrimination cases there."

Another black leader in San Francisco, Arnold Townsend, said, "If you don't count co-ops, black folks own fewer homes today than they did before redevelopment."

In the city's Western Addition redevelopment area, he said, there is a new kind of segregation: "Blacks occupy rental units, co-ops and H.U.D.-sponsored housing, while the whites live in the Victorians."

In Washington, the speed at which homes in older neighborhoods have shifted from minority rental units to rehabilitation projects has become an issue in the city's mayoral election this year.

Under pressure from representatives of the poor, the City Council there passed an ordinance two weeks ago requiring a landlord to give tenants at least six months' notice of eviction if a building is to be taken off the rental market.

Robert E. Pickeral, a senior vice president of Riggs National Bank, said there was a real estate spiral in the District of Columbia affecting low income people "that had to be dealt with by the Federal Government and the city."

John E. Jacob, executive director of the Washington Urban League, said some homes were being sold for $100,000 this year in neighborhoods "where even the police were afraid to go to two years ago," forcing poor blacks out of them.

"We're going to end up with a highly sophisticated middle-income community and no room for low-income residents," he warned. "I suppose to some people this will be very attractive; it's not attractive to me in the sense that the impact has very bad consequences for the people we are concerned about."

Forced Into Ghettoes

Where are the poor people who are being forced from home going? The answer seems to be: to other ghettoes. In Philadelphia, poor people displaced in some neighborhoods can qualify under Government programs to buy housing units in poorer neighborhoods . . . and some have begun to rehabilitate these homes. In many cities and in many neighborhoods, the displaced are simply being forced to double up with friends and relatives.

"As ghettoes get smaller and smaller, pressures build," said John Tetrault, a Washington minority housing specialist. "As whites begin to move back in, the blacks don't have anywhere to go."

Efforts to save some of the housing for the poor have begun in several cities. In Houston, for example, low-income homeowners are being urged to stay in the city and savings institutions are being solicited in a pilot program to buy some properties that would be retained as rental units for the poor.

"Once people feel they can stay here with dignity they will think twice when some entrepreneur offers them a speculative price for their homes," said the Rev. Edward Salazar, a Roman Catholic priest who is active in the program.

Some observers of the phenomenon say that it is a boon, not a problem, for many minorities. Richard Roeder, a Houston architect, said that many of the people welcomed the opportunity to move out of the city, an opportunity given to them when they can sell their homes at much higher prices than they would have in years past.

"It's presumptuous for those in ⁷Tanglewood [an affluent subdivision in Houston] to put out a prescription for others to turn down money," he said. The dream of many city residents, he said, "is to move into a ticky-tacky suburb where their neighbors don't throw old furniture out on the streets at night."

The Growing Public Stake in Urban Conservation*

Bruce K. Chapman

Two groups deserve special attention: the poor and the racial minorities. Pioneer Square is the home of the world's original "Skid Road," down which logs were skidded to Henry Yesler's waterfront mill. The road's name was applied to the whole district, which later became a tenderloin area and then a habitat for indigents.

In some cities, historic preservation is an ally of people in slums; in others it has moved them out. In Seattle, the removal of indigents from the Skid Road district was attempted in the years preceding historical designation, chiefly because of a strict enforcement of city fire codes in hotels following a major fire. However, official city policy after establishment of the historic district has been to aid and accommodate the Skid Road population, not disperse it. At worst, the panhandlers are unsightly but certainly not dangerous.

The city and county and the Seattle Housing Authority helped the Skid Road Community Council to redevelop the old Morrison Hotel as one of the nation's first municipal shelters. The state decided to maintain operation of its Skid Road branch of the Casual Labor Office, rather than consolidate it with the main office. The city council votes annual emergency appropriations to the Skid Road Community Council for winter care of indigents and supports numerous social service programs through the municipal shelter. Special parks department contracts pay Skid Roaders for part-time maintenance work in the two neighborhood parks. The city and federal government helped the Indian community establish the Indian Health Center and the Indian Social Service Center in the old Broderick Building.

The accomodation could be better, and preservation's stimulation of higher property values is an inevitable threat to the resident poor. Granted that the alternative was the urban renewal bulldozer and that government interest in the welfare of the poor is far greater than it was before district designation. But what is needed now in Seattle is a public corporation to buy and operate on a non-

*National Trust for Historic Preservation, *Economic Benefits of Preserving Old Buildings*, Washington, D. C.: Preservation Press, 1976, pp. 12-13.

profit basis the support enterprises, especially inexpensive restaurants, that permit the poor to exist. For Skid Roaders, this need is as real as that for housing.

Designation Forcing Out Families: Barrio Discovers Its History Can Hurt*

Arizona Daily Star

Tucson's Barrio Historico is being taken over by "outsiders, hip lawyers and artists, people who are borrowing others' cultural roots because they have none of their own," a county judge said yesterday.

John P. Collins, juvenile court judge, told the Democrats of Greater Tucson that property taxes and land values in the barrio south of the Community Center have increased so much that families can no longer afford to live there.

"Many families are being served with eviction notices," Collins said. "The Mexican-American families, mostly poor economically but rich in culture and tradition, are being evicted to live in housing projects. . . . These families have lived in the area for generations."

The barrio, which used to be called Barrio Libre, was designated a historical neighborhood by the City Council in 1975. It is bounded by W. 14th and W. 18th streets, S. Stone Ave. and the Southern Pacific railroad spur.

Collins' interest in the barrio comes through his work as a juvenile court judge, he said. Family disruption creates juvenile crime that puts youngsters into Collins' court, he said.

"The barrio has been a stable influence in an otherwise highly unstable community," Collins said. "The Mexican-American nuclear family is being destroyed in the name of history—so that history's form will be retained as an empty form with no content."

"If we take the barrio away from those families, we are contributing to their destruction," Collins said.

It is the city's designation of the area as historic that spurred development there, Collins said. People interested in its historic nature have bought property there and remodeled its buildings for offices and homes. That has driven property values upward, beyond the reach of the people who have given it its historical character, Collins said.

Carmen Valenzuela, 150 W. Kennedy—within the barrio—is an example. She must be out of her rented home by March 18, and doesn't know where she and her two teenaged boys will live. She is paying $48 monthly for the home, which has been sold by the owner to an artist, she said. A project development will cost her $179 monthly, she said—too much for her $300 monthly income.

"It's kind of sad," she said. "It's the house where my kids grew up. It's part of us." She and her children have lived in the house eight years, and in the barrio since 1952.

"I have neighbors in the same situation," she said. "They've had to move, too," because their homes were sold by the owners.

Her 17-year-old son, Alfredo, said, "It's just that this neighborhood has been Mexican for as long as I can remember. And it's been changing ever since they built that Community Center."

---

*March 1, 1977.

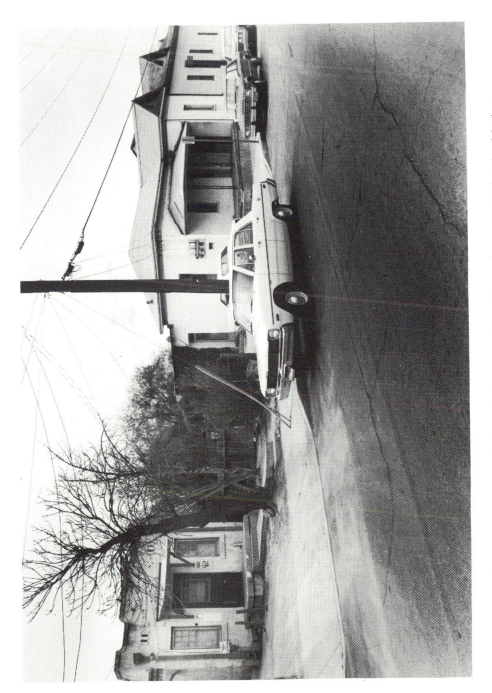

The small cottage at the left typifies the older buildings, still used as residences. The right side of the larger renovated building to the right is used partly for lawyers' offices. (The small sign says so.) *Renovation in the Barrio, Tucson, Arizona.*

James J. Matison is a real estate developer who has his office in the barrio and who is involved in several of the barrio preservation projects.

"As soon as the area got a historic designation, I'd say land values went up 50 percent," Matison said yesterday. His projects have been vacant buildings about to be condemned, he said, and there were no families living in them.

While property values and redevelopment may be forcing some barrio residents to move, County Assessor Steve Emerine speculated that tax rates are not causing an exodus.

"Taxes are not going up any more in that area than in other similar residential areas—and that's not much, only a minor inflationary increase," Emerine said. "Taxes have gone up more on commercial properties developed in the area because usage determines valuation," Emerine said.

Collins said he does not suggest that the City Council members retract the designation, but they should take the time to find out what the people want.

"It's like taking a shovel and digging up an ant den and casting it to the winds. Then ask somebody to put it back together," the judge said.

Asked about crime in the barrio the judge said, "other areas are worse." He cited a nearby housing project where family disruption has already occurred as an example of a higher crime area.

But calling the barrio a pocket of police problems is "baloney," Collins said.

"We just can't justify destroying another small neighborhood," he said.

Editors' Note: Strycker's Bay Case

The basic purpose of urban renewal operations is to revive the "normal" private real estate market in an area; and this is perhaps even more true when the emphasis is on rehabilitation rather than clearance. Now deteriorating areas (where such treatment is appropriate) have, almost by definition, substantial occupancy by the poor, and often by the minority poor; and the revival of normal market operations is likely to result in substantial displacement of these people—again, almost by definition, or at least in the absence of strong public policy measures to the contrary.

Inevitably this problem had to be faced in the West Side Urban Renewal Study for the 87th-97th Street area, carried out in the late 1950s under close and detailed supervision by the New York City Planning Department. The area as a whole was one of economic integration, for the side-street brownstones were often occupied by Puerto Ricans, and so were some tenements on some avenues (particularly Columbus and Amsterdam). A substantial controversy on basic issues resulted during the course of the study. In the New York urban context of that decade, the final decision (by consultants and top Department officials) was to propose widespread demolition and new construction of higher—income housing, quite explicitly in order to provide "good ratables"—and to provide merely token new public low-cost housing. This looked better (indeed, "more realistic") in the 1950s than it did when the City finally made its major decisions on the project, in the midst of the civil rights revolution of the mid-1960s. In the latter context, the political pressure ran precisely the opposite way, and a substantially larger amount of inexpensive housing was decided upon, in order to reduce minority relocation. (The curious thing was that those in technical charge were surprised.)

The conflict over preserving economic integration on the West Side has continued, and a recent decision in the Supreme Court points a moral which is relevant here.[1] If a substantial group of higher-income families are attracted back into such a renewal area, these nouveaux-arrivés may (as they did here) start objecting to good new housing for the (poorer) pre-renewal population.

The nature of the controversy and its background are best set forth in the long original lower-court opinion, by Judge Irving Ben Cooper.

On the city's plans:

In 1956 the City applied for, and received, federal grant funds for a demonstration study of the 20 square blocks which eventually became the West Side Urban Renewal Area.

The study was organized to determine whether realistic and meaningful proposals for renewal of the Area could be developed. James Felt, Chairman of the City Planning Commission, conducted this study and published it in April, 1958. He concluded that renewal, rather than demolition, was "desirable, practicable and economically feasible." Moreover, Commissioner Felt found that the Area, though deteriorating, had a number of residual strengths. Its proximity to public transportation and to Central and Riverside Parks as well as to many cultural and business centers had always made it a desirable residential area. In addition, much good housing stock remained, particularly along Central Park West and the numerous brownstones on the side streets.

The study also determined that the Area was maintaining a more favorable racial and economic level than was commonly achieved at the time. From 1950 to 1956, though the Area's Puerto Rican population increased almost eight-fold and the total white non-Puerto Rican population decreased by roughly a quarter, nonetheless white families constituted more than half of all families who moved in during the period. Moreover, the median income in the Area increased by more than one-third, which indicates that the white families and individuals who moved into the Area must have had above-average incomes to compensate for the low incomes of the newly arriving black and Puerto Rican families.

The study demonstrated that, though the Area was threatened by obsolescence, it had nevertheless retained the foundations of a formerly sound residential area, and that it was suited for rehabilitation rather than demolition and clearance. The objective of the renewal program envisaged by the study was not to create a new community but rather to preserve and improve the existing community so as to continue to accomodate the varied needs of its population. . . . As stated in the study: "What are the yardsticks against which a successful renewal plan should be measured? A reduction of the abnormal population turnover and elimination of the excessive overcrowding which contribute so greatly to the Area's decline. Maintenance of the economic and ethnic integration which is part of its tradition, is in accord with accepted City policy, and which will take into account the needs of its present population."

As we have discussed above, a critical issue here is the City's announced policy to provide 2,500 units of low income housing. A parallel issue, which we consider below, is the City's policy of maintaining a 70%:30% ratio of middle to low income units in middle income buildings in the Area. We find, on the basis of the history of the Plan from its initial promulgation until the present, that the 2,500 figure was intended neither as a fixed minimum nor as a maximum. Rather it was a political judgment on the part of City officials as to an appropriate number of units which would satisfy the housing needs of low income relocatees desirous of returning to the Area, while not compromising the Plan's overriding objective to create a racially and economically integrated community. No legal or binding commitment by the City was intended; the 2,500 figure was instead a statement of policy and intention. It was aimed at meeting the needs of low income relocatees to the maximum extent possible without endangering the private capital investment so necessary to economic integration. Both Roger Starr, Administrator of the Housing and Development Authority, and Walter Fried, then Vice Chairman of the Housing and Redevelopment Board (the City agency which administered the Plan), testified that balancing of these two interests was the critical factor in determining the number of low rent units to be constructed in the Area. (Tr. 397, 444, 889). Moreover, contrary to plaintiffs' assertions, the right of relocation was itself a paramount Plan objective. Though the testimony on this point is conflicting (Tr. 397, 714, 3157), the documentary history of the Plan makes clear that the City was committed to provide sufficient Area housing to low income relocatees desirous of returning. This feature of the Plan has never changed.

It is also clear that the 2,500 figure was intended as an estimate which could be modified subject to changing needs and conditions. That estimate, which was itself the product of numerous revisions, represented an assessment of low income housing needs balanced against the objective of maintaining economic integration. The assessment of such needs must inevitably vary and it has been established here that the economic conditions assumed at the inception of the Plan have themselves drastically changed. (Tr. 2660-2661). Accordingly, in order for plaintiffs to establish that the City is now violating the Plan by increasing the number of low income units in the Area, they must show that such an increase would endanger the integration of the Area and therefore the underlying purpose of the Plan.

Closely related to the 2,500 policy is the issue of the City's allegedly binding commitment to a 70%:30% ratio for middle to low income housing in the Area.[3] . . .

As of January, 1969, 1,230 public housing units had been completed. In addition, about 20% of the 1,769 completed middle income units were inhabited by low income households; this made for a total of 1,584 completed low rent units. (Ex. 65). With Section 236 subsidies in short supply and the only buildings under construction being middle income, there was a growing community sense that the commitment to provide adequate low income housing would not be met. Eventually the City converted Sites 4 and 30 from middle income to low income housing; it was this decision that precipitated the litigation before us.[4]

On the plaintiffs' claims:

Plaintiffs are a private school within the Area and a group of middle income residents, primarily brownstone home owners; they claim that these changes would violate the Plan upon which they relied in choosing their homes, and, further, that such changes would cause the Area to deteriorate and become a ghetto. Defendants are the United States Government, the State of New York, the City of New York, and a community group of Area residents; their position is that these changes are necessary to provide sufficient housing to former Area residents who were displaced by the impact of urban renewal and who therefore have a right of return to the site of their homes. Defendants further contend that the proposed changes would not adversely affect the Area.[5] . . .

Essentially, plaintiffs contend that the Area is in danger of tipping; that, given existing conditions, as more low income residents are introduced into the Area, the tipping point will be exceeded, middle income residents will flee the neighborhood, which will then rapidly deteriorate. For this reason plaintiffs ask, *inter alia*, that this Court halt the planned construction of Site 30 as low income housing. While plaintiffs recognize that tipping has been considered a racial issue, they maintain that its true characteristic is the low income of the families involved, and that the racial element is a subsidiary factor. Specifically, they assert that "the indiscriminate admission of relocatee low income families" has caused the Area to reach the tipping point. Defendants respond that the "tipping phenomenon is a racial issue which relates to economics only insofar as minority persons, i.e., blacks and Puerto Ricans, are often associated with persons of low income." We have concluded that defendants must prevail on this issue. Our reasoning, set forth more fully below, has two grounds: (1) the concept of tipping is racial and only incidentally related to income, and (2) even assuming that tipping does include economic classifications, plaintiffs have failed to show that the Area is, or is in danger of, tipping.[6]

Judge Cooper ruled in favor of the defendants (the City, and so the additional site for public housing). After six more years of litigation (and two intervening opinions), the Supreme Court upheld HUD's action in dismissing plaintiffs' environmental objections to the proposed housing, in a *per curiam* opinion which limited NEPA review to the procedural questions.[7]

Notes

1. *Trinity Episcopal School Corporation* v. *Romney*, 387 F.Supp. 1044 (S.D.N.Y. 1974), *rev'd in part*, 523 F.2d 88 (2d Cir. 1975), *sub nom. Trinity Episcopal School Corp.* v. *Harris*, 445 F.Supp. 204 (S.D.N.Y.

1978), rev'd. sub nom. Karlen v. Harris, 590 F.2d 39 (2d Cir. 1978), (appellate decision) rev'd. per curiam sub nom. Strycker's Bay Neighborhood Council v. Karlen, 444 U.S. 223 (1980).

  2. 387 F.Supp. at 1049.
  3. Id. at 1057-59.
  4. Id. at 1055-56.
  5. Id. at 1047.
  6. Id. at 1063-64.
  7. Incidentally, this opinion misstated by several years the date on which the New York City Planning Commission began formulating a plan for the renewal of this area—unlike Judge Cooper, who got it right. The West Side study was one of the first local responses to the shift in emphasis toward rehabilitation, in the Housing Act of 1954, 68 STAT. 622 et seq.

Implications of Urban Social Policy: The Quest for Community Self-Determination *

Arthur P. Ziegler

Because of our opposition to this benighted process, we almost automatically found ourselves at the outset committed to saving not only the buildings in a neighborhood but also the neighborhood's people—or at least as many as possible.

Action and Goals

One of our first areas of concentration was a decaying North Side section that we identified as the Mexican War Streets area because Gen. Alexander Hays had named the streets after battles and generals in that war. It was decaying, but not decayed. That is to say, it needed more time to become a ghetto. But long-time residents were reluctantly leaving and only the poor, the black, were replacing them. It was on the no-mortgages list of the banks. For investment it attracted only the slumlord.

---

*National Trust for Historic Preservation, Legal Techniques in Historic Preservation, Washington, D.C., 1972, pp. 36-37.

With a grant of $100,000 from the Sarah Mellon Scaife Foundation in Pittsburgh, we raised a pilot revolving fund and developed our approach as follows:

1. Buy houses in the poorest condition.
2. Restore some of them for a variety of income groups:
    A. Middle income, to try to attract persons with some financial standing, education, and vitality into the area.
    B. Moderate income, to provide decent housing for people already in the area and to prove to the Redevelopment Authority that renewal of this kind will work.
    C. Low income, to include the poor in good housing in the area.
3. Encourage our members to restore houses in the area as their homes or as investments.
4. Develop a fresh belief in the neighborhood among old-timers there and get them to restore the facades of their houses (the interiors were usually already in good condition).
5. Bind together this mixture of people—young and old, well-to-do and poor, black and white—in the cause of preserving and restoring this unique architecture and conducting this experiment of urban neighborhood renewal.

We implemented this program by purchasing a house in squalid deterioration, assembling our own restoration crew and restoring the house. Restoration for us means actual restoration of those areas on public view. Inside we alter the houses to produce apartments of a variety of sizes and rents but maintain old mantels, woodwork, hardware and any other historic fixtures. Often, if these are too sadly decayed or missing, we use replacements from houses scheduled for demolition in other areas. After 14 months of work and an expenditure of $53,000, we rented our apartments—and have continued to rent them—to young professional and semiprofessional newcomers to the neighborhood. They bring to the area a deep commitment to reinvigorating it and to participating in this urban experiment. The former residents in the building (12 people, six cats, three dogs) we relocated principally to public or other nearby housing—all except the owner of the menagerie, who, fortunately, vanished one evening. What apartment he has populated now we do not know.

The goal of renting to moderate income groups was first achieved when we purchased a house near the first one. Here we made the economics work by renewing less. While we put in new wiring, we kept most of the old plumbing. We retained the old drainboard sinks and spared ourselves a hefty plaster bill by building false drywalls in front of some deteriorated old walls. We substituted linoleum for vinyl and carpet. The rents as well as the tenants remained the same.

Low-income families also are enjoying newly restored houses. Through the leased housing program of the Department of Housing and Urban Development, we are able to buy derelict houses and fully restore them for rent to our local housing authority at a rate that returns our investment in 12 to 15 years. The authority in turn sublets to poor families at reduced rates. Their initial five-year leases, signed before we start work, enable us to obtain mortgage funds. This program is a fine one. A preservation group saves a good piece of architecture, physical improvement comes to a neighborhood, a poor family moves into a good house in an area on its way to recovery rather than on its way down, and the government adds to the available housing supply for low income families without the usual red tape.

We obtained the support of our members primarily by talking it up. One venturesome lady acquired and restored a house with reasonable financial success: her commitment helped considerably. She, too, talked it up. Then another and another, each one encouraging others by his own satisfaction, which also helped protect the investment he had made. Currently (four years after the program began), 17 members have purchased and restored or are restoring 20 houses. Rents have remained moderate for the most part. Frequently, tenants weather the restoration work and stay on.

Community Support

The old-timers in the area have stopped leaving and have started repairing and painting. They have found new heart for staying. Few really wanted to leave to begin with but they were intimidated by the decay, the fall of property value and the lack of street safety. For the first year, they listened to our glowing verbal pictures and they watched the work. Then they became acquainted with our members who were investing in their neighborhood, of all things. Then they began to follow suit, and in three years 34 of them have painted or otherwise restored facades.

To date, we have spent $225,000 in the Mexican War Streets. Every dollar we have spent has been matched by $3 in private money of members or old-time residents, and the ratio is getting steadily higher. This to us is urban renewal—through renewal not removal.

But the fifth goal, developing in all these people a new sense of neighborhood, with restoration of the houses as the unifying denominator, is perhaps the most significant one.

After we began the program, we sponsored several informal neighborhood gatherings to which we invited all residents and property owners. We discussed aspirations and afflictions and resolved on initiating such modest community ventures as a clean-up drive. After these were successfully carried out, we suggested that the area establish a Mexican War Streets Neighborhood Association to include all residents and property owners willing to pay $1 a year membership and to be operated independently of our own organization. In this way, we felt that the burden of responsibility for solving local problems would be placed squarely on the shoulders of the local people: they would have to work on their own behalf and not look to us as omnipresent problem solver and benefactor. We would receive the benefit of having the counsel of the association, which would be free to advise us on the basis of how the neighborhood saw the issues.

The group was slow in making its way, but now it has a firm foothold. At a typical meeting, we have 20 to 50 attendees. They range from widows and spinsters who have lived in the area for 30, 40, 50 years to retired couples (also old-timers) to new young tenants, to new-comer middle-aged suburbanites, young professional whites and blacks, wealthy investors, and a few representatives of both white and black poor. The latter are diffident about attending meetings, so one of our forthcoming events is to be a backyard beer party. We hope that such an environment will occasion ease in everyone.

As a group, the members have caucused with local school officials, the local police captain and a representative of speculative real estate interests in a nearby area, among others. They have taken stands on public issues (historic zoning, herringbone brick paving, trees) and they have initiated useful projects including several communal, thorough cleanings of the alleys.

Most of these people actually have little in common; however, the renewal of this historic district and the goals of this urban experiment have given them common cause, and from that has come a humanizing education. Our most notable success is that we suffer from none of the malignant hostilities that might be expected from such a mixture of people.

Community self-determination? Not exactly. We are bent on saving these buildings. To that end the Pittsburgh History & Landmarks Foundation, as an organization, pushes and prods, raises and spends funds and imposes on the neighborhood to the extent to which we own property and therefore control it and can present convincing ideas and plans to the residents and owners. But we try hard to be open minded and responsive to what advice the Mexican War Streets Neighborhood Association or individuals in the area offer to us.

Before our arrival, this neighborhood had lost its ability to determine its future. It was on the ineluctable course of going bad, like any aging organism. It had lost the means of regeneration. We provided a new injection of energy, of life, and to the extent that the injection creates certain predeterminations in the organism, we have predetermined. Essentially, however, we have really freed—or at least started the process of freeing—this area to determine what it wants for itself. Within the next few years, the area should be able to determine its own course, to go on its way—and we will then go ours.

Historic American Building Survey*

National Park Service

Black Historic Landmarks

One of the most neglected areas of historic preservation has been the role of minorities in shaping our heritage.

To help the National Park Service identify sites commemorating the role Black Americans have played in shaping this country, the Park Service called on the Afro-American Bicentennial Corporation (ABC) to select important sites for designation as national landmarks.

The Bicentennial group, led by the brothers Vincent de Forrest and Robert de Forrest, began a comprehensive three year effort to bring together scholars in Afro-American history and culture to help identify sites.

"Black Americans have played many prominent roles in the development of our country." said Dept. of Interior Secretary Rogers C. B. Morton," and it is only fitting that more of the sites involved in their efforts be recognized in this way as we approach the nation's Bicentennial."

The ABC group looks for sites which could be classified by one of three themes; development of the English colonies, 1700-1775; major American wars; and society and social conscience.

On July 1, 1974, the Secretary of the Interior announced the selection of thirteen sites associated with Black American History as National Historic Landmarks.

Of the sites nominated, four are part of the National Park System. They are: Longfellow National Historic Site in Massachusetts; Chalmette National Historic Park in Louisiana; Petersburg National Military Park in Virginia; and Perry's Victory and International Peace Memorial in Ohio. The

---

Trends, Oct. - Dec., 1974, pp. 31-32.

Longfellow Historic Site marks the meeting place of Black American poet Phillis Wheatley and George Washington in 1776, before the colonies had declared their independence. The other three sites are important in terms of the role Black Americans played in our military history.

New sites include:

- The Dexter Avenue Baptist Church in Montgomery, Alabama, the home church of the Rev. Martin Luther King, Jr.
- Ida B. Wells-Barnett House in Chicago, home of the civil rights advocate of the 1890s
- Fort Des Moines Provisional Army Officer Training School in Iowa, the first Black officers' training camp
- The Yucca Plantation, "Melrose," in Melrose, Louisiana, owned by a former slave
- Port Hudson in Louisiana, where freed slaves stormed a Confederate stronghold
- The Paul Cuffe Farm in Westport, Mass., home of one of the country's most prominent Blacks of the late 18th and early 19th centuries
- The Harriet Tubman Home for the Aged in Auburn, N.Y., home of one of the Underground Railroad's most famous conductors
- The Colonel Charles Young House, in Wilberforce, Ohio, home of the highest ranking Black officer in World War I
- The Mount Bethel A.M.E. Church, the birthplace of the first Black religion in the country and the oldest parcel of real estate continuously owned by Black people in the U.S.
- The site of the Battle of Rhode Island at Portsmouth, the only battle of the Revolutionary War in which Black Americans participated as a distinct racial group
- The Robert Smalls House in Beaufort, S.C., home of a former slave distinguished for his service in the legislature of the state and later in the U.S. Congress
- Stone River Slave Rebellion Site near Rantowles, S.C., site of one of the most serious slave insurrections of the colonial period
- Fort Pillow, Tenn., the site of the Confederate Army's prison for captured Black soldiers.

Preservation in the West*

John L. Frisbee

Sites of Significance to Ethnic Minorities

Many historic properties associated with ethnic minority groups are located in the West. Further effort is necessary to protect and develop these sites. An attempt must be made to integrate the cultural and architectural history of Western ethnic groups into the historic preservation movement. Much of the rich cultural legacy left by the Spanish, Chinese, and Japanese and by American Indians has been obliterated. Many of the historic properties associated with ethnic culture are in urban areas or small

---

*Washington, D. C.: National Trust for Historic Preservation, 1972, pp. 24-25.

towns. Because they were often the homes and shops of the working classes, the buildings were less substantial and subject to deterioration. Many have been demolished for freeways and urban renewal programs. A small number of buildings associated with the Chinese in America survive, but they are few in relation to those that once existed. The same is true of the remains of Spanish architecture in America. The building material of the early Spaniards, adobe, deteriorates rapidly under inclement weather conditions.

Some members of Western minority groups are reticent about preserving the tangible reminders of their past. Often, their memories are not pleasant ones—of degradation, virtual slave employment, hatred and poverty. It is understandable that they reject certain elements of their cultural heritage. Among other groups, the Indians of the West, the Eskimos and Indians of Alaska and the natives of Hawaii, there is a growing cultural awareness. Both Alaskans and Hawaiians expressed interest in incorporating preservation into cultural educational programs.

Much more must be done in the field of totem pole preservation, essentially a problem of Alaska and the Pacific Northwest. Southeastern Alaskans are greatly concerned with the problem of preserving their totems. In much of that area, annual rainfall may exceed 150 inches. This amount of moisture contributes to the problems of rot and insect infestation, resulting in substantial deterioration of the wooden poles in 30 or 40 years. Because the poles are made of wood, they are also easily subject to vandalism. Some efforts have been made to check deterioration and develop technical means to protect the poles in their natural outdoor setting. But much work remains to be done.

Neighborhood Conservation and Reinvestment Newsletter*

HUD last week named 155 Neighborhoods in 118 cities to receive special funds set aside under the Neighborhood Strategy Area ("NSA") program. Only 18 requests for NSA funds were rejected.

Under the NSA program, rent subsidies will go to tenants of modest incomes in housing that is fixed up through Section 8 Substantial Rehabilitation. Participating communities have designated areas for concentrated community development activity. Many cities plan to use Urban Development Action Grant or Community Development Block Grant (CDBG) money to complement their NSA allotments.

In announcing the awards, Secretary Patricia Harris described the NSA program as a major effort "to avoid displacing the poor in the name of revitalization." By paying the difference between what poorer families can afford and the market rents for renovated housing, HUD hopes to help those who otherwise couldn't keep up with rising rents and property values in revitalizing neighborhoods. If anyone is displaced due to NSA rehabilitation, he may receive compensation equivalent to payments made under the Uniform Relocation Act.

_____

*Feb. 26, 1978, pp. 1-2.

Letter to Senator Frank Church

National Trust for Historic Preservation

Dec. 29, 1978

The Honorable Frank Church, Chairman
Special Committee on Aging
United States Senate
Washington, D.C. 20510

RE: "Older Americans in the Nation's Neighborhoods"

The current unprecedented demand for housing in older urban neighborhoods has been caused by the major population phenomenon of the "baby boom" generation (peak birth years 1947-57) reaching home buying age and flooding the housing market. We believe that, in most respects, revitalization of center city housing and a reversal of the flight to the suburbs are beneficial movements. These trends give rise to new hope that our cities will regain preeminence as the cultural and economic centers of American life. The challenge to preservationists, neighborhood advocates and government officials is to utilize this unique opportunity to revitalize our cities while cushioning the impact this activity will have on low and moderate income people and the elderly, who, in many instances, are similarly affected.

Initially, most of the revitalization of cities centered in historic districts or historic areas not yet designated historic districts. Several interrelated reasons accounted for this. Action by preservationists in historic districts often eliminated blighting influences such as threat of highways or urban renewal, inappropriate zoning, negative public image and poor municipal services. In addition, preservation itself became a major component in the revitalization movement as conservation techniques such as historic designation and historic district zoning to preserve and improve neighborhoods were adopted and utilized. Overall, our experience has demonstrated that both new and long-term residents have recognized that historic preservation helps insure a positive future for their neighborhoods. It must be realized, however, that the successful revitalization of urban historic districts was as much a manifestation of increasing housing demand as it was the result of the historic status of those areas. As evidence of this, historic designation has often followed other private revitalization activity rather than preceded it.

Because it is uncertain how many elderly persons live in historic districts, the specific effect of neighborhood revitalization on older residents is difficult to evaluate. It is obvious, however, that potential negative effects include higher taxes as assessments rise, real estate speculation and high rates of property turnover. Those who rent are typically more severely affected as property values increase.

Yet, revitalization can benefit older residents in significant ways. Specifically, revitalization can mean improved property values for elderly homeowners whose homes are often their principal assets. In this regard, the development of alternative mortgage instruments such as the reverse annuity mortgage may allow older homeowners to capitalize upon the increasing value of their homes. Other benefits of revitalization include improved municipal services, reduced crime and a corresponding willingness of many elderly people to end a self-imposed isolation which is one of the products of unstable neighborhoods.

In order to mitigate the displacement problem we suggest that a strategy of dispersing the housing demand among as many neighborhoods as possible be adopted, seeking steady, carefully paced revitalization activity. This strategy should reduce the incidence of speculation and displacement that result when excessive demand is focused on just one or two areas of a city. By spreading out housing demand, such demand can be better accommodated through vacancies and normal market turn-over, thus avoiding skyrocketing prices. Programs such as that of Boston's Parkman Center to inform potential homeowners about overlooked neighborhoods should be replicated elsewhere. Additionally, to effect the dispersement of housing demand, more neighborhoods should be given recognition and protection on local, state and national registers. In this regard, the plan of the Heritage Conservation and Recreation Service of the Department of the Interior to include "Neighborhoods" as a category eligible for listing in the National Register of Historic Places should be implemented.

Further, it is essential that government programs be employed to provide housing assistance to low and moderate income residents, including the elderly, in revitalizing neighborhoods. Programs such as Neighborhood Housing Services and the Department of Housing and Urban Development's Neighborhood Strategy Areas should be utilized to help both homeowners and renters. New approaches specifically directed to the elderly should be explored, such as Detroit's Maintenance Central for Seniors. In this program HUD Community Development Block Grant funds and the Department of Health, Education and Welfare Older American funds are used to provide free home maintenance and repair services to persons age 60 and older.

Involving the Neighborhood *

Pierre Dulieu * *

Restoration of the Quartier des Brasseurs in Namur, a Council of Europe Pilot Project, Showed the Need for Public Involvement

The importance of the social and human aspects of conservation in old urban areas has been evident since the symposium organized by the Council of Europe in Edinburgh in 1974.

This new awareness stems from two factors. The first factor is that in several cases, such as the Marolles district in Brussels, the conservation scheme was decided on as the result of a reaction by the residents against "bulldozer type" urban renewal operations. They did not want to see their homes disappear, they wanted them to be rehabilitated and the cost to be borne by the authorities.

The second factor is that in this instance, and in others like it, the local authorities have been able to obtain state aid only on the ground that their aim is one of low-cost "social" [i.e., publicly

---

*Council of Europe *Forum*, 3d quarter 1979, p. vi.
* *Pierre Dulieu is Professor at the University of Namur, Belgium

assisted] housing. That is of course not so in every country, but it is the case in Belgium, where there is no legislation dealing with the problem of urban renewal in the broad sense, including rehabilitation of the heritage of existing buildings. The rehabilitation of the Quartier des Brasseurs (brewers' district) in Namur, one of the Belgian pilot projects in the Council of Europe's programme, is a hybrid operation. The inhabitants had not wanted it, but it was clearly stated at the onset that it would be carried out mainly in their interest and with their help.

Fears and Misgivings

As experience has shown, however, that is not so simple a matter. A "renovation committee" was set up, comprising representatives of the "neighborhood committee" constituted for the purpose; a social worker was appointed to assist the latter and keep the inhabitants informed; and an architect's office was installed in the street in order to facilitate contacts. Yet all these were not enough to allay fears and misgivings.

Some people attributed the mistrust to the predominance of elderly residents. Having always lived without comforts, they were more afraid of moving than interested in improving their material welfare. Other people pointed to the influence of certain landlords seeking to profit from their fixed capital and wishing neither to modernize their properties nor to sell them to the municipality, except at very high prices.

So preparations for the scheme went ahead in—at times—an atmosphere of tension, especially when the town took authoritarian measures such as the closure of insalubrious premises or the adoption of a compulsory purchase plan even though the municipal authorities explained that purchase was simply a weapon with which to stop property speculation and which it had no intention of using except in extreme circumstances.

Rumors Dissipated

Not until work began did the atmosphere change. A great many false rumors were then dissipated. Practical measures were introduced to help people required to move. Dialogue was established. Now the first batch of housing is to be let. To whom? The question is whether the town can let at least two-thirds of it (the percentage is laid down by the state) to low income households, giving priority to former inhabitants.

It is apparent at this stage that the arrangements for financing housing stock renovated by the municipality are far less advantageous than new housing built by council house contractors. If the rents are to be set at "social" levels, the town must agree to bear a significant part of the cost.

The second problem—much more complex still—is rehousing former residents. They often paid incredibly low rents. Even if those rents are doubled, when their present much higher standard of amenities is taken into account, they are still paying far less than the normal rate based on cost calculations. The state normally pays a "rent allowance" to persons moving out of substandard into good quality housing, on a permanent basis in the case of old people and for a transitional period in other cases.

But there remains a problem which the town cannot ignore. Inhabitants constantly remind the municipal authorities that they did not ask for the renovation work to be done. The town then has to handle applications for allowances and in particular has itself to settle the most difficult cases and those which are not catered for by a system devised for the purposes of a different policy.

So in spite of all the efforts made, rehabilitation remains a surgical operation which leaves scars behind it. These continue to be painful for some time. Yet the district soon comes alive again. From having been abandoned, rejected, even a place of ill repute, it suddenly discovers that it is capable of becoming a center of activity once again.

Rehabilitation is a long-term operation, especially when it tries to safeguard the interests of former residents.